Complete
Amiga C

Everything you need to start programming your Amiga in C

Complete
Amiga C

Everything you need to start programming your Amiga in C

Cliff Ramshaw

Future Leisure Books

Complete Amiga C

Book design and production Rod Lawton

Cover design Rod Lawton

Cover illustration Paul Kidby

Author Cliff Ramshaw

First published in 1994 by Future Publishing, Beauford Court, 30 Monmouth Street, Bath, Avon BA1 2BW.

ISBN 1 898275 10 6

Printed in the UK by Beshara Press

The included disks
The software on these disks is not guaranteed for use in any specific situation. The publishers accept no liability for problems arising from its use. The contents of the disk are copyright, and are not to be copied or distributed in the public domain.
If one or more of your disks fails to work, you should return the disk with a brief description of the problem to: Complete Amiga C Disk Returns, DisCopy Labs, Units 2/3, Omega Technology Centre, Drayton Fields, Daventry, Northants NN11 5RT, U.K.

Contents

About the author

Cliff Ramshaw is the editor of Amiga Shopper, the UK's best-selling serious Amiga magazine, which each month produces articles for Amiga owners who are interested in learning more about their machine. Before that he worked on the magazine for two years as first technical editor and then deputy editor.

As well as working previously as a programmer in a business environment, Cliff has also produced many commercial games and has a number of books on games programming to his credit, including Zap Pow Boom – Arcade And Other Games for the VIC-20, VIC Innovative Computing and The Commodore 64 Games Book.

After working for many years with BASIC and assembly language, Cliff finally discovered C – a damned fine language and no mistake – and has never looked back. One of his main motivations for writing this book was the feeling that other C tutorials are aimed at people already conversant with general programming techniques, whereas he feels there is no reason whatsoever why it cannot be taught to peope with no previous programming experience.

Thanks to...

The author would like to acknowledge the help of the following: Toby Simpson of Millennium, for his help in removing the bugs from the Four In A Row program, and Mark Harman of North London University for his polymorphic list code and the game engine for the Four In A Row program.

Preface

Sooner or later, most computer owners get around to programming. Maybe it's not the reason they bought the machine, and maybe it's not the first thing they wanted to do with it, but the lure of custom-designed software, the creative satisfaction out of producing a program and even the prospect of selling it usually tempt us all into dabbling with programming.

You can opt for a 'beginners' language like BASIC. Easy to learn, but slow and clunky and not remotely 'professional'. Or you can jump in at the deep end and learn assembler – the nearest you can get to raw 'machine language'. The results are as good as the machine can deliver, but you need a certain sort of mind… and have to be prepared to lose it.

Or you can learn C. C is the 'professionals' programming language. A version exists for every machine under the sun, so you only ever have to learn the language once. You write your programs in a language that the ordinary human mind can grasp, and then the C compiler turns it into fast machine language. The C programming language is the best compromise there is between understandability and efficiency.

Which is just how we like to think of 'Complete Amiga C'.

We've put everything we can into it so that you can get as much as possible out of it. Good luck, and have fun!

Introduction

We thought long and hard about a title for this book. In the end we chose 'Complete Amiga C' because we were able to put together a *complete* package – one that incorporated a book that told you how to program in C, a compiler that let you actually do so and the Commodore 'library' and 'include' files that let you use the Amiga's specific hardware features, e.g. its advanced graphics and sound.

We started off wanting to produce a book on programming the Amiga. C is the obvious language to write about – it's the professionals' choice. Then we thought, 'how can we make this book better'? Simple. By including a C compiler so that readers could not only read about C but try it out too. From there it seemed pretty logical to choose DICE, one of the best C compilers available. And rather than providing the shareware version only, we decided to go the whole hog and sort out a deal on the full, registered version.

This wasn't an especially cheap solution. But with a bit of negotiation with our various suppliers, we kept the price down to £24.95. Which, we think, is not bad for a book *and* a complete C programming environment. If you bought any of the leading commercial packages you could expect to pay up to ten times that amount. We're rather pleased with that.

What we realised we *couldn't* do, though, was produce a book containing everything there was to know about C programming on the Amiga. The subject is just too vast. And if we produced a book for experts it would be virtually meaningless to the far greater numbers of novice programmers. So if you require advanced technical information, you'll sadly have to look elsewhere.

But if you simply want to start programming your Amiga in C, everything you need is right here. And we're rather pleased with that, too.

Computers are rather precise, complicated things, and the same therefore goes for programming languages. C is not the easiest programming language to learn, but it's widely recognised to be the best. And once you've learned the basics on your Amiga, you can apply your knowledge to C programming on just about any other machine.

How to use the book

What's the best way to read 'Complete Amiga C'? Try starting from the beginning and reading through to the end! The book's been written with beginners in mind, starting with basic programming principles and gradually introducing more advanced concepts and showing how they are used in practice.

Or you can simply dip in and read the sections that offer the information you need at any one time. It works either way.

There are lots of listings in 'Complete Amiga C' to let you try sample programs and to explain how certain programming techniques work. To make things clearer, listings are printed in a different typeface with a different left-hand margin:

```
like this, in fact
```

Note that some of the program lines are too long to fit on a single printed line. When you see this character ¬ at the end of a line, *don't* start a new line when typing it in – it simply means it was too long to fit on the page.

And in the main text, where we mention C 'keywords' (variable names, or words that would appear in listings) we use a different typeface again. This makes the text much easier to understand. The words "next you define the variable **number**" are not ambiguous. The words "next you define the variable number" *are*.

And while we're on the subject, where the text describes the *contents* of variables, or function results or anything *output* by a program, we use the plain (not bold) version of this different typeface. So we might say, "the current value of the variable **number** is 14."

We also use symbols, or 'icons' in the margins to tell you, for example, what sort of listings you're looking at. They are:

Type this in This indicates a complete C program that you can type in, compile and run.

Code segment This is a part of an earlier listing that may have been revised or altered using new techniques. Or it might be an illustration of how the technique might be used in a program. Either way, these pieces of code do not run on their own, but only as part of a larger program.

We also use icons along the main text, just to highlight important pieces of information. These are the icons you will see from time to time:

Make a note This is an important piece of information you should be especially aware of

Top tip This marks a useful tip or snippet of advice. It might save time, it might save memory, it might save you tearing your hair out…

What does it mean? The most welcome icon of all! This indicates an important definition or explanation of some obscure programming term.

We've designed 'Complete Amiga C' this way to try to make it useful to all sorts of Amiga C programmers. From beginners learning the language from the ground up, to intermediate users who only need to read certain sections or who need to check up on specific details, to more advanced programmers who just want to browse through now and again in the hope of picking up little tricks or techniques they'd missed before.

What is DICE?

DICE is a C programming environment. That means it comes with an editor, where you can type programs in, a linker, which lets you 'link' your programs with other standard 'library' files (there's no point in re-inventing the wheel – if a standard screen output file exists, use it) and a compiler, which turns your raw C program (source code) into an executable machine code file (object code) that your Amiga can 'run'.

DICE is available from many PD libraries as a shareware program. That means that it can be copied and tried out freely, but if you want to carry on using it you should register with its author, which means sending you details and paying a fee (much cheaper than buying an equivalent commercial package!). In return you get the warm glow that comes from being an honest and upright citizen, plus (just as importantly) a full version of the program (the shareware version has some useful features missing).

Well you don't have to register. The version supplied with this book is the full, registered version – we negotiated a special deal with its author. We do try to think of everything.

Amiga libraries and includes

Up to a point, the C programming language is the same on all machines – Amigas, Macintoshes and PCs, for example. But only up to a point. Because although programs on all of these machines are generally constructed the same way, each machine differs in the way it handles screen displays, sound and other machine-specific things.

If all your programs ever had to do was accept text or numerical input, and display text or numbers on the screen, C programming would be easy. These things are handled in much the same way whatever machine you use and the chances are you would hardly have to change your code at all.

However, if you want to use the Amiga's Intuition interface (its standard windows-and-gadgets look) you would need to use a special 'library'. This is a file which automatically handles the Intuition interface and which can be included in your programs. The Amiga has many such libraries. The same goes for other machines, like the Macintosh and the PC. But each of these machines' libraries are unique and specific to that machine, unlike basic C code.

This means that while you can write certain basic C programs on the Amiga with just a C compiler, if you want to do anything remotely flashy, you need the full set of Amiga libraries. With the shareware version of DICE you don't get these. With the full, registered version, you do. And this is what's provided with 'Complete Amiga C'.

As well as 'libraries', you'll also come across the term 'includes'. Includes and libraries are effectively different sides of the same coin. A library is uncompiled (source) code. An include is the same code once it's compiled (object code).

The DICE disks that come with this book contain dozens of Amiga libraries. There isn't space in this book to describe all of them, which is why we've opted to demonstrate how they work with two selected examples (in chapter 15). Examining these libraries in detail is outside the scope of a book like this, but the DICE disks do contain documentation for them, and DICE's various other features.

This brings us on to another (minor) complication and a possible source of confusion. Broadly, the Amiga's operating system is in its third version. First there was v1.3, then v2 and now v3. Each version of the operating system works differently, and hence has different 'libraries'. You can get v1.3 libraries, v2 libraries and v3 libraries. The version of DICE provided with this book contains v1.3 and v2 libraries.

So what about owners of v3 machines (like the A1200, for example)? No problem! Commodore have anticipated this and been quite clever. The Amiga's operating system has been upgraded in such a way that the 'old' libraries still work. So v1.3 libraries will work fine on a v3 machine. Except, of course, that you will only be able to use features present on the original v1.3 machines. So although we have not been able to provide v3 libraries (these were only just becoming available at the time of publication), the v1.3 and v2 libraries will work on the latest machines.

Needless to say, you will not be able to use v2 libraries on your A500, since the machine will simply not have the features they use. Basically, though, we've covered pretty well every Amiga user possible (except owners of very early v1.2 machines – but there can't be too many of those about these days!).

Basic concepts

- Processors and memory: how they work together
- Programming languages
- Functions and sub-routines

In this chapter I'm going to outline some basic computing concepts. Your grasp of C and why it works the way it does will be much stronger after you've understood them. If you've already programmed in another language, or you know the basic processes underlying your Amiga's operation, then turn to chapter 2; but before doing so you might like to just glance through the contents of this chapter – it runs through the basics of programming on the Amiga, or any other machine, and it's information you need under your belt before you go on.

Your Amiga is a machine that obeys instructions given to it. It cannot act of its own volition: all it does is obey instructions. These instructions may be given by you, or by another programmer. A program is a collection of these instructions.

There are many components that go together to make up a computer, but the two most important are the processor and memory. The processor is the part of the machine that obeys (technically speaking, 'executes') instructions. It is often referred to as the computer's 'brain' because it controls all of the computer's other functions, but it is important to remember that the processor can't actually *think*, at least not in the way we understand the word.

Processors and memory: how they work together

The processor can only obey a limited range of instructions, each of which is very simple. Compared to the others, the instruction to add two numbers together is a relatively complex one. Each instruction is represented by its own unique number. The processor will only accept instructions in this numerical form: it would find the phrase 'add these two numbers together' meaningless, whereas the numerical equivalent, say '31', would have the desired effect. After receiving this instruction, the processor would of course expect a further two numbers: the two numbers that it is to add together.

Such an instruction produces a result: in this case the sum of two numbers. For this result to be useful, the processor must have some way of storing it, or 'remembering' it. The process is analogous to a human being jotting down numbers in the margin while working through a

Memory 'location'

Data is stored in RAM in individual 'addresses'. You recover or store a piece of data by specifying a memory address. Each address is a fixed size and they are numbered sequentially from 0 onwards.

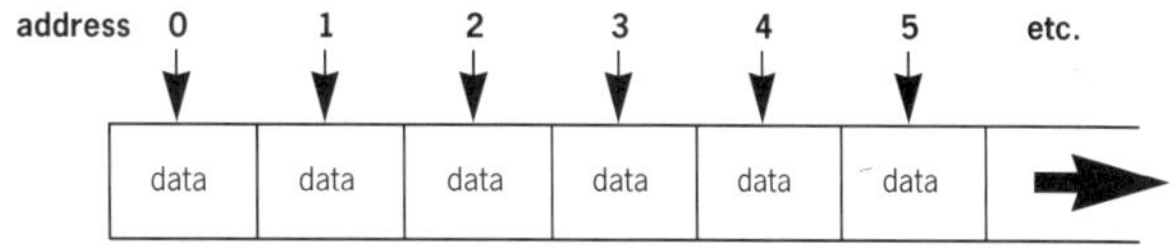

How memory (RAM) is organised

complex maths problem. Memory, the second most important component of a computer, is the place where results like these are stored, and from where, in our adding example, we retrieve the two numbers to be added.

How memory 'locations' work

Think of computer memory as a huge collection of locations, in each of which something can be stored for later recall. It's like a collection of pigeon-holes in a sorting room, with the restriction that only one letter may be held in each pigeon-hole. To make the process of storing and retrieving letters in these pigeon-holes sensible, each must have a unique tag, so that, say, a letter for Mr Hume is put in a place where Mr Hume can easily find it if he suspects a letter has been delivered to him. Pigeon-holes are usually tagged with the names of the people for whom the letters inside are addressed. If they weren't tagged in this way, our redoubtable Mr Hume would have to search through all of the pigeon-holes until he found a letter with his name on it. Computer memory is different to our pigeon-hole analogy in this respect – the stored objects themselves aren't marked with addresses – so it's essential that the places in which they are stored *are* tagged. The method of tagging is numerical: the first memory location is tagged as '0', the next as '1', the next as '2', and so on to the limit of the computer's memory.

Momory location versus contents...

Most of the processor's instructions require it to either store objects in or retrieve objects from memory. The instructions themselves are represented by numbers, and the locations in memory which they deal with are also represented by numbers. What about the actual objects held in memory? In the case of our earlier addition example, these objects are numbers too. There's a potential point of confusion here: the content of a memory location is a number, but this number is distinct from the tag or ('address'), of the location itself, also represented as a number....

Here's how it works: a typical processor instruction might be a request to retrieve an item from memory. In this case, the processor would be given the number representing the 'retrieve' instruction, followed by the number or address of the memory location it's to retrieve *from*. The content of this location, a third number, is what is actually retrieved for further processing (our addition, for example).

You're no doubt used to seeing your Amiga deal with text, sound and graphics as well as numbers. You may be surprised to learn that all of these things are actually stored in memory as numbers. As far as the processor is concerned, they *are* numbers. They're translated into other things by programs and, in the case of sound and graphics, additional hardware.

How big's a memory location?

Each memory location has a finite size, being capable of holding a number no larger than a certain value. In the case of the Amiga, this maximum value is 255 – only whole (non-fractional) numbers between 0 and 255 may be stored in a single location. Dealing with numbers within this range causes no problems. Similarly, dealing with text is no problem, because each letter of the alphabet and each punctuation mark can be denoted by its own unique number within the range.

If a programmer wants to deal with numbers larger than 255, though, or with numbers that have fractional parts, then several memory locations must be used together to hold the larger object. In the case of a graphics screen, like one created with a paint program, many thousands of memory locations are combined to store it as a single object. Nevertheless, as far as the processor is concerned each of these locations is a separate entity, holding a number in the region of 0 to 255. It has no conception of an overall object such as a graphics screen.

It's like a piano that sounds a note every time a key (analogous to a processor instruction) is struck. The piece of music in its entirety is like a program: by combining the individual notes into a whole it gives them a musical meaning.

Although each memory location can only handle whole numbers in the range 0-255, by combining four locations (which is what the processor's registers do) it's possible to arrive at much larger numbers (necessary for specifying memory addresses).

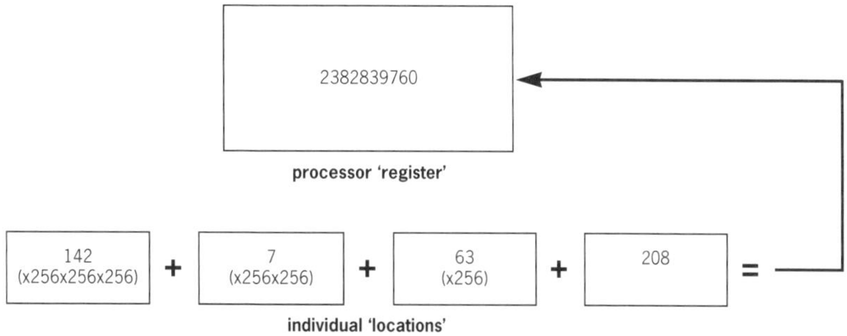

Combining four 'locations' to produce big numbers

Handling bigger numbers

Actually, in certain circumstances the processor is capable of dealing with groups of memory locations, with numbers larger than 255. It has to. Since memory locations are tagged by numbers, and it is these numbers that the processor uses to refer to the contents of the locations, if the processor were restricted to using numbers between 0 and 255 it would only be able to access a maximum of 256 locations, which would make it pretty feeble. Amigas now come with one megabyte of memory as standard – that's well over a million individual locations (each location being technically known as a 'byte'). As a solution to this addressing problem, the processor is designed to be able to deal with four locations together. Remember when you were first taught arithmetic at school, and numbers were divided up into 'units', 'tens', 'hundreds' and 'thousands'? Each of these decimal divisions is like a memory location, capable of holding a number between 0 and 9, though, instead of 0 and 255. The figure in the 'tens' location has a value ten times higher than it would if it were in the 'units' location; similarly the figure in the 'hundreds' location is a hundred times and the figure in the 'thousands' a thousand times higher than the figure in the 'units' location.

Numbers in a group of four memory locations can be handled the same way by the processor. The number in the first location has a value of 0 to 255, the number in the next location (the 'two hundred and fifty sixes', if you like) has a value 256 times greater than it would if in the first location, the number in the next location is 65536 more significant than that of the first, and the number in the final location is 256*256*256 (16777216) times more significant. If the processor were treating four consecutive locations holding the values 12, 5, 14, 7 as holding a single object, then this object would have the numerical value of 12+(5*256)+(14*256*256)+(7*256*256*256)=135202316. This final value can itself be treated as an address of another memory location. The processor may need this address for many reasons, for example to store in it the result of an addition it's just carried out.

The processor's own memory: 'registers'

The processor stores numbers in and retrieves numbers from memory, which is separate from the processor itself both physically and in principle. For the processor to do this, it must have some means of holding the numbers inside itself. For this, the processor has a small collection of its own memory locations, known as 'registers', physically built into the silicon chip. Because they're built into the processor, operations on numbers held inside these registers are carried out much more quickly than on those in ordinary memory. But because the number of registers is very small, their contents must often be passed to and from ordinary memory.

Each register is equivalent in size to four ordinary locations, so registers are ideal for holding the addresses of memory locations which the processor is to work on.

WHAT DOES IT MEAN? **RAM**

The type of memory we've discussed so far is known as Random Access Memory, or 'RAM' for short. It's called this because once you know a location's address, its contents can be retrieved immediately (or almost immediately) without having to waste time looking at any other memory locations.

WHAT DOES IT MEAN? **ROM**

The contents of RAM are erased when the computer's power is switched off, or when the computer is reset. In contrast, the contents of the second main type of memory, Read Only Memory ('ROM') are permanent. They will not be erased by a lack of power, and they cannot be changed by the processor. Nothing new can be stored in ROM: why it is useful will be explained later in this chapter.

So far I've talked about numbers being placed in memory, specifically RAM. These numbers are termed 'data'. They are the things on which the processor operates, just as numbers on a balance sheet are the things that we might add together and subtract from each other. But as I said, the processor obeys instructions, and it must be given these instructions somehow. Where are these instructions kept, and how are they sent to the processor?

Where does the processor get its instructions?

WHAT DOES IT MEAN? **Program Counter**

The instructions are also stored in memory. The processor takes an instruction from memory, does what the instruction tells it to, and then takes its next instruction from memory. One of the processor's registers, known as the Program Counter, contains the address of the location of each successive instruction. The processor uses the register like any other, retrieving the number representing an instruction from memory. Once inside the processor the instruction is carried out and the value held in the Program Counter is increased (the amount it's increased by depends on the length of the instruction previously retrieved) so that it now points to the address of the location in which the next instruction is held. This it then retrieves, and so on.

And that, basically, constitutes the life of the processor: retrieve an instruction, execute it, retrieve the next, and so on.

As you may have gathered, there is no physical distinction between data and a collection of instructions. If the Program Counter happened to hold the start address of where a graphics screen was stored, then the processor would attempt to interpret the graphics data as a sequence of program instructions. The sequence would be nonsensical, and would probably cause the computer to crash.

Now each individual processor instruction is very simple, capable of doing very little, but by combining them together great results can be achieved. The many complex applications available for the Amiga prove it. When many instructions are combined to an end, the combination is a 'program', just as a symphony is a collection of musical notes.

Storing stuff permanently

Programs, as you'll discover by working through this book, can take a lot of work to create, so you need somewhere more permanent than RAM to store them (otherwise you'd have to type them back in again every time you re-started your Amiga). That's where disks come in. For our purposes right now, there's no real difference between a floppy and a hard disk: both can store information intact, long-term. The difference between a disk and ROM is that new information can be added to a disk, and existing information can be removed or altered.

Programs, then, can be saved to disk, which can be thought of as a more permanent but slower type of memory. For a program to be run, it must first be retrieved (or 'loaded') from disk into RAM. Then, each of its instructions in turn is retrieved from RAM into the processor and executed.

But you don't just want to keep programs long-term – you'll often need to store data, too. The contents of RAM, whether they constitute a program or data such as a graphics screen, can be saved to disk. Each data 'object' is saved as a 'file', and each file has its own unique name to identify it later.

Programming languages

The collection of all the various instructions that the processor understands go to make up its 'language'. The instructions constitute its vocabulary, if you like. The language processors understand is 'machine language' – the language is the same for all computers with the same type of processor. Amigas, Atari STs and Apple Macs all share the same machine language, whereas IBM PCs and their clones, because they use markedly different processors, use a different one.

Just as in English a straightforward list of a language's vocabulary is meaningless – expecially so when you look at a list of the processor's instructions. Just as English words needed to be linked in sentences for them to make sense, processor instructions have to be linked to form programs that perform useful tasks.

Breaking down big tasks into smaller ones

Machine language programs are what is known as 'procedural', meaning that only one instruction is obeyed at a time, and when it's been carried out the next one in the sequence is started. The instructions go to make a set of 'procedures' that must be performed to carry out the program's task. The actions of instructions early in the sequence often affect the actions of later instructions.

Imagine the process of making a cup of tea. It might be broken down into the following set of 'procedures':

1 Fill the kettle with water
2 Switch the kettle on
3 Wash out the cup
4 Place a tea-bag in the cup
5 Wait for the kettle to boil
6 Pour the hot water into the cup
7 Wait for the tea to brew
8 Remove the tea-bag
9 Finally, add the milk

As you can see, each stage relies on the successful completion of the previous stage. Also, each of these stages could be further broken down into smaller sub-stages. A machine language instruction is equivalent to the smallest sub-stage imaginable.

The utter simplicity of each instruction means that very many of them must be combined to form a program that does something even as trivial as writing a message on the screen. And don't forget, all of these instructions are represented by numbers, the data they deal with is also represented by numbers, and any memory locations they use are themselves addressed by numbers.

A machine language program is nothing more than a huge list of numbers, immediately understandable to the computer but far less so to a human being. Writing one is an extremely error-prone business.

Higher-level (more understandable) languages

In order to make life easier for programmers, many other languages have been designed – C is one of them. These languages are described as being of a 'higher level', firstly because their vocabulary is closer to normal English and further removed from the 'level' of the processor, and secondly because instructions in such a language can achieve more complex and subtle results than those of machine language.

The fact remains, though, that processors understand nothing but machine language, so programs written in a high level language must first be translated before the processor can 'execute' them (i.e. follow the instructions). This translation process is dealt with by another program (itself of course consisting of machine language instructions). There are two main types of translation: interpretation and compilation.

'Interpreted' programs

Interpretation is the simpler of the two. An interpreter takes each of the statements making up a program, one at a time (a 'statement' is the high-level language equivalent of an 'instruction'). It checks the statement against its list of 'permissible' ones. If the statement isn't there the interpreter produces an error message and the program stops. If it is, then the interpreter executes a sequence of machine language instructions whose overall effect corresponds to the meaning of the statement. Then the interpreter looks at the next statement and the process repeats. As you can see the interpreter must be present whenever the program is executed, and translation occurs each time. The process of translation is part of the execution.

Also, suppose that a certain part of the program was to be executed many times, a good example being the section of a chess program that decides which move the computer is to make. If this sequence of statements was to be executed a thousand times, then each of the statements would need to be translated a thousand times during the program's execution. The translation process takes time, so the interpreter approach is clearly inefficient. The method's main advantage is its convenience. A program can be modified (as programs often need to be during their development) and then executed immediately – the effects of changes made can be seen right away. The most common interpreted language is BASIC.

'Interpreted' and 'compiled' languages

All programs written in a high-level language have to be translated into machine language before they will run on the computer. There are two ways of going about this – either translating and executing each command in turn (interpreting) or translating all the commands in one go, then executing the resulting machine language file.

Interpreted languages are easier for developing programs (changes can be tested much more quickly) but compiled programs and much more compact and run much faster.

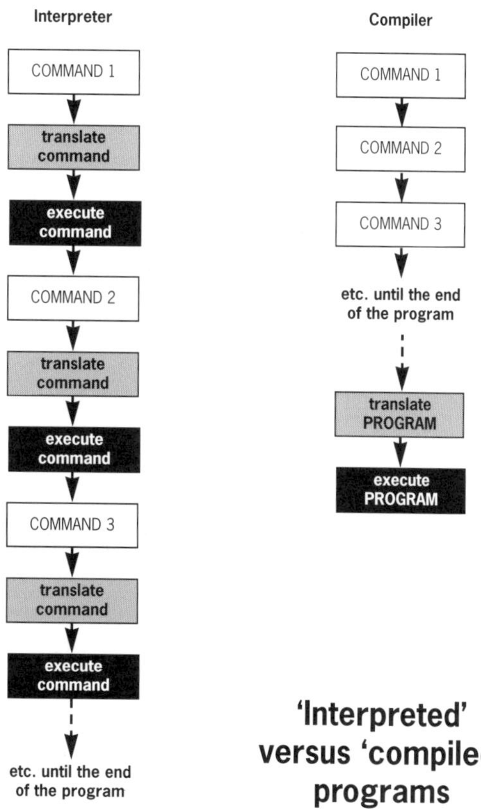

'Interpreted' versus 'compiled' programs

'Compiled' programs

With a compiler, the stages of translation and execution are entirely separate. A compiler reads in your high level program as a text file. Like an interpreter, the compiler checks each statement in the file against a list of permissible statements, and if it doesn't find the statement there it signals an error. If the statement in question *is* permissible, then the compiler creates a sequence of machine language instructions which (as with an interpreter) when executed have an effect corresponding to the statement's meaning. But the instructions are *not* executed. Instead, they become part of a file produced by the compiler. As each statement in the high-level language is in turn translated, the resulting machine language instructions are added to this file. Once the compiling process has finished, you are presented with a file ready to execute (actually, a further stage of translation is necessary, but we'll worry about that later). The new file contains nothing but machine language instructions, so it can be executed without any further intervention from the compiler – no further translation is necessary.

Because of this, compiled programs execute (run) much faster. Also, since compiled programs run independently of the compiler they tend to be smaller in size than their interpreted counterparts (interpreted programs must also contain the interpreter itself).

Compilation has its disadvantages, though. Programs of any complexity go through many versions before they are finished. Errors must be corrected, and modifications must be made to increase efficiency and usability. If you're using a compiler, each modification means your program has to be re-compiled (a time-consuming process) before your modification can be checked by re-executing the program. This requires patience...

Error correction is also harder with a compiler. A compiler, like an interpreter, can spot many errors, but many more can only be spotted by a human being. A translator can only pick up 'grammatical' errors – cases in which a statement has been mis-spelled, a non-existent statement has been used or a statement has been used in a context which makes it nonsensical.

But consider the sentence: "Eat lurid frying pans to sail the sands of time." It's grammatically correct, but complete nonsense. The programming equivalent would be translated without question by a compiler *because it's 'grammatically correct'*, each of the statements leading to a legitimate set of machine language instructions. But the effect of their combination would not be apparent until they were executed. To make matters worse, these sort of errors can often be very subtle, requiring the program to be tested many times before they're discovered. Yet these disadvantages are outweighed in the long run by the advantages. Most professional programmers use compilers.

C is a compiled programming language, and the most popular one on the Amiga.

Functions and sub-routines

Here's the secret of programming: learn how to analyse things in terms of their components. Take our earlier example about making a cup of tea. The task was broken down into several smaller, simpler instructions: wash out the cup, fill up the kettle and so on. Each of these could be broken down further: "fill up the kettle" becomes "Unplug the kettle, place it under the tap, turn the tap on, wait until the kettle is filled to a certain level, turn off the tap, plug the kettle back in." You get the idea...

Program instructions are the equivalent of these very basic instructions. It's the programmer's job to take a problem and reduce it to successively smaller parts, until each of these parts is itself a program instruction. Knowing what the program instructions do, in our case knowing C, is only the basis for good programming skills. The real skill lies in being able to reduce problems effectively. To make matters more interesting, there are usually many ways in which a problem can be broken down. In other words, you could write many different sets of instructions (i.e. programs) to carry out a particular task. Choosing the best one, or at least a *good* one, is a matter of experience.

Simply learning C will not make you a good programmer – practice and experimentation are essential. But the language does offer some help, in the form of 'functions'. Now functions are quite an advanced concept, so I won't go into their details until much later in the book, but the basic concept behind them is so fundamental its worth introducing now.

A 'function'

What is a function? A function is a thing that does something; more accurately, it is a thing that takes data, does something to it and produces data as a result. This result depends on the initial data. Back to the real world: an oven is a function which takes raw food as its data and produces cooked food as its result.

'Source' code 'object' code

Programs themselves are essentially functions; they takes data as their input and produce data as their output. A compiler is a perfect example. Its input is a program written as an ASCII text file ('source code') and its output is an executable machine language program ('object code').

The elements of a program may also be functions, whose combined effects go together to produce the program's effect. Each of these functions in turn may rely on several smaller functions. An example of a particularly fundamental function is addition, a function which takes two numbers for its input and produces as its output their sum. As you can see, 'functions' are ideal tools for reducing a problem to its components.

Unlike some more dogmatic languages, not every instruction in C is a function. The instruction to store a numerical value in memory, for example, is not a function. You could say it was taking the number as its input, but it would be stretching the definition too far to suggest that the storage of the number in memory was in itself an output. Such instructions are termed 'statements'; they do things, they produce effects, but they do not yield results in a strict sense. There'll be more on this later in the book.

Setting up your system

- Backing up your DICE disks
- Floppy disk installation
- Hard disk installation
- Final steps
- What you've got

In this chapter you'll learn how to set up your DICE compiler so that you can create C programs. You'll also learn something about the various processes involved in translating a program from C into machine language.

Hardware requirements

DICE requires a minimum of 1Mb of memory to run, and even then you are going to find yourself hampered until you get more memory. If you are running with only 1Mb, I strongly recommend you get more – it will make life so much easier.

DICE will run from floppy disk, but again you will find life so much easier if you get yourself a hard disk.

What follows is an explanation of how to install DICE on your system. You must do this before you can write any C programs. Follow the instructions carefully: once you are familiar with the environment, you can read the extensive documentation with DICE (in the doc directory) to find out how you can customise the system as you wish.

Backing up

Before you go any further, make copies of each of the four disks that come with this book. Once you have done so, put the originals away and work only with the copies. Floppy disks, alas, are not perfect: if you lose some data on a copy, you can always revert to an original; if you lose data on an original, you're stuck. You can make copies of the disks either by using the **`Diskcopy`** command from the Shell, or by using a Workbench menu option (don't use the Shell command **`Copy`**, as most of the DICE files are compacted and copy will fail to give accurate duplicates). Either way, be sure to give the copies the same names as their originals: the names will play a significant part in what follows. If you're copying from Workbench, you'll find that the text '`copy of`' appears in front of the name of each disk copied. Use the Workbench menu command **`Rename`** to remove this part of each name.

Having made back-ups of the disks, you are now ready to follow whichever procedure applies to the machine you own:

Floppy disk installation

If you are running from floppy, then you can run DICE as is. Boot from the first disk in the set. This will give you access to all the commands you need, and automatically load the DICE text editor, dme.

Most of the files on the supplied floppy disks are compressed. You can get to the uncompressed versions by using the ARCH: handler. Accesses to any files on the disk via ARCH: will mean that the files are decompressed before reading; similarly they will be compressed before they are written back to the disks, should you choose to modify them.

The actual disks are named XDCC1:, XDCC2:, XDCC3: and XDCC4:.However, you can get to them via the assignments DCC1:, DCC2:, DCC3: and DCC4. These assignments include the ARCH: handler, so accessing any files with them will result in them being decompressed first. (Assignments let you use a simple name to refer to a file and its directory path.)

Files in the c, s and l directories are not compressed, and can be directly modified (without the aid of ARCH:) if you so wish.

Important note

You must have the first dice disk (XDCC1:) in your drive before attempting to execute any of the DICE compiler commands outlined later in this chapter (`dcc` and `dme`), otherwise you will be given a "command not found" error message. AmigaDOS will not recognise the commands unless it can immediately see them on the current disk.

Workbench 1.3

Manual assignments

If you're working with a single floppy drive, you'll find that the assignments DCC2:, DCC3: and DCC4: are not made. This is because AmigaDOS 1.3 will only make assignments if the disks involved are present at the time.

After boot-up you can manually make the assignments from the Shell by typing, for example:

```
resident c1.3/assign
```

Then put XDCC2: into your drive and type:

```
assign DCC2: ARCH:XDCC2
```

Then put in XDCC3: and type:

```
assign DCC3: ARCH:XDCC3
```

Now put in XDCC4: and type:

```
assign DCC4: ARCH:XDCC4
```

Finally, replace your first DICE disk in the drive and type:

```
resident assign remove
```

The installation process is now complete. Go to 'What You've Got'.

Workbench 2 and above

With Workbench 2, all the correct assignments are made at boot-up time. You have a ready-to-run system. Go to the 'What You've Got' section.

Hard disk installation

Because you have a hard disk you have the space to store all of the DICE files in their de-compressed form. This will mean that their execution is quicker, because they do not have to be decompressed each time before they are run.

To obtain the de-compressed version of DICE, you need to copy each of the files individually via the ARCH: handler. This will automatically decompress the files before putting them on your hard disk.

If you've booted from your hard disk, rather than the DICE floppy, then you'll first need to set the ARCH: handler running with the following Shell command:

```
run <nil: >nil: xdcc1:l/fsovl-handler
```

You then need to create a directory on your hard disk in which to store the DICE files. The directory name 'dice' seems appropriate, and for the sake of argument I've created it on the partition called 'WORK':

```
makedir WORK:dice
```

All of what follows assumes you have made such a directory. If, for example, you have instead created a directory called 'compiler' on partition dh0:, then replace every occurrence of 'work:dice' in what follows with 'dh0:compiler'

You then need to copy the contents of each individual disk into this directory. Remember to use the ARCH: handler to de-compress everything before it is written to hard disk. To do this, type the following commands:

```
copy ARCH:XDCC1 work:dice ALL CLONE
copy ARCH:XDCC2 work:dice ALL CLONE
copy ARCH:XDCC3 work:dice ALL CLONE
copy ARCH:XDCC4 work:dice ALL CLONE
```

Having done this, you'll have copied a few files that you don't need. These are necessary only for those booting DICE from floppies, so you can delete them with the following command:

```
delete work:dice/(l1.3|l2.0|c|libs1.3|libs2.0) all
```

There are a number of DICE files stored within archives. With the luxury of a hard disk, you can afford to de-archive them with the following commands:

```
cd work:dice
bin/dzrestore libsrc.bak
bin/dzrestore dlib.orig.bak
cd include
work:dice/bin/dzrestore amiga13.bak
```

```
work:dice/bin/dzrestore amiga20.bak
work:dice/bin/dzrestore amiga30.bak
```

Workbench 1.3

You will need to copy the contents of DICE's libs: directory to that of your hard disk. Do so with the following Shell command:

```
copy XDCC1:libs/#? libs:
```

which assumes that you have booted from your hard disk.

You will need to modify your startup-sequence so that a script called startup-dice is also executed when the Amiga boots. This script makes the necessary assignments for DICE usage. Add the following line to your startup-sequence file, just before the loadwb line:

```
execute work:dice/s/startup-dice work:dice
```

You can add the line by using the Shell-based editor Ed, which is invoked with the following line:

```
ed s:startup-sequence
```

Typing [Esc-X] will save your changes. Consult your manual for more information on using Ed.

Minor bug

There is a small bug in the file startup-dice which also must be corrected if you are using Workbench 1.3. Open the file up with an editor such as Ed, for which you can use the command:

```
ed work:dice/s/startup-dice
```

and enter the following line just before the one that reads **resident >nil: force**:

```
failat 21
```

Now save the changes with [Esc-X]. Go to the 'Final Steps' section.

Workbench 2 and above

Enter the following line into your user-startup file, contained in the s: directory of your hard disk:

```
execute work:dice/s/startup-dice work:dice
```

You can do this by editing the file with the Shell command:

```
ed s:user-startup
```

and pressing [Esc-X] to save your changes.

Final steps

Whether you're using Workbench 1.3 or 2.0 and above, there's one more thing to do if you're using a hard disk. There's a file, called .edrc, that lives in DICE's s directory. This is an initialisation file for the DICE editor, dme. Without it, dme won't function properly. You therefore need to copy it into the s directory of your system disk with the following Shell command:

```
copy work:dice/s/.edrc s:
```

What you've got (and how to use it)

DICE isn't just a C compiler, but a complete development system. With it you can create and run just about any program for the Amiga. The three main components of the system (there are more: consult DICE's on-disk documentation for more details) are the editor, the compiler and the linker:

The editor

A text editor is supplied with DICE. All C programs are written initially as ASCII text files. If you have an editor which you like and which you are used to working with, then by all means use this in preference to the one supplied with DICE; but be sure that you save your files out in standard ASCII format. This is normally the default option with editors, but some word processors may be different.

You can call up the DICE editor with the following command, typed from the Shell:

```
dme <filename>
```

where <filename> is the name of the file you wish to edit. If no such file exists, then dme will create a new one. It's standard practice to put a '.c' at the end of C source code files.

You'll find all the usual editing options in dme. Hitting function key F9 will save your work, while key F10 will save and quit from the editor. If you're using more than 1Mb of memory, you'll find it more convenient to run the editor in conjunction with the compiler (the compiler will reveal an awful lot of errors that will require you to change the source file). In this case, you can multi-task dme by running it from the Shell with the command:

```
run dme <filename>
```

The compiler and linker

Once you've created your source code file with an editor, you'll want to translate it into machine code. This is primarily the responsibility of the compiler - the main component of DICE – but, to a lesser extent, the linker too.

Typically, C programs rely on pre-written code. Even the most trivial program, such as the first in the next chapter, will rely on some pre-written routines. Printing text to the screen, for example, is actually a very complex task, and one with which, thanks to somebody else's endeavours, we won't have to concern ourselves with. We simply need to make use of the already-existing code.

The linker and libraries

The linker is the program that lets us do this. The compiler translates a program into machine language, producing an intermediate file known as an 'object' file (usually given the prefix '.o' when saved). The linker joins an object file with any pre-written code that the file may require to run. Such commonly used pre-written code is stored in 'library files'. Two types exist: library files that supply all the functions common to C on any platform; and library files specific to the platform – those that, on the Amiga, enable you to use the machine's special features. Happily, you don't as a rule have to worry about the linking stage with DICE: it's all taken care of. To compile a program with DICE, simply type:

```
dcc <filename>
```

from the Shell. DICE will then go off and compile and link your program, producing an executable (i.e. a runable program) with the same name minus the customary '.c' at the end. For instance:

```
dcc hello.c
```

would produce the output file:

```
hello
```

More often than not, you'll end up with a list of errors instead, which is why it's nice to be able to multitask dme so you can go straight back to your source code and attempt to eliminate their causes.

You can make DICE produce an executable file with a different name by using the -o option. The text following -o is the name by which you want the executable to be called. The following:

```
dcc hello.c -o fred
```

would cause the source code to be compiled into an executable called `fred`. You would then run `fred` simply be typing:

```
fred
```

The same applies for any executable, but note that you must be in the directory that contains the executable, or its directory must be within the path that AmigaDOS searches when attempting to execute commands.

If you want to just compile a file, and not link it into an executable, then you can do so by adding the -c option to the command line:

```
dcc -c fred.c
```

would produce an object file called 'fred.o'. This will come in useful when you begin to compile your own libraries. You won't actually need to link them until you've written a program that calls functions that they contain. If you have, you can compile your program and link it with a library as follows:

```
dcc program.c fred.o -o program
```

which will compile program, link it with the library **fred**, and produce the executable file program.

You'll find that DICE's linker is largely transparent: unless you need to link programs in with your own libraries, you won't have to be aware of its existence. You'll even find that those programs in this book that call on Commodore's pre-written libraries will be compiled and linked without problem by the **dcc** command.

MAKE A NOTE!

Floating point maths

The one exception comes about with floating point maths. Floating point is the means by which C deals with non-whole numbers, those that contain fractional parts. Because such numbers are stored and dealt with in a special way by C compilers, and because they are largely unused in most practical applications, DICE treats them as a special case. If any of your programs, and that includes the examples in this book that include variables of type **float** or **double**, make use of floating point numbers, then you must specifically link your program with a maths library when compiling and linking. You can get DICE to do this by including the -lm option. If program fred.c made use of floating point numbers, and you wanted to compile it into a program called vincent, then you would type:

```
dcc fred.c -lm -o vincent
```

You now should be able to use DICE to create your own programs. All of the examples in this book can be compiled with the information given. If you want to know more about how DICE works, or the options it offers, consult the text files in the doc directory.

Basic C programming

- Analysing a simple program
- Numbers and variables
- Variable types
- Expressions, operators and operands
- Handling user input
- Mixing variable types

All of what's gone so far may have given you the impression that programming is complicated. In fact, it's fairly straightforward, as you'll discover once you get those basic concepts under your belt. And the best way to do that is to start programming.

Analysing a simple program

The first thing to attempt is a program to print a message to the screen. There's hardly any problem-solving to be done at all: we already know that there's a C library holding a function to do the printing for us, so all we need to do is make use of that function. Everything else is just the basic framework which must surround all programs.

Run your editor and enter into it the following lines of code:

```
#include <stdio.h>

/* program to print a message to the screen */
void main()
{
    printf("Hello from planet C\n");
}
```

Now save the text file, compile it and run it (you'll find instructions for using DICE to do this in chapter two).

You should see the text below printed on your screen:

```
Hello from planet C
```

I'll go through the program line by line to explain what's going on. The first line tells the compiler that we want to use some code that's already been written, collected in what is called a 'header file'. It tells the compiler to include this code as part of our own program. The name of the file to be included is held within the angled brackets. **Stdio.h** (for standard input and output) is a file provided with all C compilers, containing a set of functions to perform simple printing operations, retrieve entries from the keyboard and the like. We need to include it because it contains the function to print information to the screen.

The next line has been left blank. It isn't necessary, but has been put there to aid clarity. So far is C is concerned, all white space is the same. It does not distinguish between a space character, a tab or a return character. They are all used merely as separators. It's possible, though confusing to read the result, to write C programs as a single line with only single spaces separating the statements.

Use comments in your code

The next line is a comment. It's a message from the programmer to him or herself, and to any other programmers who may look at the code. It's a signpost that explains what's going on. Using comments in your programs is a good idea: you'll be surprised how confusing your own programs can appear when you come to look at them some time after you first wrote them. Comments help you to unravel the knots. In C, the two characters `/*` together denote the beginning of a comment, and the characters `*/` denote its end. Anything between them is ignored by the compiler, and is not translated into machine code. In other words, comments don't waste space and don't detract from the efficiency of your programs. On the other hand, they do improve the efficiency with which you can root out program errors and make changes.

After the comment comes a function definition. The function is called **`main`**; every C program has a function with this name. This is the function that gets used when the program is executed. The reason such a function needs defining will become apparent if you consider that many more function definitions may be contained in a program; the computer must be told which to execute first, which is the 'top level' or 'main' function. The word **`void`** before the function's name indicates that the function does not produce a result. It has an effect – that of printing text to the screen – but no result is produced in the strict sense. The parentheses after the function name let the compiler know that it is a function that is being defined, and the fact that there is nothing between them indicates that the function does not require any input.

The opening and closing curly brace are used to bound the contents of the function. Everything between them, in this case just one statement, is defined as the block that comprises the function. They are just part of the grammatical structure that C expects, in much the same way as English requires reported speech to be enclosed by inverted commas.

Finally, we get to the statement that actually *does* something. What it does is to make use of (or "call" in technical parlance) a function named **Printf**. **Printf** is a pre-written function that writes information to the screen. Its definition is provided by the inclusion of the **stdio.h** header file. The "**f**" in its name stands for "formatted"; **printf** is a clever little function that can, if used properly, write all sorts of information to the screen in all sorts of different formats.

In this case our use for **printf** is straightforward. The information enclosed in the parenthesis is the input for the function (known as the function's "parameter"), for our purposes a segment of text. Enclosing items within quotation marks ensures the compiler treats them as text.

The two characters at the end of the text – **\n** – are instructions that tell printf to print a newline character, in other words to skip to the next line, at the end of its printing. It's one of the elementary formatting instructions that **printf** obeys. You'll soon learn how useful it is to be able to do this.

When **printf** is called it takes the text as its input and has the effect of writing this text to the screen. It also, separately, comes up with a numerical result, which can be used by a program to determine whether or not the function was successful. This result is ignored by our program, which stops once **printf** has done its work.

The final thing of note is the semi-colon at the end of the **printf** line. It's another one of those grammatical aspects of C – it marks the end of a statement for the compiler, letting it know that what follows is either another statement or, as in this particular case, the end of a block, as denoted by a closing curly brace. And the closing of that curly brace marks the end of your first program. Not a very complex one, granted, but the first step towards great things.

Numbers

One of the more important things that C can do is deal with numbers. Even the most un-numerical of applications will rely heavily on numbers. Although these numbers and their manipulation (usually pretty basic in mathematical terms, don't worry) may be hidden from the program user's view, you as the program's creator must deal with them. Here's how.

Integer

C divides numbers up into several different types, the most common of which is a type called "integer". An integer is a whole number, positive or negative in value. There's a limit to its size, but we'll go into more detail about that later. All the usual mathematical operations can be performed on integers, but if you divide one integer by another you'll end up with an integer result, a whole number. The "remainder" will be forgotten. Dividing three by two will yield a result of one.

Storing numbers – variables

Variable

As I said in chapter one, for numbers to be of any use there must be a means of storing them. For this purpose, and for the purposes of storing other things too, C supplies things called variables. You can think of a variable as the memory location, or more accurately the collection of memory locations, in which the number is held. But rather than using a numerical address, the programmer can access the number stored by means of the variable name, which can be an intelligible word decided on by the programmer.

Variables are akin to the Xs and Ys of school-day algebra. Numbers may be stored in them and altered. In other words, their contents "vary" throughout the time the program is executing (running).

Why is it necessary to refer to numbers via variables rather than as numbers themselves? Imagine you were writing a spreadsheet program, and that you needed to total up all the numbers in a column. You could define a variable called `total`, and set its value to zero. Then you could add the number in the first column to it. Then the second number would be added, and the third, and so on. After all the additions were complete, the value held in the variable `total` would contain the sum of the column. It would be impossible to write a program to do this if it only referred to numerical values, since these values would be unalterable once the program was running. Nor could any of the numbers in the column be written into the program simply as numbers. If they were, then the spreadsheet would contain exactly the same numbers every time it was run. Their values must be decided by the user when the program is running, in other words they too must be stored as variables, with their values either typed in by the user or loaded in from a file on disk.

To help clarify the above, let's take a look at a simplified program to do the spreadsheet totalling:

```
#include <stdio.h>

/* program to total four numbers */
void main()
{
    /* first declare variables */
    int first, second, third, fourth, total;

    /* set the total value to zero */
    total=0;
    /* now assign arbitrary values to the other variables. In a real-
world example these values would be entered by the user running the
program */
    first=23;
    second=-5;
    third=42;
    fourth=1;
    /* now perform the addition to find the total */
    total=total+first;
    total=total+second;
    total=total+third;
    total=total+fourth;
    printf("The total is ");
    printf("%d\n",total);
}
```

The program begins in the same way as the last, by calling on the services of **stdio.h** (because we'll be needing the **printf** function again) and by defining the function **main**. Once again, **main** returns no result (although it has the effect of printing something to the screen) and requires no inputs, so the word **void** appears before it and the parenthesis after it (which let C know that it is a function) are empty.

Declaring variables & variable 'types'

After the curly brace comes the line which 'declares' our variables. To declare a variable means to let the compiler know what its name is, and what type it is. In C, all variables must be declared before use. They are usually declared at the beginning of a function, before any of its real "meat".

MAKE A NOTE!

Variable names

We are using integers exclusively, represented by the C word **int**, so this word precedes the names of the variables we want to use. The names of variables can be anything you decide, according to certain restrictions. The first character in the variable's name must be a letter, either upper or lowercase (the two are seen as different, so the names **fred** and **FRED** refer to different variables). The following characters be made up of letters, numbers or underscore characters "_". It's conventional to use predominantly lower case letters for variable names. You cannot use words that represent C instructions.

In the above example, all of the integers were declared in one line, with commas separating them. Instead the declaration could have been written as many lines, like so:

CODE SEGMENT

```
int first;
int second;
int third;
int fourth;
int total;
```

The two styles can be mixed and matched as you see fit, but note that you can only declare several variables with a single type specifier (**int**, in our case) if they are all of the same type.

The next line after the comment is used to set **total**'s value to 0. In C, the equals sign means "set whatever is to the left of the equals sign to the value of whatever is to the right".

The next few lines assign arbitrary values to the other variables in much the same way. The assignment to the variable called second makes use of the - sign; as you might expect this means that the value stored in the variable is a negative one, in this case **-5**. As it says in the preceding comment, for the program to be of any practical use these values would need to be entered by the user while the program was running. Note how the comment can be split across more than one line without ill effect.

Expressions

The next line is where the real work begins. Again, it contains an equals sign, so an assignment is being made to the variable on the left, i.e. **total**. The value being assigned is the result of an "expression".

An expression is just like a sum in maths; it relies on "operands" and "operators". In our example the operands (that is to say, the things to be operated on) are variables, or more correctly the numbers held in the variables, and the operator is the plus sign, representing addition. C has many such operators, including ones to carry out all the basic mathematical tasks.

The result of the expression is gained by applying the operator or operators to the objects supplied. We are adding the values held in **total** and **first** together (0 and 23 respectively) and getting the result 23, which is stored in **total**, erasing the old value of 0. Notice how if a variable is being assigned the result of an expression, and that expression itself contains the variable, then the variable's old value is used in computing the expression, and the variable's value is not changed until the expression has been fully evaluated.

The following three lines add each of the next variables in turn to the value held in **total**. When they have all been added, **total** holds the sum of all of them, the value 61.

An expression can contain more than one operator, and more than two operands. All of the above additions could have been compacted into the following line with the same effect:

```
total=total+first+second+third+fourth;
```

CODE SEGMENT

The final two lines are there to print out the result. The first one prints a text message, as in our first example. The second is more interesting.

Passing parameters

For a start, two "parameters", or values to be given to the function, are included between the parentheses. **Printf** is an exception among C functions in that it can accept a variable number of parameters. The first parameter is a piece of text, the last two characters of which mean, as you know, print a newline at the end. The first two characters inform **printf** that it is to expect a second parameter, and that it is to treat it as an integer.

Different letters after the percentage sign are used for different variable types. The two print statements could have been combined into a single one as follows:

```
printf ("The total is %d\n", total);
```

As you can see the "**%d**" formatting command tells **printf** whereabouts within the printed text to include the value of the integer. If you changed the line to:

```
printf ("You have %d in total",total);
```

The output produced would be:

```
You have 61 in total
```

The "**%d**" need not appear at the end of the segment of text to be printed.

Type in the above program, compile it and get it running. Once you have done so, try experimenting with the **printf** statement, splitting it across more than one line, varying the position in which **total** is included in the message, and printing other variables too.

Another thing to experiment with is different types of expressions. As well as additions, you can perform subtractions with the - operator, multiplications with * and divisions with /. Try them and see the results.

Operator 'precedence'

Modulus

If you try mixing several different operators on the same line, you might notice some odd results. For one thing, there is the consequence of integer division as mentioned earlier, meaning that the expression **third/first** (i.e. 42/23) would give the result 1, rather than the expected 1.826. To compensate for this, C provides an operator called the "modulus", that will find the remainder. It is written as a percentage sign, and used just like the operators already discussed. For example, the expression **42%23** would give the result 19, the remainder of 42 divided by 23.

That's division taken care of, but there some more anomalies waiting to be uncovered. What result would you expect from calculating the expression **23-1+42**? There are two possible ways to go about this: you could subtract 1 from 23, giving 22, and then add 42 to arrive at the result of 64; or you could add 1 to 42, giving 43, and then subtract this from 23 to arrive at the result of -20. To resolve this apparent ambiguity C has the rule that expressions with multiple operators are evaluated left to right, so the correct answer in this case would be 64.

Using parentheses

You can force a different order of evaluation using parenthesis. If the above expression were re-written as **23-(1+42)**, the right answer would be -20. Any operations inside parentheses are carried out before the others. If there is more than one set of "nested" parentheses – i.e. one set enclosed within another, as in the example **23-(1+(42-7))** – then the expression within the "deepest" set of parentheses, the one most enclosed, is evaluated first.

Here's another tricky one: **23+1*42**. Is the answer to this found by adding 1 to 23 and multiplying the total by 42, or by multiplying 42 by 1 and adding the result to 23? In fact, the latter is the correct method. Multiplication, division and modulus are said to have a higher "precedence" than addition and subtraction. This simply means that sub-expressions involving them are evaluated first. Once the question of precedence has been dealt with, then the simple left to right rule is followed. So 1+42*23-5 gives 962.

As before, parentheses can be used to change the order of precedence. As a rule, it's a good idea to use them in complex expressions, that way you can be sure that C is evaluating your expressions in the order you want.

Real numbers and user interaction

There are two modifications that could be made to the previous example which would greatly improve its usefulness. One would be to make it able to handle real numbers, the kind with decimal points and non-whole values; another would be to let a user enter values to be totalled, rather than the program totalling the same four numbers every time it's run.

Floating point variables

The first modification is straightforward. Happily, C provides a variable type, distinct from `int`, which can hold non-whole values. It is signified by the keyword `float` before the variable's name in the declaration. `Float` is short for "floating point", which is a reference to the way such numbers are stored inside the computer's memory. The specifics of this don't concern us; suffice to say that `float`s can contain a whole part, a decimal point, and a fractional part. If we wanted to use `float`s instead of `int`s, the declaring line in our totalling example could be written as follows:

```
float first, second, third, fourth, total;
```

One thing to note is that if a number is assigned to a `float`, then it should include a decimal point within it, even if it is zero or a whole number. So the initial assignment for `total` becomes:

```
total=0.0
```

This is to help distinguish between floating point variables and integer ones. DICE won't complain if you assign a `0` to a `float`, but it's better to stick to the convention of assigning a `0.0`.

A natural result of using `float`s rather than `int`s is that divisions yield the correct answers. There is a limit to the accuracy of variables, though, so a certain amount of rounding takes place, but `float`s are accurate to a

Modulus operator and floats

sufficient number of decimal places to make this rounding inconsequential in most circumstances. Using the modulus operator on floats will result in an error, since a non-integer division does not produce a remainder.

To get some input from the user we use another function from `stdio.h`, a close cousin of `printf` called `scanf`. `Scanf` essentially performs the reverse of `printf`: instead of printing the program's output, it takes the program's input. Like `printf`, there are many subtly different ways in which `scanf` can be used. Some of them are quite complex, so we won't go into them at the moment.

We want to use `scanf` to get a user-entered value for subsequent storage in a variable. To do this we must supply `scanf` with two parameters: the first is a format command, telling it to treat the input as a certain type, analogous to the "`%d`" telling `printf` to treat a variable as an integer; the second is the variable in which the result is to be stored.

Variables and functions

The format command we will be using is "`%f`", which tells `scanf` that it is dealing with a `float` variable. "`%f`" must also be used with `printf` when we come to print out a `float`. The second parameter, the variable in which the input is to be stored, must have a "`&`" character before its name. There's no space for a full explanation here, but for now suffice to say that ordinarily when a variable is given to a function as a parameter, only the value held by the variable is given, not the variable itself. What this means is that the function may modify this value without affecting the variable – it is only modifying a copy of the variable which is private to itself. For the purposes of `scanf` this is no good – we want the variable itself to be modified. By prefixing its name with "`&`" we let the function know where exactly in memory the variable is stored, meaning that the function can directly alter the number held in memory and thus the value held in the variable. `Scanf` can store its result. Don't worry if you don't really follow this; you'll understand it better once we've dealt with several other, related concepts. For now all you need to know is that integer and floating point variables must be prefixed by "`&`" when they are used as parameters for `scanf`. The line to get a user-entered number into the `float` variable called `first` looks as follows:

```
scanf("%f",&first);
```

Like **printf**, **scanf** also produces a numerical value, independent of the one assigned to the variable called **first**. This value is the number of items that were input. It could be assigned to an integer variable, possibly to help with error-checking, as follows:

```
was_an_error=scanf("%f",&first);
```

but for now we'll ignore it.

The modified spreadsheet is shown below. Type it in and try it.

```
#include <stdio.h>

/* program to total four non-integer numbers */
void main()
{
    /* first declare variables */
    float first, second, third, fourth, total;

    /* set the total value to zero */
    total=0.0;
    /* Now get the numbers to be added from the user */
    printf("Enter the numbers to be added\n");
    printf("Enter the first number ");
    scanf("%f",&first);
    printf("\nEnter the second ");
    scanf("%f",&second);
    printf("\nEnter the third ");
    scanf("%f",&third);
    printf("\nAnd the fourth ");
    scanf("%f",&fourth);

    /* now perform the addition to find the total */
    total=total+first+second+third+fourth;
    printf("\nThe total is %f\n",total);
}
```

To compile this successfully you'll need to include the maths library at the linking stage – it's needed by both **printf** and **scanf** to handle **float**s successfully. If you're compiling with DICE, and have named the file **spread2**, then using the following line will do the trick:

```
dcc spread2.c -lm -o spread2
```

Notice how I've used the "**\n**" formatting command in the program's **printf**s to keep the screen from getting too cluttered when the program is running. Notice also the use of the "**%f**" command in the final **printf** to let the function know it is dealing with a **float** variable.

Feel free to modify the program as you see fit. In particular, try altering the expression to include multiplication and division. The more you experiment, the more you learn.

Mixing variable types

You may be wondering what happens if both **int** and **float** variables are used in the same expression. In general, **int**s are "promoted" to the accuracy of **float**s, so that in an expression involving both, the integer value is treated as a **float** with zero after the decimal point. For example, the result of the expression **32.3+5** is 37.3, not 37. Similarly, if an integer value is assigned to a **float** variable, then it is first converted into a floating point value.

If a floating point value, which may be the result of an expression mixing **int**s and **float**s, is assigned to an integer variable, then the fractional part of the value is lost.

Decision-making

- Reducing statements to 'true' or 'false'
- 'Switching' statements
- 'If' statements & 'logical expressions'
- Relational operators
- Loops
- 'Goto' statements and 'labels'
- 'Do while…' and 'while…'
- Logical operators (AND, OR, NOT)

If there is one thing about computers that makes them more than glorified adding machines, and one thing that leads to the popular misconception that they can think, it is their ability to make decisions. This ability in no way implies that computers have free will, but is nevertheless so important, so fundamental, that all but the most basic programs rely on it.

So far we've dealt with programs that follow a single course of action, where each statement within a program is executed in sequence. Decision-making involves us in providing more than one possible course of action. Which of these two courses is taken depends on whether or not a set of circumstances, as defined by the programmer, have been met. Think of a requester that asks a user whether or not the program it belongs to should continue, a good example being a simplified "`are you sure? (1 for yes, 2 for no)`" requester that appears before a disk is formatted. If the user enters a 1, then one course of action, that of the program going on to format a disk, occurs; if the user enters a 2, then another course is taken, that of the program stopping; if the user enters anything else, then the question is asked again.

The circumstance on which the decision depends is the user's input. This would be taken from the keyboard, perhaps using the **`scanf`** function introduced in the last chapter, and stored in a variable. The decision is then made by looking at the contents of this variable, and seeing if they are the same as any of the expected responses.

In fact, all computer decision-making comes down to the examination of variables, and there is only a small number of ways in which these examinations can be done. Before we look at these, though, let's talk about truth....

True or false?

A statement can be either true or false; the computer has no conception of things being *partially* true. For the example above, we could make the statement, "`The user entered a 1.`" It may be true, but if the user entered something else, then it is obviously false. Decision-making involves asking the computer whether or not a particular thing is true. We might, in English, write the decision-making part of the program as,

A program can be designed to follow more than one course of action depending on the user's input. In this case, if the user doesn't want to format the disk, the program simply skips that step.

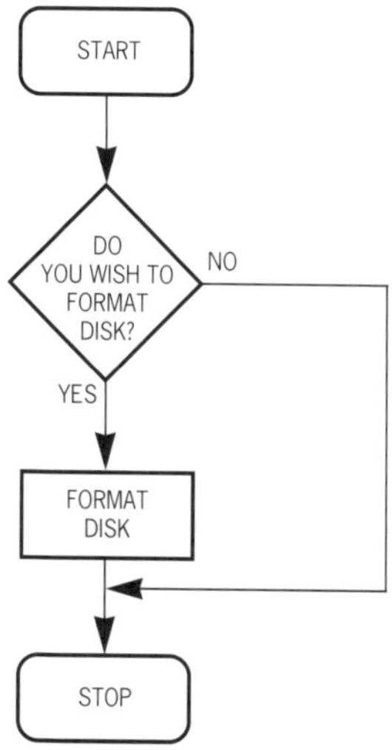

Simple 'Yes/No' decision-making program design

"**`Did the user enter 1? If so, format the disk.`**"

What we would actually do is look at the variable – let's assume it's called **`reply`** – in which the user's input was stored. We would compare the contents of the variable with the number `1`, which is a "constant expression" – its value, unlike that of the variable, never changes. We would test to see if the contents of the variable and `1` are one and the same thing, to see if they are equal. The test for equality is the simplest of the possible examinations performable on variables.

Imagine a simple calculator program. It asks the user to enter two numbers, say floating point numbers, and then asks what operation it is to perform on them: addition, subtraction, multiplication or division. For simplicity's sake, let's make the last input a number, too. We'll use a simple menu system, using '`1`' for addition, '`2`' for subtraction, and so on. (See diagram opposite.)

The first part of the program is executed no matter what. It gets two numbers from the user. The second part asks the user for a third number, and then, depending on what that third number is, one of four actions is taken. Finally, the result is printed out to the screen. This last part, like the first, is executed no matter what the user enters. Here's the program:

```
#include <stdio.h>

/* simple calculator */
void main()
{
    /* declare the variables */
    float first, second, result;
    int reply;

    /* get the user to enter the numbers */
    printf(“Enter the two numbers to be operated on \n”);
    scanf(“%f”,&first);
    scanf(“%f”,&second);
    /* print up the menu and get user’s choice */
    printf(“Which operation do you require?\n”);
    printf(“1 - addition\n2 - subtraction\n3 - multiplication\n4 ¬
- division\n”);
    scanf(“%d”,&reply);

    /* now to make the decision */
    switch (reply) {
        case 1: result=first+second;
            break;
        case 2: result=first-second;
            break;
        case 3: result=first*second;
            break;
        case 4: result=first/second;
            break;
        default:
            break;
    }
    printf(“\nThe result is %f\n”,result);
}
```

Everything up to the line which begins with **switch** should be familiar now, but the decision-making part introduces new elements.

Not all decisions have to be of the simple 'YES/NO' variety.

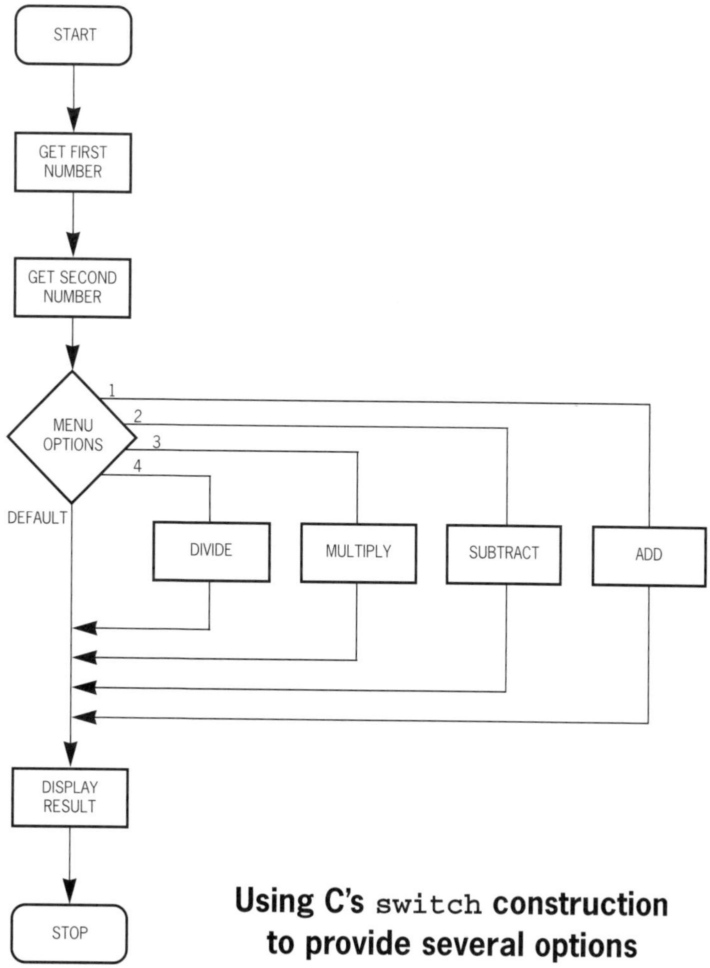

Using C's `switch` construction to provide several options

The **`switch`** statement means "switch execution to one of the following groups of statements, depending on the result of the expression inside the parentheses." The expression in this case is simply the variable **`reply`**, but it could be more complex. The body of the **`switch`** statement is in curly braces – this means the body constitutes a statement block.

Just in case

Each of the lines beginning with the word "**case**" also represents an expression. If the expression held in the parentheses after the **switch** statement is equal to the expression following **case** (in this "case", ahem, one of four numbers or the word "**default**"), then the statements following **case**'s colon are executed. In our example, the first **case** statement is asking whether or not the variable **reply** holds the value `1`. If it does, then the sum of the variables **first** and **second** is stored in the variable **result**, by a statement that ought to be familiar – **result=first+second**. It is followed by a semi-colon, as are all statements that aren't followed by a block enclosed in curly braces.

Break

The next statement – **break** – is an interesting one. It tells the computer to "break out of" the **switch** statement, to ignore all other statements in the block, and continue execution at the next statement not associated with the **switch** statement, in this instance the **printf** that outputs the result of the calculation.

The reason for the **break** is that otherwise execution would continue at the next available statement, which is a check to see whether or not **result** holds the number `2`. If the addition statement has been executed we already know that **result** holds the number `1` and we've done everything we want to do that depends on the fact, and that there's therefore no need to perform any further checking, and it's time to get on with the rest of the program.

Default

For the same reason, the **break** statement follows the statements to be performed after each of the checks for the other possibilities (`2`, `3`, `4` and the mysterious "`default`"). The last one – `default` – is used to catch any unexpected result. If, in our example, the user had entered anything other than `1`, `2`, `3` or `4`, then execution would end up here. You could put a statement that prints out an error message here, something like, "`You have not entered a valid option.`" Try it.

As it is though, there is no statement following **default:**, other than **break**. It's still important to put this segment in, though. Although a **break** after **default:** isn't necessary, it's a good idea to include it. Apart from its inclusion being a convention, it's a good guarantee against your introducing a bug should you decided in the future to add another case to the end of your **switch** statement, e.g. an option 5 to find percentages in the above program. (Otherwise your program would find a percentage whether its user entered 5, 6, 7 or any other invalid option.)

Switch statement

The **switch** statement provides a good way of performing one of several actions, depending on the contents of a variable. A common use for it, as above, is in responding to a user's menu selection. There are many more uses for it, however, as you'll discover. An important point to remember is that more than one statement can come between a particular case and the next, so it offers a great deal of flexibility.

ifs but no buts

Sometimes, though, you may want to make simpler decisions, with fewer possible outcomes, or decisions that rely on a variable holding something other than integer numbers (for that is all **switch** can decide between). In these situations it's more sensible to use C's **if** statement.

With **if**, you can ask whether something is true, and if it is, then do something. If it isn't true, then the statement, or series of statements enclosed in curly braces, that comprise the "do something" bit are ignored. Here's a quick example:

```
#include <stdio.h>

/* Quick demo of if */
void main()
{
    int reply;
    printf("Enter the code number\n");
    scanf("%d",&reply);
    if (reply==999)
        printf("Correct\n");
}
```

OK, it doesn't do very much, but I've kept it simple to illustrate the point. The bit inside **if**'s parentheses is a "logical expression". If it is true, then the statement immediately following is executed. If not, it's ignored and, in this example, the program finishes.

The expression here is a comparison between two smaller expressions (the contents of the variable **`reply`** and the number `999`). The program is testing to see whether or not they are equal.

In C, the test for equality is done using two equals signs (==) together, with an expression on either side. If the results of the two expressions are the same, then the test is said to be true, otherwise false. For example, **`2==3`** and **`7.9==7`** are false, while **`1==1`** and, if the variable **`reply`** holds the number `1`, **`reply==1`** are true. Two equals signs together are used because one on its own, as you should remember, is used to store the result of an expression (which may be a simple expression, such as a number) in a variable. Confusing = and == is one of the most common mistakes made by C programmers.

The comparison as a whole, made up as it is of two expressions and the test for equality (known as a "relational operator", since it examines the relationship between two expressions), can also be viewed as an expression. Unlike other expressions, which can have a whole range of values, this kind of expression can have only one of two logical values: truth and falsity. Falsity is represented by the number `0`, any other number is equivalent to truth. This means that you could have an **`if`** test without using a relational operator. In other words, you could substitute a simple expression for a logical one involving a relational operator.

It would come in handy for a program dividing two integers. As you may know, there's no sensible result gained from dividing any number by zero. The answer tends towards infinity, and always generates a computer error. So your program would need to check to make sure the divisor was something other than zero. You could write it like this:

```
#include <stdio.h>

/* simple division program */
void main()
{
```

```
    /* declare variables */
    int dividend, divisor, result;

    /* get their values from user */
    printf(“Enter the two numbers to be divided\n”);
    scanf(“%d”,&dividend);
    scanf(“%d”,&divisor);

    /* test to see if divisor is not zero */

    if (divisor) {
    result=dividend/divisor;
    printf(“The answer is %d\n”,result);
    }
}
```

You could, if you liked, streamline this a bit as follows:

```
#include <stdio.h>

/* simple division program */
void main()
{
    /* declare variables */
    int dividend, divisor;

    /* get their values from user */
    printf(“Enter the two numbers to be divided\n”);
    scanf(“%d”,&dividend);
    scanf(“%d”,&divisor);

    /* test to see if divisor is not zero */

    if (divisor)
    printf(“The answer is %d\n”,dividend/divisor);
}
```

It needs one less variable, and loses a line of code. **`Printf`** only requires a value to be passed to it, not necessarily a variable. So here we've given it the value found by evaluating an expression. Notice also how the curly braces surrounding the consequences of the **`if`** statement can be dropped if the consequence is only made up of a single statement.

Relational operators

Different kinds of logical expressions can be formed by using different types of relational operators. As well as testing to see whether two things are equal, you can test to see if one is larger than the other, or if one is smaller than the other.

The symbols used for these are as follows:

`>` Pronounced "greater than", which tests to see if the expression on the left is numerically bigger than the one on the right

`>=` ("greater than or equal to") Tests to see if the expression on the left is at least equal to, if not bigger than, the one on the right

`<` ("less than") tests to see whether the expression on the left is smaller than that on the right

`<=` ("less than or equal to") tests to see whether the left-hand expression is smaller than or at most equal to that on the right.

You already know about `==` ("equals") which tests to see if the two expressions are equal. There's a similar, but opposite operator, which tests to see if the two expressions are *not* equal. It is written **`!=`** (and is pronounced, unsurprisingly, "not equal to").

In the last example, we used the test **`if (divisor)`** to ensure the division is only performed if divisor equals something other than zero. It might be clearer to write the test out more explicitly:

CODE SEGMENT

```
if (divisor!=0)
    printf("The result is %d\n",dividend/divisor);
```

The other relational operators ("less than" and the rest) are useful in a whole range of circumstances, but, rather than concoct an artificial example right now, I'll use them as they become necessary in later programs.

Doing it again (and again)

Let's go back to the first example of the chapter, the simple calculator. We left it by saying some sort of error message segment would be useful if the user entered a number other than `1`, `2`, `3` or `4`. If you modified the program yourself, then the last part of your switch statement will look something like this:

```
default:
    printf("You have not entered a valid option\n");
    break;
}
```

(If you did do it yourself, I hope you didn't miss out the semi-colons at the ends of **`printf`** and **`break`**; and if you didn't do it yourself, why not?) This solution is all very well, but the program will, if the user enters an invalid choice, give him a result of `0` and has to be run again before he can enter the choice he actually wants. What we need is an opportunity for error recovery, like this:

```
default:
    printf("You have not entered a valid option ¬
    - try again\n");
    printf("1 - addition\n2 - subtraction\n3 ¬
    - multiplication\n4 - division");
    scanf("%d",&reply);
    break;
}
```

Have you seen the problem with this approach? If not, add it to the calculator program and run the whole lot. Although we've given the user the opportunity to correct his mistake and enter a new option, we haven't modified the program so that it will do something *with* this new option.

One particularly clumsy solution is to include a copy of the whole of the unmodified **switch** statement after the first **switch** statement's **default**, so the whole decision process could be made again, depending on the new value of reply. It would look something like this:

```
default:
    printf("You have not entered a valid option ¬
    - try again\n");
    printf("1 - addition\n2 - subtraction\n3 ¬
    - multiplication\n4 - division");
    scanf("%d",&reply);
    /* now to make the decision again */
    switch (reply) {
        case 1: result=first+second;
           break;
        case 2: result=first-second;
           break;
        case 3: result=first*second;
           break;
        case 4: result=first/second;
           break;
        default:
           break;
    }
    break;
  }
  printf("\nThe result is %f\n",result);
}
```

Now, this is an example of pretty bad programming. It will work – add it to the original, and see – but not particularly well. If the user enters an incorrect value twice, then he'll still end up without a proper result, and he'll have to run the program again (you might argue that, after two chances, he deserves all he gets, but it's just as easy to write a program that gives him as many chances as it takes).

Secondly, we've had to write out the majority of the program twice. The logical extension of this is that for every chance we give the user to rethink his input we're going to need a corresponding piece of code, even though it is the same as all the others.

It might be a bad solution, but it does at least illustrate one point: that you can embed, or "nest", **case** statements inside other **case** statements. You can also nest **if** statements in this way, so you can test for conditions only if certain other conditions have already been met. This sort of thing comes in useful in more complex programs. For now, back to the error recovery problem.

Jump to it

Goto statement

A slightly better solution is to use a jump. C provides a statement called **goto**, which enables you to transfer execution to anywhere else in the program. The point you want execution to continue from is marked by a label, a piece of text that obeys the same rules as the name of a variable, followed by a colon. The same label also appears immediately after the **goto** statement.

You can use **goto** to jump forwards in the program, skipping intervening statements, or backwards, to execute a segment of code for a second time. It's here that it becomes useful for our calculator program. Take a look at this latest version:

```
#include <stdio.h>

/* simple calculator for careless users */
void main()
{
    /* declare the variables */
    float first, second, result;
    int reply;

    /* get the user to enter the numbers */
    printf("Enter the two numbers to be operated on\n");
    scanf("%f",&first);
    scanf("%f",&second);
    /* print up the menu and get user's choice */
    /* next lines is the label - control jumps back here if the user
```

```
enters anything other than 1, 2, 3 or 4 */
    try_again:
    printf("Which operation do you require?\n");
    printf("1 - addition\n2 - subtraction\n3 - multiplication\n4 ¬
- division\n");
    scanf("%d",&reply);

    /* now to make the decision */
    switch (reply) {
    case 1: result=first+second;
        break;
    case 2: result=first-second;
        break;
    case 3: result=first*second;
        break;
    case 4: result=first/second;
        break;
    default:
        printf("You have not entered a valid option - try again\n");
        /* jump to the part of the program that reads the user's menu
selection */
        goto try_again;
        break;
    }
    printf("\nThe result is %f\n",result);
}
```

Now this is much more elegant. We don't even need two segments of code to input the user's choice – the first instance just gets used again. Also, the user can enter as many wrong values as he likes, and the program will continue patiently asking for another until a valid one is input.

The situation is still not ideal, however. **Goto** statements are generally frowned on by programmers, the reason being that you have to look pretty hard at a program using them to see what's going on. In the above example, having seen the **goto** statement you then have to go searching through the listing to find out to where the jump is made. It isn't until

The goto command is useful for going straight to a specific point in the program. In this case, if the user doesn't enter one of the menu options he's taken straight back to the menu again. The only way out is to choose a 'valid' menu option.

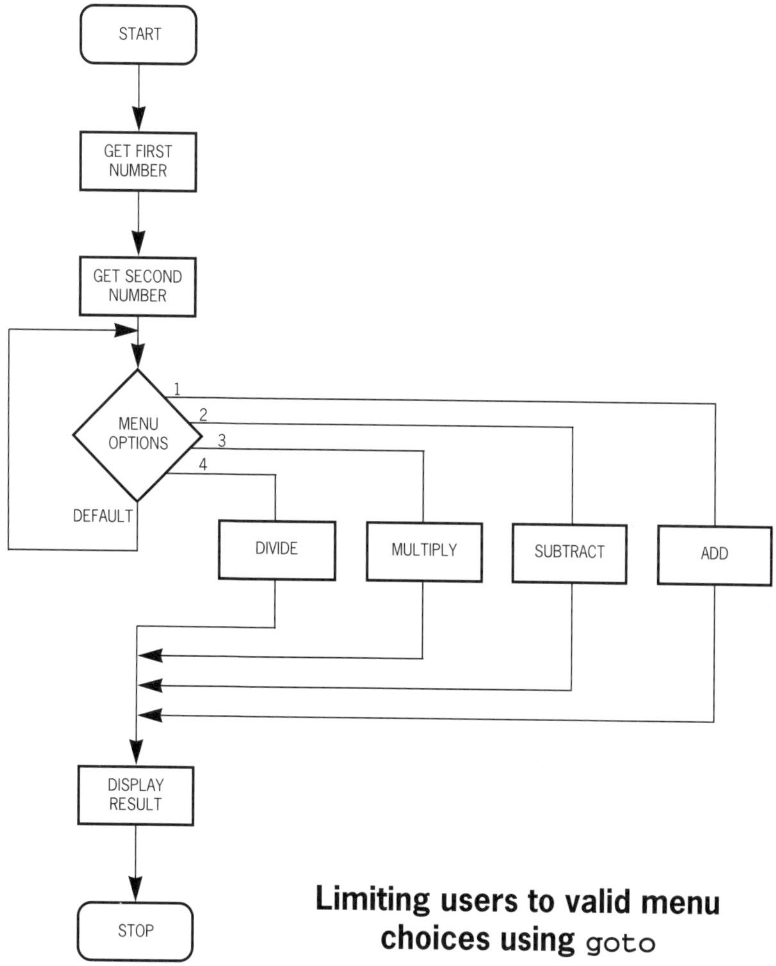

Limiting users to valid menu choices using `goto`

you've also examined the **`switch`** statement that the logic of the loop becomes apparent.

C provides a few ways in which you can make this logic, and the logic of similar repeating segments, explicit.

Doing the do

The method that's of most use here is made up of two statements: **do** and **while**. They surround a statement (or several statements grouped into a block by curly braces) which is executed for as long as the logical expression contained within the parentheses that follows **while** is true. For this loop (as segments of code that are executed more than once are called) to be of any use, the intervening statements must modify the variable used in the expression, otherwise the loop may be repeated indefinitely.

Here's how we would use it with our calculator program:

```
#include <stdio.h>

/* simple calculator for careless users */
void main()
{
    /* declare the variables */
    float first, second, result;
    int reply;

    /* get the user to enter the numbers */
    printf("Enter the two numbers to be operated on\n");
    scanf("%f",&first);
    scanf("%f",&second);
    /* print up the menu and get user's choice */
    /* This next statement marks the beginning of the loop, which will be
executed over and over until the user enters a valid menu selection */
    do {
        printf("Which operation do you require?\n");
        printf("1 - addition\n2 - subtraction\n3 - multiplication\n¬
4 - division\n");
        scanf("%d",&reply);
    } while (reply<1 || reply>4);

    /* got a decent reply - now to make the decision */
```

```
    switch (reply) {
        case 1: result=first+second;
            break;
        case 2: result=first-second;
            break;
        case 3: result=first*second;
            break;
        case 4: result=first/second;
            break;
        default:
            /* no need for anything here, since this part of the program
should never be executed */
            break;
    }
    printf("\nThe result is %f\n",result);
}
```

This looks much clearer. From this it should be obvious that the bit in curly braces is executed for as long as the logical expression after the **`while`** statement is true. Quite what this expression is I'll come to in a moment, after I've pointed out the lack of any statements other than **`break`** following the **`default`** clause in the **`switch`** construct. There's no longer need for any, since we've already checked that result holds one of the four valid numbers. Nevertheless, we have included **`default:`** and **`break`**, by convention.

Logical operators

OR locigal operator

Now to the expression. It is actually a combination of two, joined together by a logical operator called "**`or`**". The "**`or`**" operator is written as `||`. It combines the expression on its left with the one on its right (in the example **`reply<1`** and **`reply>4`**) in such a way that if either of the expressions is true, then the total, overall expression is true. If both are false, then the expression containing them is also false. You might express the logic of the loop in words as, "Carry out the segment within the loop for as long as **`reply`** is less than one or it is greater than four." Only when it is one of the correct values will the loop be left and the rest of the program, the calculation, be executed.

Notice that the expression is only tested for its truth after the statements within the loop have been executed at least once. A consequence of this is that, in a longer program, it is conceivable that the variable **reply** might already hold a valid value before the loop was entered, yet the program would still ask the user to enter another. You could avoid this situation by placing the expression at the beginning of the loop. Change the loop segment to the following:

CODE SEGMENT

```
while (reply<1 || reply>4) {
    printf("Which operation do you require?\n");
    printf("1 - addition\n2 - subtraction\n3 - ¬
    multiplication\n4 - division");
    scanf("%d",&reply);
}
```

It's similar to the previous loop, but no **do** keyword is required. The end of the loop is marked by a closing curly brace. The contents are only executed if the condition after the **while** keyword is true. This isn't a particularly good example of the **while** loop's use, since the variable **reply** doesn't hold anything before it is tested. You would need to set it up with a dummy value beforehand, with a statement such as **reply=0**;. Once variables are declared, and before you've put into them, their values are said to be undefined, which means, practically speaking, they can contain any old value. In our example it's possible that **reply** could contain one of the four valid values, in which case the program would go off and carry out a calculation without the user being given a choice as to which one.

WHAT DOES IT MEAN?

DO WHILE and WHILE loops

The difference between the **do while** and the **while** loops is whether or not the loop is executed at least once as a matter of course, or whether the test has to prove true before the loop is executed at all. The **do while** loop ensures the former, the **while** loop the latter. In our example, we want the loop always to be executed at least once, in other words for the user to have at least one chance to enter an option, so the best of the two is the **do while** loop. There are circumstances in which the **while** loop will prove more convenient, but we'll come on to these in due course.

*The logical operator AND returns true if **both** expressions are true. OR returns true if **either** of the expressions is true. While NOT simply returns the **opposite** of an expression.*

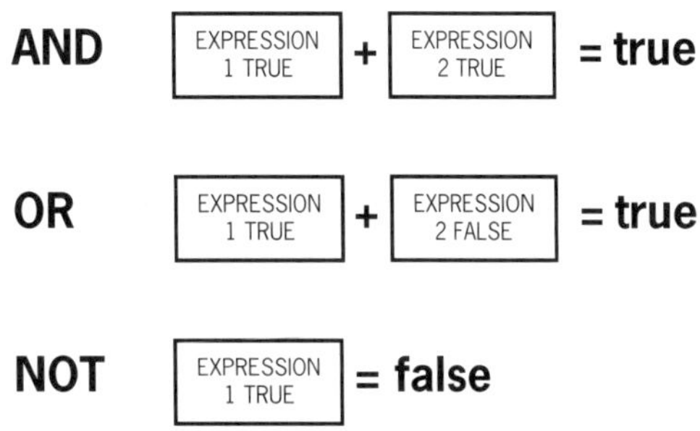

Logical operators

AND logical operator

There's another logical operator, similar to the "`or`" used above, called "`and`". It is written as `&&`. Logical expressions using "`and`" are only true if both the expression on the left and that on the right of the `&&` sign are true. If either or both are false, then the overall expression is also false.

The final logical operator, "`not`", is different in that, rather than combining two smaller logical expressions, it operates on only one. The result of an expression involving `not` is the logical inverse of the expression following the symbol. It turns a true expression into a false one, and vice versa. It is written as `!`, followed by a logical expression.

We could combine the "`and`" and "`not`" operators to come up with a different approach to the loop logic in the above example. Whereas the logic of the `do while` loop was expressed as, "Carry out the segment within the loop for as long as reply is less than one or it is greater than four," we could write a loop with the logic, "Carry out the segment within the loop for as long as reply is not greater than or equal to one and less than or equal to four." The C equivalent would look as follows:

```
do {
    printf("Which operation do you require?\n");
    printf("1 - addition\n2 - subtraction\n3 - ¬
    multiplication\n4 - division");
    scanf("%d",&reply);
} while (!(reply>=1 && reply<=4));
```

Let's look at the expression within the deepest set of parentheses. It is true only if **reply** is greater than or equal to 1 *and* **reply** is less than or equal to 4. It is enclosed in parentheses, and its result is converted to its opposite by the "**not**" operator that precedes it. The loop therefore executes so long as the result of the inner logical expression (which is checking for a correct user-entered value) is false, that is to say so long as the user has entered an incorrect value.

You'll find that "**not**", "**and**" and "**or**" are used a lot, not just in **while** and **do while** loops, but also in **if** statements and a new statement to be introduced next chapter. They enable more complex decisions to be made by a single statement, that is to say they enable different actions to be performed based on more subtly distinguished criteria. You'll find yourself using them more and more as you create more involved programs.

Loops elaborated

- Arrays
- Symbolic constants and pre-processing
- Loop counters – the 'for' loop
- Character variables
- Escape sequences
- String variables
- Initialising arrays
- Handling string arrays

I'm going to return to the spreadsheet program introduced in Chapter 3. As you may remember, we had to declare a variable for each number that was to be totalled. We also needed a succession of **scanf** lines to get the value for each for variable from the user. That's all very well if all the program has to do is total a few numbers, but what if 50 or so have to be totalled? Things begin to get out of hand.

After our brief flirtation with looping in the last chapter, you may be thinking that therein lies the solution. Well, if you are then you're right. But that's not the whole answer. Remember that the code inside a loop can't be modified, just repeated. So although we could set a loop up to enter a succession of values from the user, requiring but a single **scanf**, we have as yet no mechanism for storing them in anything but the one variable. It'll come as no surprise for me to tell you that C does in fact provide such a mechanism.

Array

The mechanism comes in the form of arrays. An array is a way of grouping a whole set of variables together with a single name (the concept originates with the mathematical objects matrices). The variables are numbered in sequence, so you can access the value in any particular variable by means of both the array name and the number of the particular variable, or "element".

You declare an array just like you declare any other variable, but you must follow its name with square brackets and the number of elements it is to have. This number must be a positive integer (obviously); its maximum size is usually determined by the compiler you are using and available memory.

Arrays can be of any variable type, but each element within an array must be of the same type. Here's how you would declare an integer array with 10 elements:

```
int numbers[10];
```

To access any particular element, whether it be to store a value there, use the value held there as part of an expression or whatever, you use the array name with the number of the element of interest enclosed in the

An array lets you group many variables together under a single name. You refer to them by the array name followed by the relevant element number.

A 10-element array

square brackets. Here's an example of assigning a value to the first element of the above array:

```
numbers[0]=72;
```

Numbering

Notice there's something funny about that? The first element is numbered 0. That's weird, but at least the next one is numbered 1, and the next 2, as you might expect. The last element in this array is numbered 9. The reasons are historical, and relate to the way memory addressing and the way the original compilers worked. The convention of numbering arrays from 0 instead of 1 has stuck with us. It's another one of those little tricks that can often catch out even experienced C programmers, so watch out for it.

OK, now we know enough to have another stab at that spreadsheet program. Below is the latest version:

```
#include <stdio.h>
/* This next line defines a constant */
#define MAX_ELEMENTS 10

/* program to total ten non-integer numbers */
void main()
{
    /* first declare variables */
    float numbers[MAX_ELEMENTS];
    float total,entry;
```

```
    int next;

    /* set the total value to zero */
    total=0.0;
    /* set the loop counter to zero */
    next=0;

    printf("Enter the numbers to be added\n");

    /* set up our loop to be executed MAX_ELEMENTS times */
    do {
        /* Now get numbers to be added from user */
        printf("Enter number %d ",next);
        scanf("%f",&entry);
        numbers[next]=entry;
        /* add the next number entered on to total so far */
        total=total+entry;
        /* increase loop counter to index next element of array */
        next=next+1;
    } while (next<MAX_ELEMENTS);

    /* print out result held in total */
    printf ("\nThe total is %f\n",total);
}
```

Before I explain the important part of the program, the loop, I'd better own up about that statement I sneaked in at the third line, the one that says: **#define MAX_ELEMENTS 10**.

Symbolic constant

What it does is define a symbolic constant. This means that wherever, within the program, the compiler sees the symbol **MAX_ELEMENTS**, it replaces it with **10** before compiling. I say the compiler, but it is actually a part of the compiler known as the C pre-processor that performs this and similar processes such as loading in the **stdio.h** library before the compiler gets stuck in translating the program into machine code. Instructions to the C pre-processor, distinguishable from ordinary C statements by the **#** sign that precedes them, are not terminated by a semi-colon.

Symbolic constants follow the same rules for names as variables do. They're usually written in upper case, though, to distinguish them from variables.

Using symbolic constants offers two benefits: readability and ease of modification. By using the **MAX_ELEMENTS** symbol in the **while** part of the loop instead of **10**, I've made it clear that the variable **next** is being compared to the maximum number of elements in the array. As for ease of modification, try turning the above program into one that deals with 20 numbers.

All you have to do is go to the **#define** line and change the number at the end from **10** to **20**. Without the **#define**, the **while** statement would read **while (next<10);** and the **10** would have to be changed to a **20**. That's fine, but in a month's time you may find that you have to look long and hard at the program before discovering which bit depends on the array size and therefore has to be changed. You may also forget to modify the size of the array in its declaration. It's easy to conceive of more complex programs where several operations are performed on arrays, and where the size of the arrays is going to become a consideration; in cases like these the value of symbolic constants becomes obvious. Changing a symbolic constant is effectively asking the C pre-processor to change the rest of your program for you.

Before going on to the loop in our spreadsheet program, I'll just point out that not only integers can be represented by symbolic constants. The C pre-processor performs a text substitution; wherever it sees the constant being used it simply substitutes whatever followed the constant when it was defined by the **#define** statement. You can use constants for all sorts of substitutions (although none with white space in them – including a tab or a carriage return – since these are used to separate the constant name from the text to be substituted, and also to separate this text from the next statement).

The key variable in the spreadsheet program (discounting the array, which is used to store the numbers to be totalled) is the integer **next**. It performs two closely-linked functions. Its first use is as a counter. It is given an initial value of zero. Then, once the **do... while** loop is entered, a value of one is added to **next** each time the loop is repeated. The loop continues so long as **next** has a value less than 10. In other words, the loop finishes once **next** reaches 10. So **next**'s use as a counter ensures that the loop is executed exactly ten times.

The second use of **next** is as an "index" into the array. An element of an array is accessed by use of the array name and the element number. The variable **next**, within the loop, always has a value between 0 and 9, conveniently the numbered elements of the array. So **next** is used within the loop to fill up with user-entered numbers each element of the array in turn. You'll find this combination of loop counter and array in an awful lot of programs.

The final point of note in this program is the part where the value of **total** is computed. Rather than having an expression at the end combining all the elements of the array numbers, I've added each number as it is entered to **total** during the loop. This means that when the loop is exited, **total** already contains the correct value.

For loop

The combination of a loop with a counter variable is such a common one that C provides a special looping construct just for the occasion. It's the **for** loop, and you could use it in the above program by replacing the loop and its body with:

```
/* set up our loop to be executed MAX_ELEMENTS times */
for (next=0; next<MAX_ELEMENTS; next=next+1) {
    /* Now get numbers to be added from user */
    printf("Enter number %d ",next);
    scanf("%f",&entry);
    numbers[next]=entry;
    /* add the next number entered on to total so far */
    total=total+entry;
    /* increase loop counter to index next element of array */
}
```

All of the controlling logic of the loop has been removed to the top, in the parentheses following the **for** statement. Notice that each of the three elements – the initialisation of **next** to 0, the test to see if it is less than **MAX_ELEMENTS** and adding 1 to it – is separated by a semi-colon. The first part is executed just the once, when the loop is first executed. Then the truth of the second part is established. If the value in **next** is less than 10, then the expression will be true. So long as it is true, the body of the loop will be executed. Each time the loop has been executed, the final part of the **for** statement is executed – a 1 is added to the value held in **next** (this eliminates the need for the addition statement in the body of the loop). The loop is then executed again, beginning with the test to see whether or not **next** is less than **MAX_ELEMENTS**.

As you can see, the **for** loop is similar to the **while** loop in that the condition for looping is tested before the loop itself is executed. In both cases it is possible for the loop to be skipped entirely if the condition is not met. In the case of **do... while**, the loop is always executed once before the condition is tested.

Notice how the body of the loop is again a block, enclosed in curly braces. If only one statement forms the body of the loop, then the braces are not necessary, it must only be terminated by a semi-colon. To demonstrate, here's a quick program that will print out the numbers between one and ten:

COMPLETE LISTING

```
#include <stdio.h>

void main()
{
    /* declare variable */
    int number;

    /* loop to print out numbers */
    for (number=1; number<=10; number=number+1)
        printf("%d\n",number);
}
```

I've used **<=10** here rather than **<11** to make it clear that we're interested in the values between 1 and 10 inclusive.

In a couple of chapters' time we'll be ready to write something that's beginning to look like a *real* spreadsheet, but first, there's some more you need to know about variables.

Char variable

As well as numerical variable types – integers and **float**s – that we've talked about, there is a type known as **char**, short for character. It will hold a single symbol, a letter, numeral or punctuation mark, for instance.

The values held by **char**s are written in C by enclosing them in single quotes. To declare the **char** variable **choice** and assign the letter a to it, you would do the following:

```
char choice;
choice='a';
```

Char variables can be used in logical expressions in much the same way as others. You could re-write the calculator program of chapter 4 so that it expected an alphabetical entry rather than a numerical one for the user's menu selection.

```
#include <stdio.h>

/* simple calculator with alphabetical menu */
void main()
{
    /* declare the variables */
    float first, second, result;
    char reply;

    /* get the user to enter the numbers */
    printf("Enter the two numbers to be operated on \n");
    scanf("%f",&first);
    scanf("%f",&second);
    /* begin loop by printing up menu */
    do {
        printf("Which operation do you require?\n");
        printf("a - addition\nb - subtraction\nc - multiplication\nd ¬
- division\n");
```

```
        scanf("%1s",&reply);

    } while (reply<'a' || reply>'d');

    /* Got a decent reply - now to make the decision */
    switch (reply) {
        case 'a': result=first+second;
            break;
        case 'b': result=first-second;
            break;
        case 'c': result=first*second;
            break;
        case 'd': result=first/second;
            break;
        default:
            /* No need for anything here, since this part of the ¬
program should never be executed */
            break;
    }
    printf("\nThe result is %f\n",result);
}
```

The usage of **char** is pretty straightforward, apart from a couple of anomalies which you may have noticed. For one thing, I've used the less than and greater than relational operators on **char**s, yet they only work with numerical values. Secondly, I've used **char**s as labels for the **case** statements in my **switch** statement, yet these labels should be either integer values or constant expressions evaluating to integers (for example, **2+1** is a constant expression, evaluating to 3).

MAKE A NOTE!

Chars

The truth of the matter is that C treats **char**s as numbers. A character is represented internally by a code, an integer with a value between 0 and 255. This set of codes comprises the ASCII code, a standard across computers for representing text. You'll find a full list of ASCII codes in your Amiga manual.

C uses characters and the numbers by which they are represented interchangeably. So when **reply** is compared with 'a', what in fact is happening is the ASCII code of the character in **reply** is being compared with the ASCII code for the letter a, 97. Similarly with the check against 'd', and also the use of the character constants in the switch statement. Because the letters of the alphabet are numbered consecutively, a check for reply being less than 'a' or greater than 'd' picks up any entries outside the required range just fine.

Escape sequences

As well as the various symbols available from the keyboard, other "invisible" characters can be stored in **char** variables. The ASCII codes for these characters are not used to display things on the screen, but to perform functions such as skipping to a new line or moving to the next tab stop. The '**\n**' combination often used at the end of **printf** statements is one such character – although written as two symbols within a C program, it is turned into a single ASCII code by the compiler when the program is translated. The character representing a tab is written as '**\t**'. The combination of **** and a following character is known as an "escape sequence" – they provide a convenient way of writing otherwise un-writeable ASCII characters. If you wanted to store the character **'** itself in a **char**, for instance, you would need to include it as part of an escape sequence to distinguish it from the single quotes used to surround it. The correct escape sequence for a single quote is **\'**, and it would be used in an assignment as follows:

```
char quote_character;
quote_character='\'';
```

If you look at the **scanf** line used to input a character into the variable **reply**, you'll notice that the control string **"%1s"** has been used – this ensures that **scanf** returns the next non-white space character input by the user. The **s** referes to a "string", a concept we'll discuss in a moment, while the **1** means that we only want a single character. If we'd given scanf the control string **"%c"**, asking for a character input, it would have failed to wait for the next non-white space character entered by the user. Try it.

One thing you may notice about the previous calculator program is that it will not recognise user entries in upper case as valid, because upper case letters have quite different ASCII codes to lower case ones.

You could solve this problem by converting any upper case characters to lower case characters before the value held in reply is checked. Because it is possible to perform arithmetic on **char** variables, the conversion can be done by adding 32 to any upper case entries. Here's the menu selection loop with the appropriate modifications:

CODE SEGMENT

```
do {
     printf("Which operation do you require?\n");
     printf("a - addition\nb - subtraction\nc - multiplication\nd - ¬
division\n");
     scanf("%1s",&reply);
     if (reply>='A' && reply<='Z')
          reply=reply+32;
} while (reply<'a' || reply>'d');
```

WHAT DOES IT MEAN?

STRING variable

Just like **int**s and **float**s, **char**s can be used to form arrays. An array of **char** has a special name – it is called a "string". The primary use of string variables is to hold words. But strings needn't be used as variables, they can also appear as literal constants. All of the **printf**s used so far have contained string constants – the segments of text inside double quotes. It is these sets of double quotes that are used to mark out strings in C. You would declare a string variable called **word**, and assign the value `elephant` to it with the following segment of code:

CODE SEGMENT

```
char word[20];
word[0]='e';
word[1]='l';
word[2]='e';
word[3]='p';
word[4]='h';
word[5]='a';
word[6]='n';
word[7]='t';
word[8]='\0';
```

Here, the character '`e`' is assigned to the first element of the array (numbered element 0, remember) '`l`' to the 2nd, '`e`' to the third and so on. After the letter '`t`' is stored in the 8th array element, a further value is

String arrays can hold whole words by assigning each letter to one of the array elements. The \0 character (element 9) marks the end of the word.

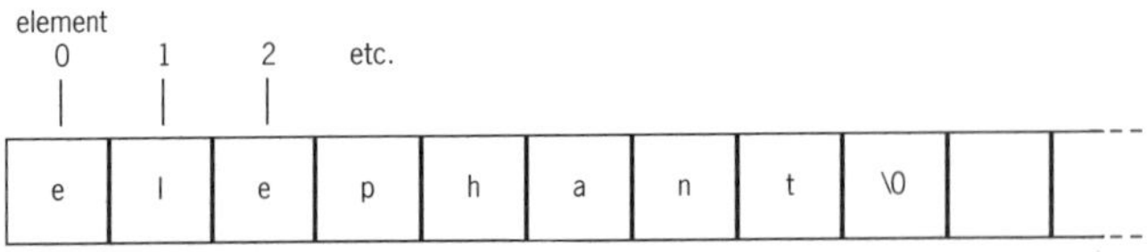

A string array

Null character

stored. This is the number zero, representing the "null character". I've written it as a character escape sequence, but it could also be written as the number 0 without single quotes. It needs to be there to mark the end of the string, to ensure that the remaining elements of the array (whose values are undefined, i.e. garbage) are not considered part of the string, for example when it comes to be printed out. As a result, a string is always one character longer than the number of characters appearing in the quotes surrounding its contents. Therefore, the maximum number of characters a string can ever contain is always one less than the number appearing in the square brackets of the array definition. As with any array, writing to string elements whose number exceeds the stated maximum when the array was defined will cause an error.

Assigning values to strings in this way can be something of a hassle. With simple variables, it is possible to declare them and assign a value to them at the same time.

The two lines we used to declare a **char** variable called **choice** and assign the letter a to it, can be combined into one:

```
char choice='a';
```

The same applies for **int**s and **float**s; and C lets us do a similar thing with arrays, including strings. Here's a quicker way of assigning the value "elephant" to an array called **word**:

```
char word[]="elephant";
```

This time the square braces don't contain a number. When C creates the array, it makes it of the required size, depending on the string to be

MAKE A NOTE!

String terminators

placed in it. As well as the characters contained within the double quotes, C also adds the obligatory '\0' string terminator, meaning that in this case the array **word** consists of 9 elements.

Incidentally, a similar technique can be used for initialising other types of array when they are declared. For these, and **float**s, the values are all enclosed in curly braces and separated by commas. Here's how you would declare an array of five integers and assign it the values **32**, **29**, **11**, **4** and **7** respectively:

```
int numbers[]={32,29,11,4,7};
```

EXAMPLE CODE

Again, there isn't a number between the square braces. The compiler automatically counts the number of elements (five, because we don't need a null character at the end – that's only for strings) and creates the array at the required size. You can include a number if you want – if it is greater than the number of elements you've defined, the rest will be left containing zero; if it is less, then you'll get an error.

As you can probably see, the method used for initialising strings is a convenient shorthand of the method used for initialising other types of array. It means you don't have to define the elements as individual characters surrounded by single quotes and separated by commas, and enables you instead to write the string out as a segment of text.

WARNING

Handling strings

Strings are incredibly useful things, probably the most common form of the array in C. But, like other arrays, they suffer because they are not simple variables. It's not possible to assign a value to a string with a simple equals sign, except for when the string is being declared. The assignment operator assigns a single value to a single variable, but a string consists of several variable elements, each of which holds a separate variable. Similarly, it's not possible to simply add two strings, or any two arrays, together, or to compare two strings with the == relational operator.

But to be useful strings need to be manipulated in many different ways. C provides a standard set of functions to provide these manipulations, saving you from having to re-write such obviously necessary functions as the one to see if two strings contain the same thing. We'll come on to these functions, and consequently demonstrate the real power of strings, later. For now, though, here's a quick demonstration of string basics:

```
#include <stdio.h>

/* set up symbolic constant for newline character */
#define NEWLINE '\n'
/* set up maximum length of user's input */
#define LINE_LENGTH 80

void main()
{
    /* declare variables */
    char text[LINE_LENGTH];
    int position=0;
    int index;
    char input;

    printf("Type a line of text\n");
    /* set up loop to read line from keyboard */
    do {
        input=getchar();
        text[position]=input;
        position=position+1;
    } while (position<LINE_LENGTH && input != NEWLINE);

    /* Now convert NEWLINE character at the end of text to a ¬
string terminator */

    position=position-1; /* because it points to one after the last ¬
character */
    text[position]='\0';

    /* Now convert lower case to upper case */
    for (index=0; index<position; index=index+1) {
        if (text[index]>='a' && text[index]<='z')
            text[index]=text[index]-32;
```

```
    }
    /* Now print out the result */
    printf("\n\nYour line in upper case is:\n%s\n",text);
}
```

It's a program to take a line of input from a user and convert any lower case letters to their upper case equivalents. The user signals that his input is finished by typing carriage return, which the computer perceives as a newline character, '**\n**'. For this reason we've set up a symbolic constant called **NEWLINE** with this value. It's a good example of how you can make your programs that little bit more readable.

We've also defined a symbolic constant called **LINE_LENGTH**, which represents the maximum number of characters the user can type in. I've chosen 80 as an arbitrary limit; the largest array you can have depends on the memory of your machine and the compiler you are using but you're unlikely to find yourself restricted. Once this has been defined, we can declare the array **text[]** to be of the appropriate size. Notice that there's no point initialising it with anything, since its contents are to be supplied by the user.

I've used three other variables. **Input** is of type **char**, and it is used to accept the user's input one character at a time. It's used as a temporary variable, holding the character before it is stored in an element of text. The other two, both **int**s, are index variables, pointing to elements inside **text**. One is needed for each of the two main sections of code.

The first main section inputs a succession of characters from the keyboard, typed by the user. I've chosen to use a new function, **getchar**, rather than the more familiar **scanf**. For the purposes of this program, **scanf** isn't as useful as it might be. You *can* use it for inputting strings (using the **%s** formatting sequence), but it treats any white space character as signifying the end of an input string, meaning that our user would only be able to enter a single word rather than a whole line of text. It can be used to input individual characters (using the **%1s** formatting sequence), but **getchar** is simpler to use and quicker.

Getchar gets the next character typed from the keyboard. It doesn't need anything between its parentheses for this simple task. Unlike **scanf**, which needs the variable to be included in parentheses as an argument, and which as well as modifying this variable produces a "result" used to count the number of elements input, **getchar** produces the character typed as a "result". We'll talk about results in more detail in the next chapter. For now, just be aware that the result from a function can be treated as the result of an expression. In other words, you can compare it using relational operators, or assign it using the assignment operator:

```
input=getchar();
```

Once we've got a character from the keyboard and stored it in **input**, it is then stored in the element of **text** marked by the index variable **position**. Having done this, the program adds one to the value of **position** so that it is pointing to the next free element in **text**.

Finally, the loop is closed with the **while** statement. Inside **while**'s parentheses are two conditions that must be met for the loop to continue. The variable position must have a value less than **LINE_LENGTH**, in this case 80, *and* the character entered by the user, held in input, must not be a **NEWLINE** character. The first condition makes sure that the length of **input** doesn't exceed what the array can cope with; the second ensures that when the user types a carriage return it is understood to mark the end of his input.

Once the loop has ended, the program knows that the string **text** contains the user-entered line. The variable **position** is pointing to the next free element in the array, in other words to one more than the last-used element. For this reason, one is subtracted from its value.

The last element currently contains a **NEWLINE** character, the last assignment made during the loop – unless the user's input was too long, in which case he'll lose a character. Each string must be terminated with a null character – '**\0**' – so the **NEWLINE** character is replaced with this.

The array **text** now contains a bona fide string, so it's time to convert each of its elements in turn into upper case. This is done using a **for** loop. These kind of loops are useful when you know how many times round the loop (or the "number of iterations", to get technical) you need to go. The first time round we didn't – it's decided by the user each time the program is run – but this time we do. The number of iterations is the same as the length of the string, not counting the terminating character (there's no point in trying to convert that into upper case).

Conveniently, the variable **position** already points to the last-used element, the one containing the null character, so we can set up a loop that indexes from 0 to one less than the value of **position**. We need another index variable here, which I've actually called **index**, because, since we're using **position** as a check, it's value must not be altered. The value of **index** must be increased by one each time the loop is executed. All of this results in the **for** loop above.

The contents of the loop – the **if** statement – are similar to the example before that changed upper to lower case. Here, we're operating on successive elements of a character array, and subtracting 32 rather than adding, since we're converting from lower to upper case.

After the loop comes a **printf** statement, which is used to output the string. Notice that the formatting sequence to output a string variable is "**%s**". The **printf** could have been replaced with another **for** loop and the function **putchar** – the opposite of **getchar** – which prints a single character, given as an argument enclosed in parentheses, to the screen. You could shorten things further by including the **putchar** function in the previous **for** loop:

```
    /* Now convert lower case to upper case  and print out result*/
    printf("\n\nYour line in upper case is:\n");
    for (index=0; index<position; index=index+1) {
        if (text[index]>='a' && text[index]<='z')
            text[index]=text[index]-32;
        putchar(text[index]);
    }
}
```

You don't need to print out the null character (it's non-printable anyway), but you might want to put a **printf**("\n\n"); between the two closing curly braces to tidy the output up. Notice how this statement and the introductory **printf** can't be included in the loop.

While we're on the subject of improvements, let me mention a way in which you could tighten up the first loop in the program. As it stands it makes two assignments and then a conditional check:

```
do {
    input=getchar();
    text[position]=input;
    position=position+1;
} while (position<LINE_LENGTH && input != NEWLINE);
```

You could make this much shorter as follows:

```
while (position<LINE_LENGTH && (input=getchar()) != NEWLINE) {
    text[position]=input;
    position=position+1;
}
```

The first thing to notice is that it now makes its conditional check at the beginning, rather than the end, of the loop. A consequence of this is that the last character entered, whether it be **NEWLINE** or one that exceeds the permitted string length, is not stored in **text**. Once the loop has been exited **position** still points to the next free element within the array, but because there is no **NEWLINE** character to be replaced with a null terminator, the terminator must be tacked on to the end of the string, in the next free element. For this reason, you have to delete the line following the loop that says: **position=position-1;**.

Changing the logic of the loop around in this way hasn't made things any more complicated – just different. What it has enabled us to do, though, is include one of the assignments in the part where the loop is set up, rather than in the loop body.

The reason this is possible is because we've used the assignment **input=getchar()** as an expression. First of all the result of the function **getchar()** is placed in the variable **input**. The whole lot, enclosed in parentheses to make sure the assignment is carried out before anything is compared with **NEWLINE**, is then treated as an expression in its own right. The value of such an expression is the value of the assignment made, in other words, the variable **input.** We can then use this value in the same line and check that it's not equal to **NEWLINE** before deciding to go on with the loop.

It's possible to dispense with **input** altogether and store the results of **getchar()** directly into the text array:

```
    while ((position<LINE_LENGTH-1) && (text[position]=getchar()) != ¬
NEWLINE)
        position=position+1;
```

We don't need curly braces around the block making up the loop body if it is just one statement long. If you're going to type this version in, then you can remove the declaration of **input** from the beginning.

One thing to note here is that, unlike in the previous two versions, in this one when the loop is terminated **position** already points to the last-used element of **text**, rather than to the next free one. And in this case, because, as with the original version and unlike the last one, the last character entered – usually a **NEWLINE** – is stored in **text**, we need to replace it with a null terminator rather than tag one on to the end of the string. Hence there is no need for a **position=position-1;** line at the end of the loop.

This time, we need to check that **position** is less than **LINE_LENGTH-1**, rather than **LINE_LENGTH**. Why? Well, suppose that the user had been merrily typing away without pressing carriage return, and the loop was about to be executed with **position** holding a value of **LINE_LENGTH-1** (that is, 79). If we were checking against **LINE_LENGTH**, the first part of the condition would be true, and the second part would then be checked (it wouldn't need to be if the first condition were false), resulting in a character being stored in **text[79]**.

If this character was anything other than **NEWLINE**, the body of the loop would be executed, increasing the value of **position** to 80. The loop would exit next time OK, but when the program came to tag a null character on to the end of the string it would try to do it at element 80, which doesn't exist. We need to check for 1 less than **LINE_LENGTH** to prevent this happening.

Changing the logic of your loops in this way can, as you've seen, subtly alter the way in which your indexing variables need to be used, and the way in which you check for loop ending conditions. Be on the watch for bugs that you might introduce in this way.

It's possible to shorten the loop even further, and it's in this form that you'll most often see it in other people's programs:

```
while (position<LINE_LENGTH && (text[position++]=¬
getchar()) != NEWLINE)
    ;
```

Variable increments/ decrements

Here the loop has no body at all. The statement terminator – **;** – still needs to be included, to ensure that the compiler doesn't take the following statement to be the loop body. The entire body of the loop has been incorporated into the loop definition. The only remaining part from the previous example – **position=position+1;** – has been replaced by one of several bits of shorthand that C provides. If you want to add 1 to a variable in C, you can do so simply by writing:

```
variable_name++;
```

Similarly:

```
variable_name–;
```

will subtract one from the value in **variable_name**. In the above loop, I've used the **++** shorthand (pronounced "increment", while **–** is pronounced "decrement") to add one to the value of **position** while it is being used to index an element of text. Note: it is both making an assignment and being used as an expression.

The way increment has been used here, the result of the expression is the old value of **position**, which is used as an array index, before **position** is assigned a new value, 1 greater than its old. This means that, if **position** has a value of 0 before the loop is entered, the first input character will be stored in element zero. Immediately afterwards, **position** will point to the next free element.

For the boundary check it is safe to compare **position** against **LINE_LENGTH** rather than **LINE_LENGTH-1**, because once the loop has been exited, **position** will point to the next free element of **text** and not the last filled one. The line **position=position-1;** must be replaced at the end of the loop, leaving **position** pointing to the final character in the string. You could, of course, write **position–;** instead of **position=position-1;**.

Pre-increment & post-increment

The kind of increment used here is known as "post increment", which means the result of the expression is the old value of the variable, before it is incremented. It is also possible to perform "pre-increment" and "pre-decrement", in which the assignment is performed and the variable's new value becomes the expression's result, by writing them as:

```
++variable_name;
```

and

```
–variable_name;
```

It would have been wrong in the above example to have used pre-increment:

```
while ((text[++position]=getchar()) != NEWLINE && ¬
position<LINE_LENGTH)
    ;
```

It would mean that, the first time through the loop, **position** would have been given a value of 1 before anything was stored inside **text**, missing out the first element of the array. The choice between pre and post increment or decrement depends on the logic of the loop structures you've employed. Say, for instance, you wanted to alter the upper case converter to print out the **input** line backwards. If you go back to the original program, and replace the final **printf** line with the following, you've got it:

```
/* now to print the line backwards */
printf("\n\nYour line in upper case and backwards ¬
is:\n");
for (index=position; index>0;)
    putchar(text[--index]);
```

Notice how the final third of the **for** loop definition – the bit that is used to alter the index variable – has been left blank, because **index** is being decremented in the loop body. It's also possible to leave the first or second parts blank, but creating a loop without an exit condition is a good way to trap your program in an infinite loop. Notice also how the routine automatically misses out the terminating character when outputting.

Before going on to the next chapter, try incorporating this and the upper case conversion into the one loop. Also try removing the decrement operator from the body of the loop and putting it in the final part of the loop definition. You'll also have to modify the rest of the loop structure – either body or definition – in some way to get it working properly.

Functions

- Modular program planning
- Functions, and how they're constructed
- Prototyping functions
- Function 'side effects'

Functions are the means by which you keep sane when writing complicated programs. They are the building blocks from which larger and larger programs can be built.

Function

As was explained in chapter 1, functions enable you to break a task down into its component parts. Instead of having one long program to solve a problem, you can have lots of little sub-programs, each devoted to solving *part* of the problem. One strength of this approach is that things become more manageable. At any one time you are only trying to make a small section of code work, rather than a whacking great program.

Another good thing about functions is that they can be re-used. Once you have written a function that will, say, find a percentage of a value, you can use that function in any program that needs to be able to do this. And once you've got it working correctly, you can use it in any other programs sure in the knowledge that it does what it is supposed to do.

Having written and tested a function, you need no longer concern yourself with exactly what it does to achieve its effect. All you have to remember is the information you need to give it, and the information it will give you in return. It doesn't matter how many loops, arrays or whatever are used inside the function – they have no impact on the rest of your program.

With C you get a lot of pre-written functions, which you can access by including various header files, **`stdio.h`** being a good example. **`Printf`** is one such function. It is available with every C compiler for every computer, and its use is just the same on all. Any of the programs that you have written so far will compile happily on any computer with any C compiler. Yet the mechanics of printing to the Amiga's screen are quite complicated, and certainly different to those for other computers. These mechanics are all dealt with by the code that makes up **`printf`** – code which will be different for different versions of **`printf`** on various machines – and need not concern you. In fact, if instead of dropping in a call to **`printf`** you had to write code to output characters to the screen each time you wanted some output, you'd be faced with quite a job.

'Functions' are small programs or sections of code that you can 'call' within your main program. Using functions makes your program easier to write and understand, and lets you use useful routines in many different programs.

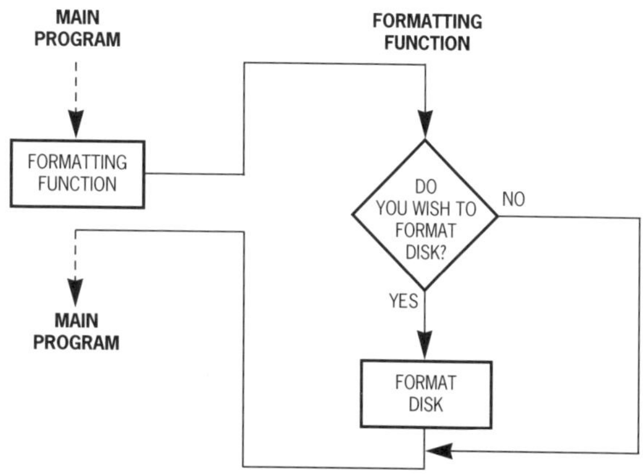

A disk-formatting 'function'

Not only can **printf** be used by many programs, it can, like any other function, be used several times in the one program, as we've already used it in previous chapters. It would be difficult enough having to write out all the code to do the job of **printf** rather than just a single line – a "function call" – but imagine having to write this out several times within one program. With C, you just write the function out once, name it, and use this name to call on its services from anywhere within your program. Part of the trick, when it comes to writing functions, is to write them so they are re-useable. **Printf** has been written with so many options, it is generalised to fit so many cases, that it proves very useful.

For the time being we'll stick to functions that are to be used only within the program that defines them. We'll go on to writing functions that are accessible by many programs in Chapter 11.

How programs are built

A program file in C consists of one or more function definitions. All of the programs written so far have contained only one (remember that **printf** is used, but not defined, by us – it comes from **stdio.h**). That function is called **main**, and every C program must have one. It is the function that is "called" (the technical word for getting a function to do its stuff) when the program is run. Other functions are called by **main**, and others, in turn, may be called from within one of these functions.

From a look at any of the programs so far you should learn how functions are constructed. The first line consists of a variable type, the name of the function and a pair of parentheses. Functions have names (following the same rules as variable names) so that they can be referred to and called from other parts of the program; the variable type and parentheses parts are used to communicate information between the function and the part of the program that called it – we'll go into more detail in a moment. Finally, the actual statements that make up the body of a function follow the first line, all of them enclosed as a block in curly braces. Note that the C pre-processor instructions (**#define**s, **#include**s and so on) are not part of any function. The effects of these instructions are applicable throughout the file that contains them.

Time for an example. Let's write a program that asks the user for two numbers and prints out the biggest. We'll divide it into two parts – the main bit that handles all the input and output, and a function that decides which of two numbers is bigger. Here's the listing:

COMPLETE LISTING

```
#include <stdio.h>
/* declare function to be used */
int biggest(int a,int b);

void main()
{
    /* declare three variables */
    int first,second,answer;

    /* get users input */
    printf("Enter two numbers\n");
    scanf("%d",&first);
    scanf("%d",&second);
    /* find biggest of two and put it in answer */
    answer=biggest(first,second);
    printf("The biggest of the two is %d\n",answer);
}

/* function definition */
int biggest(int a, int b)
```

```
{
    /* define function's own variable */
    int big;

    /* now to choose biggest between a and b */
    big=a;
    if (b>big)
        big=b;
    return big;
}
```

The definition of our function appears in the latter part of the program. It's supposed to choose the biggest of two integers and give this as a result, so the result too will be an integer, hence the int specifier at the start of the definition. Following the function name, enclosed in parentheses are two variable definitions. These define the function's "parameters" – they make the function behave in different ways depending on their values. Called `a` and `b`, both are `int`s. They are the means by which information is passed to the function. When it is called from within the main program, the values held within the parentheses after the function name in the calling statement are stored in the variables `a` and `b`.

The statements within the function body are straightforward. The first defines another `int` variable. It is used to hold the biggest of the two numbers. The way its value is chosen by the `if` statement should be readily understandable.

Variables in functions

The variable `big`, like `a` and `b`, belongs to the function. None of them can be read by any other functions. Likewise the variables `first` and `second` in `main`. They are not normally "visible" to `biggest`. The only reason they become visible is because they are copied into the function's parameters when it is called.

The variable `big` isn't visible to `main`, yet it contains the answer that `main` needs. `Biggest` makes this result visible to `main` by means of the `return` statement. The expression or, as in this case, variable following

return is defined as the function's result. It must be of a particular type, as defined by the type specifier preceding the function name at the top of the definition. In this case it is of type **int**. If a function isn't going to return a result, then it should be declared of type **void** at the start, as **main** generally is.

The result of a function can be used as an expression. In this example it has been assigned to the variable **answer**. Notice that **main** still has no access to the variable **big**, only to its value. The value is effectively substituted for any part of code where the function is called.

Handling arguments

Argument

In the line where **biggest** is called we've had to enclose the two values to be passed to it in parentheses. These two values are called "arguments" (they're arguments so far as the part of the program calling the function is concerned, and they get stored in variables that become the function's parameters when it is being executed). Because it's only the values of these two variables that are passed, and not the variables themselves, you could replace them in the call with any integer expressions. Try replacing the line with:

```
answer=biggest(57,3*4);
```

And because the function call results in a value, this value can be used directly without first being assigned to a variable. You could, for instance, remove the line assigning the function result to **answer** and replace the following **printf** with:

```
printf("The biggest of the two is %d\n",¬
biggest(first,second));
```

In cases where one of the arguments for a function is itself the result of a function call, the second function will be evaluated before the first is called.

The last line of note comes near the top of **main**, the line that reads

```
int biggest(int a,int b);
```

It looks a little like a variable declaration, and it is similar. Instead, it is declaring the function **biggest**, and it's called a "function prototype". With it you declare the function that **main** is going to be calling on (in case you were wondering, functions such as **printf** are declared within the header file **stdio.h** that is loaded in by **#include**, so there's no need to re-declare them). You say what type of value it will return with the type specifier before its name, and what type each of its parameters will be with type specifiers inside the parentheses.

Function prototypes

Prototyping

Prototyping your functions ensures that you don't use them incorrectly – you don't expect one type of value when it in fact returns a different type and that you don't supply it with the wrong kind or number of arguments – because the compiler can check the prototype against the function's usage in the part of the program that calls it, and also against the function definition itself. This is especially useful for programs that use functions from other files, but also for large programs whose function are defined in the same file, but whose details are easy to forget.

I said earlier that the arguments supplied in a function call are copied to the function's parameters, and that these parameters are invisible to the rest of the program. In fact, they can even have the same names (though this is liable to lead to confusion), and will still be treated as different entities. Try entering this to clarify the point.

```
#include <stdio.h>
/* function declaration */
void Out_Number(int number);

void main()
{
    /* variable declaration */
    int number;

    printf(″Enter a number \n″);
    scanf(″%d″,&number);
    Out_Number(number);
    printf(″After the function call, your number is now %d\n″,number);
```

```
}

/* define function */
void Out_Number(int number)
{
    printf(“The number is %d\n”,number);
    number=number+10;
}
```

Even though `10` is added to the function parameter **number**, this addition has in no way affected the variable **number** within **main**, which still retains the original value entered by the user.

If you used different names in **main** and the function body, and tried to access the function's variable from **main** or vice versa, you'd get an error. Try this:

```
#include <stdio.h>
/* function declaration */
void Out_Number(int fred);

void main()
{
    /* variable declaration */
    int number;

    printf(“Enter a number \n”);
    scanf(“%d”,&number);
    Out_Number(number);
    printf(“After the function call, your number is now %d\n”,number);
    printf(“And the value of fred is %d\n”,fred);
}

/* define function */
void Out_Number(int fred)
{
    printf(“The number is %d\n”,fred);
    fred=fred+10;
```

```
    Printf("And the value of number is %d\n",number);
}
```

Each of the variations on **Out_Number**, unlike **biggest**, are declared as type **void** and return no results. Yet they all – well, the working ones at least – have an effect. They alter the contents of a variable and print some information to the screen.

The variable in question is local to the function – it has no impact on the rest of the program and can safely be ignored. The writing of text to the screen, however, is a noticeable effect. It is called a "side effect."

Side effect

Functions are normally designed so that they are given information via their parameters, and they give information back via the expression following their return statement. Any other information given or altered by the function is done so as a side effect of the function.

Handling side effects

Sometimes, you may need a function to provide more than one result, or it may need access to more information than is practical to give as arguments. In these cases it is necessary to use side effects. **Printf** is once again a good example. Its side effect is to write information to the screen; the actual result it returns has so far been ignored by our programs. It can be used to count the number of elements printed out.

Later on I'll show how you can give a function access to variables outside its ordinary scope. But you should make use of side effects only where necessary – a function that can alter more than just its own variables can so easily be badly written and made to alter variables in the main program that it shouldn't, introducing a bug that can be very difficult to track down.

Handling other variable types

Functions can return more than just **int**s. Similarly, they can accept more than just **ints** as their arguments. It's also permissible to use **float**s and **char**s. Arrays are a special case which we'll go into in the next chapter.

Let’s take another look at the calculator program from chapter 5. The first thing we could do is section off the bit that asks for the user’s menu selection as a function:

```
#include <stdio.h>
/* declare selection function for later use */
char selection(void);

/* simple calculator with menu function */
void main()
{
    /* declare the variables */
    float first, second, result;
    char reply;

    /* get the user to enter the numbers */
    printf(“Enter the two numbers to be operated on \n”);
    scanf(“%f”,&first);
    scanf(“%f”,&second);
    /* print up menu */
    printf(“Which option do you require?\n”);
    printf(“a - addition\nb - subtraction\nc - multiplication\nd - ¬
division\n”);
    reply=selection();

    /* Got a decent reply - now to make the decision */
    switch (reply) {
        case ‘a’: result=first+second;
            break;
        case ‘b’: result=first-second;
            break;
        case ‘c’: result=first*second;
            break;
        case ‘d’: result=first/second;
            break;
        default:
            /* No need for anything here, since this part of the ¬
program should never be executed */
```

```
            break;
    }
    printf("\nThe result is %f\n",result);
}

/* now to define menu selection function */
char selection(void)
{
    /* declare local variable */
    char input;

    /* body of function takes input, converts it to upper case and ¬
checks its within acceptable bounds */
    do {
        scanf("%1s",&input);
        if (input>='A' && input<='Z')
            input=input+32;
    } while (input<'a' || input>'d');
    return input;
}
```

All we've done here is isolate the part of the program that accepts the user's input, converts it into upper case and checks to see if it's within the required range. If not, more input will be asked for. A consequence of separating the selection loop from the printing of the menu is that the menu is not re-drawn each time an incorrect entry is made.

The function **selection** returns a value of type **char** rather than **int**. Both the function prototype at the top of the program and the function definition at the end confirm this. It doesn't need any parameters, so the word **void** is placed in parentheses in both the declaration and definition.

The only benefit we've gained by using a function is taking all that messy loop business away from the main program. But the value of the functional approach becomes more obvious if we want to add an extra capability to our calculator.

Let's add an option, e, that computes percentages. It'll be a function that takes two floating point numbers as its parameters, and provides one floating point number, the answer, as its result. The prototype for such a function is as follows:

```
float percentage(float x, float y);
```

Put this line in at the top of the program, beneath the one that declares **selection**. Now we need to define the function. Place the following code at the end of the program file, after the closing curly brace of the **selection** definition:

```
/* definition of percentage function */
float percentage(float x, float y)
{
    /* define variable local to function */
    float result;

    /* compute x percent of y */
    result=(x/100.0)*y;
    return result;
}
```

Notice how the literal constant `100` has been written with a decimal point; this clarifies that it is being used as a floating point value in the expression.

Now we need to alter our menu display segment so that it reflects the new ability. Change the **printf** line that displays the menu to:

```
printf("a - addition\nb - subtraction\nc - ¬
multiplication\nd - division\ne - percentage\n");
```

The **switch** statement in main doesn't as yet take account of our new option. We need to alter it so that it calls **percentage** if the user enters an '`e`'. Change it to this:

```
switch (reply) {
    case 'a': result=first+second;
        break;
    case 'b': result=first-second;
        break;
    case 'c': result=first*second;
        break;
    case 'd': result=first/second;
        break;
    default:
    /* No need for anything here, since this part of the ¬
    program should never be executed */
        break;
    case 'e': result=percentage(first,second);
        break;
}
```

Notice that, because of the **break** following **default**, we can just add our new **case** in at the end of the **switch**, and still be sure that it will be chosen if and only if the user enters an 'e'.

At the moment, though, the **selection** function won't accept the letter 'e' as a valid input. It's a simple matter to change it so that it does. Just change the line ending the loop to:

```
} while (input<'a' || input>'e');
```

Easy. A better solution, though, would be for the main program to pass two arguments to **selection**. These arguments could be used as lower and upper bounds on valid input. That way our **selection** function would be of use in any circumstance where menu selection was required, no matter the number of options available. All we need to do is give the function two parameters of type **char**, and use these in the conditional part of the loop rather than the literals 'a' and 'e'.

Here's the new function:

```
char selection(char lower, char upper)
{
    /* declare local variable */
    char input;

    /* body of function takes input, converts it to upper case ¬
    and checks its within acceptable bounds */
    do {
        scanf("%1s",&input);
        if (input>='A' && input<='Z')
            input=input+32;
    } while (input<lower || input>upper);
    return input;
}
```

Don't forget that you'll have to change the function prototype at the top of the file to read:

```
char selection(char lower, char upper);
```

and the line that calls **selection** will have to be changed to:

```
reply=selection('a','e');
```

Just to prove that doing this is useful, here's a version of the program that will make two uses of the **selection** function. The first use will be as before, to enable the user to choose a calculation, with five options ranging from `a` to `e`. The second will be to ask the user if another calculation is required, with two options – `a` for yes, and `b` for quit.

To do this the main body of the program is enclosed within a **do... while** loop. At the end of the loop the user is presented with the choice of continuing or quitting. The loop goes around again so long as the user enters an '`a`', and stops as soon as a '`b`' is entered. By virtue of the **selection** function, no other entry is allowed.

Here's the listing:

```
#include <stdio.h>
/* declare functions for later use */
char selection(char lower,char upper);
float percentage(float x,float y);

/* simple calculator with menu function */
void main()
{
    /* declare the variables */
    float first, second, result;
    char reply;

    /* begin calculation loop */
    do {
    /* get the user to enter the numbers */
        printf("Enter the two numbers to be operated on \n");
        scanf("%f",&first);
        scanf("%f",&second);
        /* print up menu */
        printf("Which option do you require?\n");
        printf("a - addition\nb - subtraction\nc - multiplication\nd - ¬
division\ne - percentage\n");
        reply=selection('a','e');

        /* Got a decent reply - now to make the decision */
        switch (reply) {
            case 'a': result=first+second;
                break;
            case 'b': result=first-second;
                break;
            case 'c': result=first*second;
                break;
            case 'd': result=first/second;
                break;
            default:
                /* No need for anything here, since this part of ¬
the program should never be executed */
                break;
```

```
            case 'e': result=percentage(first,second);
                break;
        }
        printf("\nThe result is %f\n",result);

        /* give user chance for another go */
        printf("Another calculation?\na - yes\nb - no, quit\n");
        /* now close loop by getting and checking user's response */
    } while (selection('a','b')=='a');
    /* loop ends once user enters a 'b' */
}

/* now to define menu selection function */
char selection(char lower, char upper)
{
    /* declare local variable */
    char input;

    /* body of function takes input, converts it to upper case and ¬
checks its within acceptable bounds */
    do {
        scanf("%1s",&input);
        if (input>='A' && input<='Z')
            input=input+32;
    } while (input<lower || input>upper);
    return input;
}

/* definition of percentage function */
float percentage(float x, float y)
{
    /* define variable local to function */
    float result;

    /* compute x percent of y */
    result=(x/100.0)*y;
    return result;
}
```

Pointers

- More about decision-making
- Modifying arguments with pointers
- Pointers and arrays

Before going on to the main subject of this chapter – pointers – I first want to talk a little more about decision making. As you no doubt remember from chapter five, there are two ways in C to make decisions explicit (if you think about it, the loop control structures such as **do... while** are making implicit decisions) and those are the **switch** and the **if** statements.

More about decision-making

If and else

Switch is useful for deciding between one of a number of possible courses of action, but is limited in that decisions can only be made on expressions that evaluate to one of a set of constants. **If**, on the other hand, is capable of evaluating more subtle and complex expressions, by virtue of the various relational and logical operators. So far, though, we've only seen how it can be used to optionally perform a single course of action. But, like **switch**, it can in fact be used to decide between several courses.

The keyword **else** makes this possible. Type in the following quick example, which, rather usefully, decides whether or not the user has entered the letter 'a':

```
#include <stdio.h>

void main()
{
    char entry;

    /* get users input */
    printf("Enter a letter\n");
    scanf("%1s",&entry);

    /* print out appropriate message depending on value of entry */
    if (entry=='a')
        printf("You have entered an 'a'\n");
    else
        printf("You have not entered an 'a'\n");
}
```

Conditional 'if' statements can be nested within each other, in the same way you can nest parentheses.

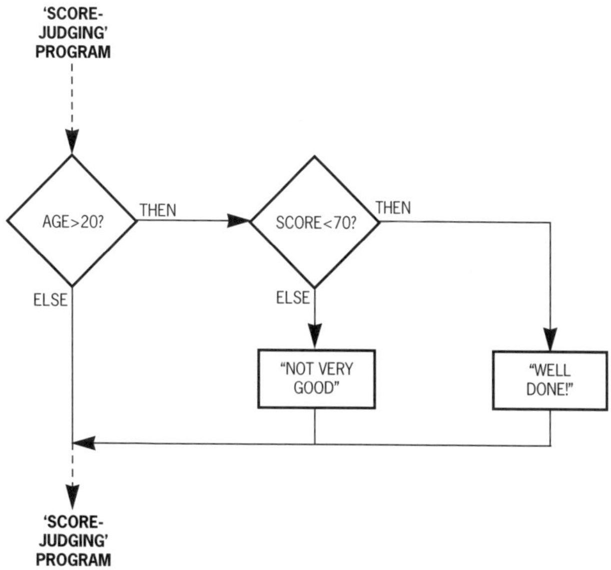

Nested 'if' structure

The **else** comes after the block defining the action to be taken if **if**'s expression evaluates to `true`. In this case the block consists of a single statement, so no delimiting curly braces are necessary. Following **else** is the block to be executed if the expression proves false. As with the previous block, it can consist of more than one statement, so long as they are all enclosed in curly braces.

'Nested' ifs

It's possible to place **if** constructs inside each other, so that a following **if** is only executed if its preceding one proves true. This is occurrence is known as a set of "nested" **if**s, and looks like this:

```
#include <stdio.h>

void main()
{
    int age, score;
```

```
    /* get info from user */
    printf("Please enter your age\n");
    scanf("%d",&age);
    printf("Please enter your percentage score\n");
    scanf("%d",&score);

    /* make decision on info */
    if (age>20)
        if (score<70)
            printf("That's not very good, is it?\n");
        else
            printf("Well done\n");
}
```

As it stands, the program will only judge the scores of users above the age of 20. It judges any score below 70 as being poor, and scores of 70 or higher as good. Notice how the **else** statement belongs to the **if** statement directly above it, rather than the previous one.

Using braces

Else statements are always taken to belong to the closest previous **if** that doesn't already have an associated **else**. The underlying logic of nested **if**s can sometime be hard to comprehend; enclosing the various consequential blocks in braces helps to make the logic more explicit. Here's the modified form of the decision making part of the above program:

CODE SEGMENT

```
    /* make decision on info */
    if (age>20) {
        if (score<70) {
            printf("That's not very good, is it?\n");
        } else {
            printf("Well done\n");
        }
    }
}
```

It now becomes obvious which **if** the **else** belongs to. If you wanted to change the program so that it chastised people over 20 who scored less

Conditional 'if' statements can also be used in series using the 'else if' construct.

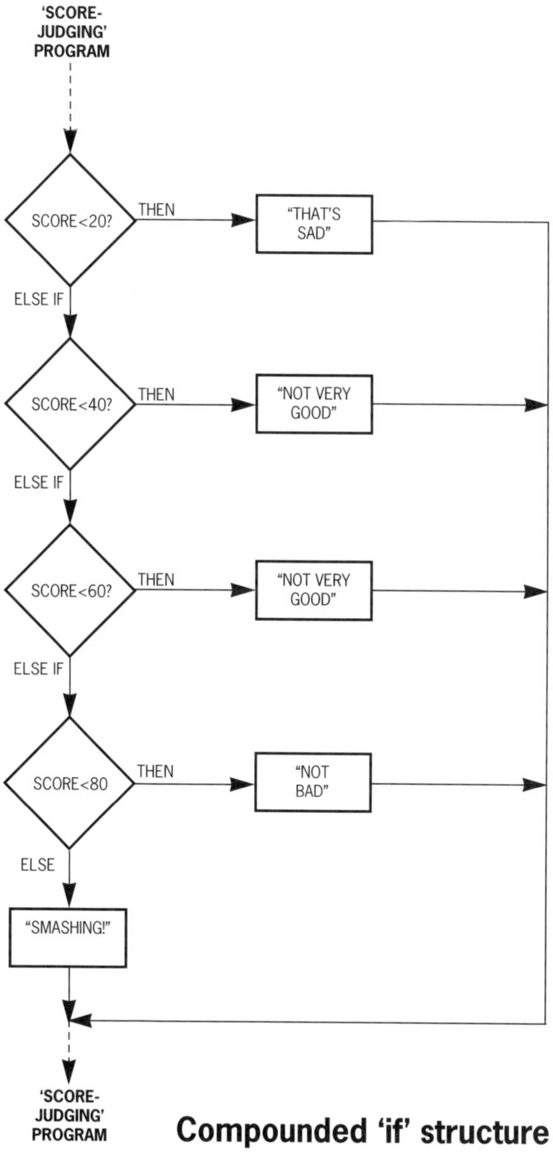

Compounded 'if' structure

than 70 and left them alone otherwise, while praising people of 20 years or less regardless of their scores (I know you wouldn't really want to, but it illustrates a valid point), you would need to use braces to force the **`else`** to associate with the first **`if`**:

```
    /* make decision on info */
    if (age>20) {
        if (score<70) {
            printf(“That’s not very good, is it?\n”);
        }
    } else {
            printf(“Well done\n”);
    }
}
```

It’s also possible to compound **if**s so that one is only executed if its predecessor proves false. Take a look at the following example:

```
#include <stdio.h>

void main()
{
    int score;

    /* get user’s score */
    printf(“Enter your score\n”);
    scanf(“%d”,&score);

    /* make decision on info */
    if (score<20)
        printf(“That’s sad\n”);
    else if (score<40)
        printf(“Not setting the world alight, are you?\n”);
    else if (score<60)
        printf(“Could do better\n”);
    else if (score<80)
        printf(“Not bad\n”);
    else
        printf(“Smashing!\n”);
}
```

As with the previous example, the consequences of each **if** must be enclosed with braces if they extend to more than one statement, and braces may also be used to increase the logic's clarity. They're not necessary in this example, though.

The sort of logic supplied by the **`if... else if`** construct is very similar to that supplied by the **`switch`** statement. Both enable the program to choose between one of several possible courses of action. But with **`switch`** we could have only tested for one of five possible values for **`score`**, rather than testing for its lying in one of five ranges as we do here. In fact, the expression in each of the **`if`** statements can be completely different from any of the others, giving you much more freedom in the kind of decisions you can get your programs to make.

With this sort of construct, each **`if`** is only tested if the one preceding it proves false. Once an **`if`** proves true, then the code forming its consequence is executed, and the entire construct is finished – no further **`else if`**s are tested (remember that to achieve the same effect with **`switch`** each set of statements must be terminated by a **`break`** statement).

The final **`else`**, without a following **`if`**, is equivalent to the **`default`** label with **`switch`** – the statement(s) following it are only executed if *all* of the previous **`if`**s have evaluated to false. Its use is optional.

It's also possible to include nested **`if`**s inside an **`if... else if`** construct – and here curly braces really *are* necessary to help you keep track of the decision-making logic. I'll wait until we're dealing with a program of sufficient complexity to justify its use before introducing an example of this.

WHAT DOES IT MEAN?

Conditional expression

C also provides something called a conditional expression. It's a shorthand way of deciding between one of two expressions, on the basis of a third, logical, expression. It's more succinct than **`if`**, and can sometimes come in handy. Here's a short example. It expects the string variable **`name`** to contain someone's name, and the character variable **`sex`** to contain either '`m`' or '`f`'. The following would print the person's name, preceded by either "`Mr`" or "`Mrs`" depending on the person's sex:

```
#include <stdio.h>

void main()
{
    char sex;
    char name[10];

    printf("Enter name\n");
    scanf("%s",name);
    printf("Enter sex\n");
    scanf("%1s",&sex);

    printf("Dear Mr%s %s.\n", (sex=='m') ? ("") : ("s"), name);
}
```

The conditional expression is the

```
(sex=='m') ? ("") : ("s");
```

bit in the **printf** statement (remember that in this example, because of the two **%s** sequences in the **printf** string, it is expecting two string expressions to print out). The first part, the expression preceding the question mark, is evaluated as a logical expression, yielding a value of either true or false. If it is true, then the value of the overall expression becomes the value of the expression immediately following the question mark, in this case an empty string. If it is false, the vale of the overall expression becomes the value of the expression following the colon. Notice that the type of the variable tested in the logical expression need not be the same as the type of the overall expression.

In this case we are using a character variable to decide which of two strings the overall expression will become. If **sex** contains 'm', then **printf** will take the first string, as denoted by **%s**, to be nothing, otherwise it will print an 's' immediately after "Mr".

A common use of the conditional expression is to assign one of two values to a variable. Here's a a segment that would assign the smallest of two integers to a third:

```
minimum = (first<second) ? (first) : (second);
```

The parentheses around the expressions aren't necessary, they just help to make things clear. The logical expression is (**first<second**). If it is true, that is to say, if the value of **first** is less than that of **second**, then the overall expression evaluates to **first**, and this value is assigned to **minimum**. Otherwise, the overall expression evaluates to **second**, and this value is assigned to **minimum**. The equivalent of this using an **if** and an **else** is as follows:

```
if (first<second)
    minimum=first;
else
    minimum=second;
```

Modifying arguments with functions

I don't know if you noticed, but I tried to slip something past you in that earlier Mr and Mrs example. If you look back to the **scanf** statement that was used to enter a value into the string called **name**, you'll notice the lack of the now customary **&** sign before the variable's name. What follows will explain this omission, and why the **&** sign has been necessary in other instances.

Let's take a look at a statement designed to input an integer:

```
scanf("%d",&entry);
```

Scanf is a function, and as such it returns a result. This result is *not* the value stored in **entry**. It is the number of assigned input items – useful because **scanf** can be used to input several items with a single call, but we won't go into that now.

That's the function's result, in the strict sense of the word, but the effect that we have so far used **scanf** for is the modification of a variable, i.e to have the user's input stored in such a variable. As I said in chapter 6, functions can normally return only one result, yet **scanf** returns a result *and* modifies one of its arguments.

When a function is called, any values passed are ARGUMENTS. These arguments become the function's PARAMETERS. The function acts on the parameters and returns its RESULT. But the original argument, e.g. a variable, remains unaltered.

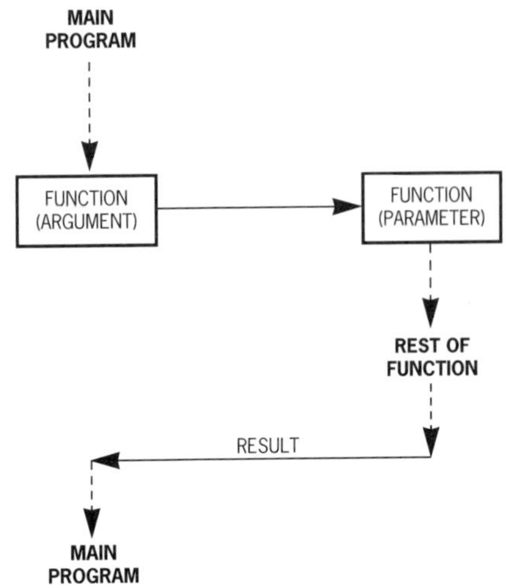

Functions, arguments & parameters

Normally, once an argument is passed to a function, that function gains a copy of the argument, known as a parameter. The function can modify the parameter without affecting the value of the original argument. Yet in the case of **`scanf`**, the function is modifying one of its arguments.

This is done by passing **`scanf`** not the contents of the variable to be modified, but the variable's address. The address, remember, is the location in memory that the variable is stored. Once **`scanf`** has this information, it can manipulate the contents of the relevant memory locations directly, so that once the function has finished the contents of the original variable are quite different.

You can get the address, rather than the value, of a variable by preceding its name with the "**`&`**" sign.

Pointer

Now that you can give your C programs direct access to memory locations, you also need a method to manipulate the contents of such locations. This is done by a device called a "pointer", which is one of the most potentially confusing areas of the language. It is also one of the aspects that give C its real power.

Instead of using variables, you can use 'pointers to variables'. These don't refer to the contents of the variable itself, only its current position in memory. If the variable is a large string, this can save a great deal of processing time.

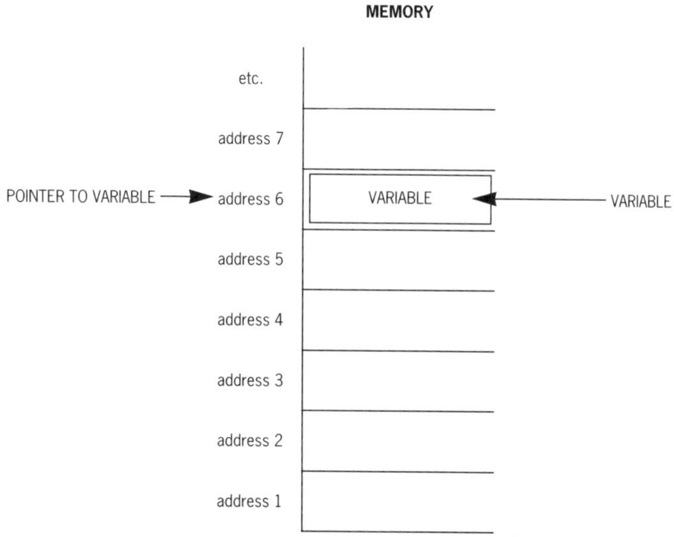

Variables and 'pointers to variables'

A pointer is a variable that contains a memory address. The variable "points" to an area in memory. You declare a variable as a pointer as follows:

```
int *pointer_to_integer;
```

Using pointers

The asterisk before the name in the declaration is the thing that distinguishes it from an ordinary integer. The declaration defines the variable as not only containing an address in memory, but also defines that the value held in that address should be of type integer. It is possible to declare pointers that point to other variable types. The reason C requires you to specify the type of information you're pointing to is that, once you start messing around with memory, it is important to have some sort of check that you are messing around with the right part of memory. Mistakes with pointers in C can cause your program to write to unpredictable memory locations, resulting in system crashes.

You could define an integer, and then an integer pointer to hold its address, with the following short segment:

```
void main()
{
    int number;
    int *pointer_to_number;

    pointer_to_number=&number;
}
```

The reason the usage of pointers and address can seem so confusing is because the whole thing is quite self-referential. The above example helps distinguish the elements. The variable **number** is an integer variable. The name **number** is a tag to indicate the contents of the variable at any given time. It is similar to, but not the same as, the address of the memory location where these contents are physically stored. Whenever the name **number** appears in an expression, the value used will be the variable's contents, an integer. The variable **pointer_to_number** contains the address of a memory location which in turn contains an integer value. The value of **pointer_to_number** is not of type integer, it is of type pointer. Here it is given the address of the variable **number**, obtained by preceding **number** with the "**&**" sign.

Often, as in the code internal to **scanf**, it is necessary to examine or modify the contents of the memory location that a pointer points to. This might have to be done because the variable name that also enables the program to access this memory location is not available.

For example, when a variable is passed to a function as a parameter, the function's parameter contains only the same value as the variable. Modifying this value will not modify the original value. And that's why a variable's address, rather than its value, must be passed to **scanf**. The address is stored by **scanf** as a pointer, and by making use of this pointer it alters those memory locations directly that comprise the variable in which the input is to be stored.

A program can access the contents of memory that a pointer points to by the following means:

```
#include <stdio.h>

int calculation(int first, int *pointer_to_number2);

void main()
{
    int number1,number2;

    /* get two numbers from user */
    printf("Enter two integers\n");
    scanf("%d%d",&number1,&number2);

    /* call function */
    printf("The product of the two numbers is %d\n",¬
calculation(number1,&number2));
    printf("And the first divided by the second gives %d\n",number2);
}

int calculation(int first, int *pointer_to_number2)
{
    int second;

    second=*pointer_to_number2;
    *pointer_to_number2=first/second;
    return (first*second);
}
```

Here we're expecting the function **calculation** to give us two values – that of its arguments multiplied together and that yielded by dividing the first value by the second value. The first value is returned as a simple result, so the function is defined as being of type **int**. In order to get the function to produce a second value, we pass it the address of the second number rather than the value itself as its second parameter (this is done in the first **printf** line), which enables it to directly alter the value of the integer.

This address is stored in a pointer, defined as the second parameter in the function's definition. Because the variable it points to is going to be modified for one calculation but its original value is also needed, a temporary variable, **second**, is also defined.

The asterisk in front of a variable name at declaration time is used to define the variable as being a pointer. When it is used at any other time it means that the value of interest is not the contents of the variable – a memory address – but rather the value stored in the memory address pointed to by the variable's contents. In this case, that memory address is where the contents of the variable **number2** is stored.

This value is first stored in **second**, because it will be needed again, after the contents of **number2** have been modified to be that of the variable first divided by second, in the line:

```
*pointer_to_number2=first/second;
```

The next line returns the value of the variables **first** and **second** multiplied together. This becomes the value of the expression, the function call, in the first **printf** line of the main program, and it is printed out.

The second **printf** line prints out the value of the variable **number2**, which has now been modified by the function **calculation**.

Arrays and pointers

That explains the use of the **&** character when getting **scanf** to input integers, floats or single characters, but why was not **&** necessary when we were calling **scanf** with a string array? The reason comes about because of the very close association between arrays (of any kind of variable) and pointers.

An array name is also the address of the first element in the array (the element numbered zero, that is). If we define a string array as:

```
char animal[]="elephant";
```

Then we can assign a pointer to point to the first element with:

```
char *pointer_to_character;
pointer_to_character=&animal[0];
```

But, because the array name, without any element of the array being specified, is itself the address of the first element, this assignment could also be made with:

```
pointer_to_character=animal;
```

Having performed either of these assignments, the first character of the array can be accessed either by the expression **animal[0]** or the expression ***pointer_to_character**. If you wanted to print out the second character in the array, (the letter 'l', element number 1) you could use the line:

```
printf("The second letter is %c\n",animal[1]);
```

but you could also use the line:

```
printf("The second letter is %c\n",*(pointer_to_character+1));
```

Here we're asking for the value held in the next address *after* the one pointed to by **pointer_to_character**. This is done by the addition of 1 to **pointer_to_character** (note that the parentheses are necessary, otherwise the compiler would retrieve the first letter via **pointer_to_character** and then add a value of 1 to it, turning it into the letter 'f').

MAKE A NOTE!

Accessing array elements

Adding 1 to the pointer before retrieving the value it points to is the same as accessing element 1 of the same array. Different types of variables taking up different amounts of space in memory. The elements of an array of **int** each take up four consecutive addresses, while those of an array of **char** only take up a single address each. Nevertheless, adding 1 to a pointer for either will still point at the next item in the array. It doesn't mean "look at the next address" but "look at the address where the next item in the array begins".

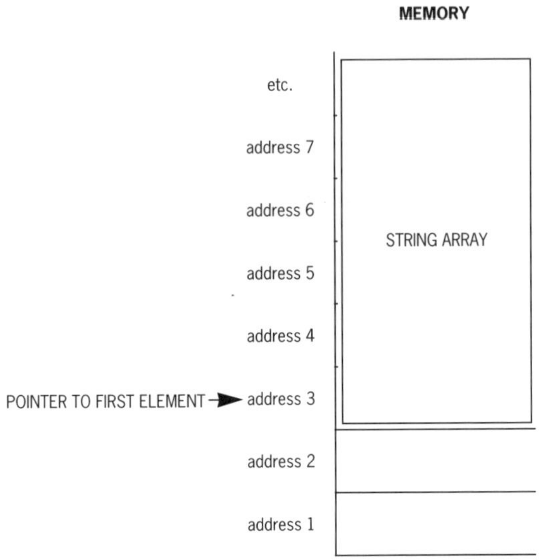

A string array may take up many memory addresses, but the array pointer always points to the address of the first element in the array.

Pointers to string arrays

Similarly, you can access element number **n** of an array (where **n** is of type **int**) either by writing **array_name[n]** or ***(pointer_to_array+n)**.

As you can see, when a string array, declared as

```
char name[10];
```

is passed to **scanf** with a line such as:

```
scanf("%s",name);
```

then it is the address of the string that is being passed, enabling **scanf** to modify the string's contents as it would the contents of any other type of variable passed. The line could be re-written as:

```
scanf("%s",&name[0]);
```

to achieve the same effect.

An array pointer points to the address of the first element (element 0) of the array. Add 1 to this pointer to point to where the next element in the array starts, add 2 to point to the next and so on. Adding 1 to the pointer always points to the next ***element****, not the next* ***address****.*

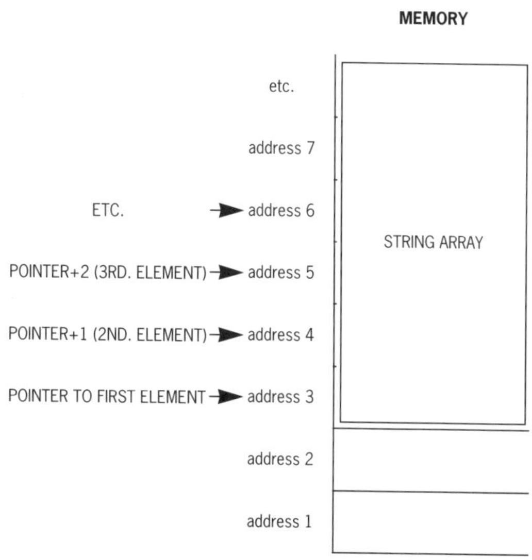

Pointers to successive array elements

You needn't pass the whole of an array to a function. You could, if you wished, pass it the address of a later element, perhaps because you wanted to preserve the first few characters of a string and get **scanf** to add the users input to the end. You could get **scanf** to input from element five onwards with the line:

```
scanf("%s",&name[5]);
```

which is equivalent to writing:

```
scanf("%s",name+5);
```

Let's take a look at a short example. This one will take ten integers and sort them into ascending order. We'll divide it into three main functions: **input**, which gets the ten numbers from the user; **sort**, which sorts them; and **output**, which prints out the result on the screen.

All three functions require the array to be passed to them. An array has to be passed as an address, rather then by having its values copied as is the

Our sort function works very simply. In stage 1 it goes through the elements in the array, comparing consecutive pairs and swapping them round so that the highest value is the second of the two. By the end, the highest value in the array is the last element. In successive stages, the number of comparisons is one less, and the array is sorted progressively from the 'top down'.

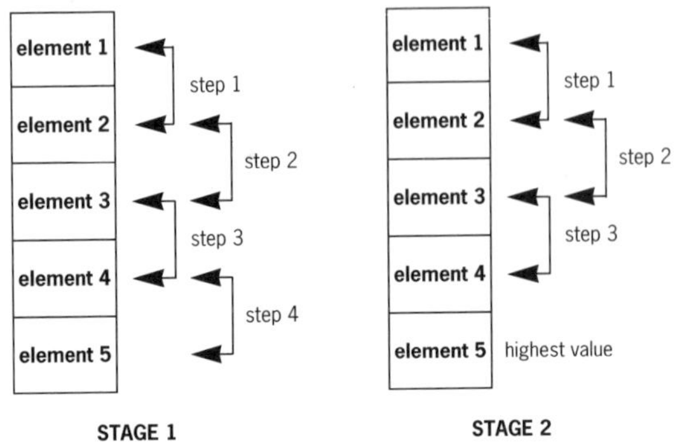

Basic sort function

case with other variable types. Arrays can be very large, and to copy them each time they were passed to a function would be expensive in terms of time and memory. This method of passing the address is the only solution. The function called can treat the address either as a pointer, or as an array name. It's usual to choose the method that makes the program clearer.

The `sort` function we're going to use is a simple one. It looks at successive pairs of the array. If the first is larger than the second, then the function swaps the two around. It then goes on to look at the second compared to the third, the third compared to the fourth, and so on. When it has gone through the entire array once, the highest of all the numbers will have been moved to the final element. The whole pair-checking procedure is then carried out again, with the final element being omitted. We can now be sure that the second largest number is stored in the penultimate array element. The pair-checking repeats, looking at progressively less and less of the array, until only the first two elements are compared, and if necessary changed.

Once this stage has been reached, the entire array has been sorted. See the diagram above for an example with five integers.

Now here's the source code to do it. Type it in and try it:

```
#include <stdio.h>

void input(int *numbers);
void sort(int *numbers);
void output(int *numbers);

void main()
{
    int data[10];

    input(&data[0]);
    sort(&data[0]);
    output(&data[0]);
}

void input(int *numbers)
{
    int counter;

    /* get elements 0 to 9 */
    for (counter=0; counter<10; counter++)
        scanf("%d",&numbers[counter]);
}

void output(int *numbers)
{
    int counter;

    /* output elements 0 to 9 */
    for (counter=0; counter<10; counter++)
        printf("%d\n",numbers[counter]);
}

void sort(int *numbers)
{
    int counter, limit, temp;

    /* work initially through elements 0 to 8, then 0 to 7, 0 to ¬
```

```
6... 0 to 0 */
    for (limit=8;limit>=0;limit-)

        /* work through sub-group of elements specified by outer limit */
        for (counter=0;counter<=limit;counter++)
            /* compare an element with the next in sequence */
            if (numbers[counter]>numbers[counter+1]) {

                /* if it is greater than its successor, then swap ¬
them both */
                temp=numbers[counter];
                numbers[counter]=numbers[counter+1];
                numbers[counter+1]=temp;
            }
}
```

Notice that in the function definitions, the parameters were declared as being of type pointer to integer, rather than of type array of integer, which would have been written as:

CODE SEGMENT

```
void output(int numbers[])
```

This is also acceptable, but the definitions in the example above make it clearer that it's a pointer being passed, and that the array is *not* being passed by value, a copy is *not* being made.

The functions themselves deal with the array as an array, rather than using pointer notation. In this particular instance, it's clearer that way, but here it is using pointer notation instead, so that you can compare:

COMPLETE LISTING

```
#include <stdio.h>

void input(int *numbers);
void sort(int *numbers);
void output(int *numbers);

void main()
{
```

```
    int data[10];

    input(data);
    sort(data);
    output(data);
}

void input(int *numbers)
{
    int counter;

    /* get elements 0 to 9 */
    for (counter=0; counter<10; counter++)
        scanf("%d",numbers+counter);
}

void output(int *numbers)
{
    int counter;

    /* output elements 0 to 9 */
    for (counter=0; counter<10; counter++)
        printf("%d\n",*(numbers+counter));
}

void sort(int *numbers)
{
    int counter, limit, temp;

    /* work initially through elements 0 to 8, then 0 to 7, 0 to ¬
6... 0 to 0 */
    for (limit=8;limit>=0;limit—)

        /* work through sub-group of elements specified by outer limit */
        for (counter=0;counter<limit;counter++)
            /* compare an element with the next in sequence */
            if (*(numbers+counter)>*(numbers+counter+1)) {
```

```
                    /* if it is greater than its successor, then swap ¬
them both */
                    temp=*(numbers+counter);
                    *(numbers+counter)=*(numbers+counter+1);
                    *(numbers+counter+1)=temp;
                }
}
```

Compare both versions, to be sure you understand the correspondences between arrays and pointers. Pay particular attention to the uses of **scanf** in both, and how they differ from the uses of **printf** – **printf** requires a value to be passed to it, whereas **scanf** requires the address of a value.

Pointers enable functions to modify variables they wouldn't otherwise be able to, thus enabling functions to return more than a single result. They also enable large amounts of data – in the form of arrays and other data types we've yet to discuss – to be passed to functions without massive memory overheads. These attributes make pointers ideal for operating

*Passing pointers to arrays to functions is not only quicker (the pointers may be many times smaller than the arrays themselves), it also lets the called function modify the array directly, not just a **copy** of the array.*

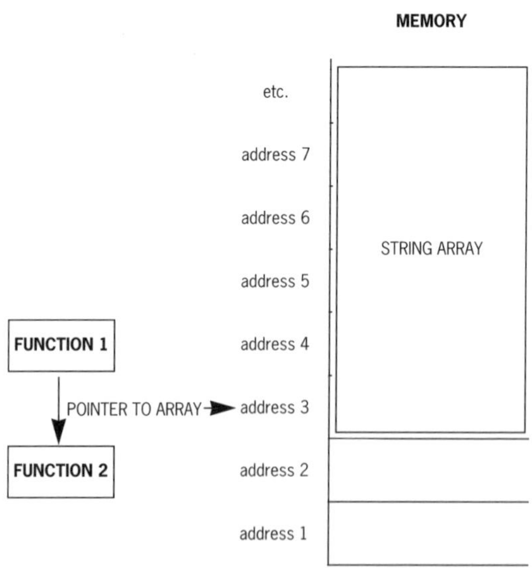

Passing pointers to functions

system use, and necessary for when you want to interface your programs to the Amiga's operating system. It's important to be reasonably comfortable with pointers, because you won't open any screens or windows without them.

Pointers and strings

- Two-dimensional arrays
- Modifying our 'sort' program
- Standard library string functions
- Initialising arrays on declaration
- Sharing variables amongst functions

Before going any further, we'll look into another very common use of pointers – when they are used to access strings.

String

A string is an array of characters, so all of what was said in the previous chapter about the correspondences between pointers and arrays holds true for strings, too. In addition, you may remember the shorthand notation for both declaring a string and defining its contents:

```
char animal[]="elephant";
```

in which the array is declared to be of the necessary size to hold the string – in this case 9 elements, numbered from 0 to 8. Remember that the final element of the string contains the '\0' character, or integer value 0, to mark the string's end. You could also define the string as a constant with a pointer pointing to it:

```
char *pointer_to_string="elephant";
```

Again, the string is terminated by a '\0' character. The difference, though, is that **animal** always references the same string. Its contents can be changed, but it always indicates the same area of memory, and an array of the same size. The variable **pointer_to_string**, although it begins by pointing to a string constant, can be modified so that it points to another area of memory entirely.

Passing strings

When you pass a string constant, enclosed in double quotes, as an argument to **printf**, what **printf** actually receives is a pointer to that string constant. There is no mechanism for passing strings directly between functions, they must be passed as pointers. It's possible to group strings together, just like simple variables such as **int**s, into arrays. But since each string is itself an array, an array of strings is in fact an array of arrays.

Two-dimensional arrays

Arrays of arrays are more usually called two dimensional arrays. Their original use was to store matrices, which you may have come across in maths. If you declare an array as follows:

```
int numbers[10][20];
```

You've created an array called **`numbers`**, with 10 elements. Each of these 10 elements contains a further 20 elements, all of which can be used to hold an integer **`number`**. There are in total 200 elements. You can think of the array's two indices as co-ordinates, referencing a particular point on a two-dimensional grid. The array is the grid, and each point on the grid can contain an integer value. Such an array is useful for storing something such as a chess board, which would be an array of 8 by 8 elements.

The same applies to strings. The declaration for an array of 10 strings, each no longer than 20 characters, would be as follows:

```
char words[10][20];
```

Each of the 10 elements of words is itself made up of 20 characters, which can be individually accessed by providing a number between `0` and `19` as the second index.

This is an array of 10 elements, each of which contains its own array, of 20 elements. Each element can be accessed by quoting its 'grid reference'.

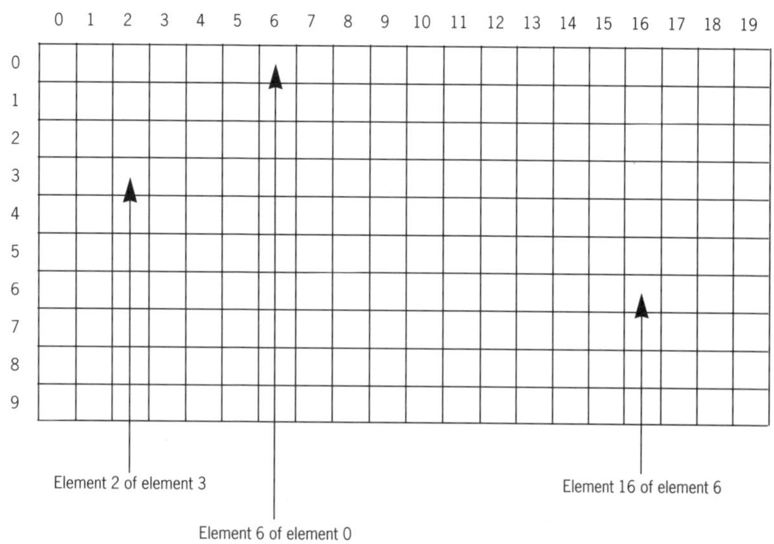

A two-dimensional array

Notice how the space for the strings is here fixed in advance. No strings longer than 20 characters (including the terminating '\0') can be stored. Similarly, no space is saved if the strings held are shorter than the size of the array – the extra elements are filled with garbage.

Modifying our 'sort' program

To illustrate the use of string arrays, we'll convert the sorting program from the last chapter to sort words instead of numbers. Here's how the string arrays are implemented in the sort example:

```
#include <stdio.h>

/* declaration of a handy string function */
int stringlarger(char first[], char second[]);

/* and the three main functions of the program */
void input(char words[][20]);
void sort(char words[][20]);
void output(char words[][20]);

void main()
{
    char words[10][20];

    input(words);
    sort(words);
    output(words);
}

int stringlarger(char first[], char second[])
{
    /* returns a value of 1 if the first string is alphabetically ¬
after the second, 0 otherwise */

    int counter=0;

    while (first[counter]!='\0' && second[counter]!='\0' && ¬
```

```
first[counter]==second[counter])
        counter++;
    if (first[counter]=='\0' || first[counter]<second[counter]) return 0;
    return 1;
}

void input(char words[][20])
{
    int counter;

    /* get elements for 10 strings */
    for (counter=0; counter<10; counter++)
        scanf("%s",&words[counter][0]);
}

void output(char words[][20])
{
    int counter;

    /* output elements 0 to 9 */
    for (counter=0; counter<10; counter++)
        printf("%s\n",&words[counter][0]);
}

void sort(char words[][20])
{
    int counter, limit,i;
    char temp;

    /* work initially through elements 0 to 8, then 0 to 7, 0 to ¬
6... 0 to 0 */
    for (limit=8;limit>=0;limit–)

        /* work through sub-group of elements specified by outer limit */
        for (counter=0;counter<=limit;counter++)
            /* compare an element with the next in sequence */
            if (stringlarger(&words[counter][0],&words[counter+1][0])) {
                /* if it is greater than its successor, then swap ¬
```

```
them both */
                for (i=0;i<20;i++) {
                   /* work through all elements of the ¬
string - 0 to 19 */

                   /* swap each character in turn */
                   temp=words[counter][i];
                   words[counter][i]=words[counter+1][i];
                   words[counter+1][i]=temp;
                }
            }
}
```

Converting the program to sort strings rather than integers has added a number of complications. For one thing, we've needed a support function to help us in manipulating the strings. **`Stringlarger`** takes two strings as its parameters and decides which is the greater, or which comes last alphabetically. Because of the way the ASCII character code is mapped out, upper case letters are treated as being lower in the alphabet than lower case ones.

The function searches through each element of both arrays in turn. If it finds a difference between the two arrays, or if it comes to the end of either, then the loop will exit. Once this happens, a result of `0` is returned if the value of the last element checked is less for the first array than for the second, or if the end of the first array has been reached. Otherwise, a value of `1` is returned. A consequence is that if two arrays are otherwise the same, the shorter of the two will be considered to be the lowest in value.

The three main functions, **`input`**, **`sort`** and **`output`**, have had to be modified extensively. All now accept an array of **`char`** arrays as a parameter. In the function definitions, and in any functions which accept two-dimensional arrays as parameters, the number of sub-elements making up each array element must be declared. The functions can be passed arrays with any number of primary elements, but the number of sub-elements of which they consist must be defined in advance.

Modifying 'input'

The function **input** uses the integer variable **counter** to work through each of the array elements in turn, from 0 to 9. For each, **scanf** is called to get a string from the user. We want the string to be copied into the sub-elements numbered 0 to 19, so we must pass **scanf** the address of the first (or, more correctly, zeroeth!) sub-element of the string referenced by **counter**. This is done with the '**&**' character. Notice that just passing **scanf** the array name, **words**, would give it a pointer to the first element of the first string of the array – it would be equivalent to writing **&words[0][0]**, which is no good for our purposes.

Modifying 'output'

The function **output** should seem straightforward, the main difference from the earlier version being that instead of passing an integer to **printf** it now passes a pointer to a string (the string again being chosen by the integer variable **counter**).

Modifying 'sort'

The modifications to **sort** are the most dramatic. The comparison between the two elements here cannot be done by a relational operator like '**<**', which can only be applied to simple types such as **int** or **char**. Instead, **sort** calls the function **stringlarger** to make the decision. Notice again how pointers to the first element for each string, as referenced by **counter** and **counter +1**, are given by using the '**&**' sign. If **stringlarger** returns a value of **1**, meaning the first string is larger than the second, then **sort** must swap the two strings around. Doing this involves swapping each of the character elements of the strings separately.

To this end, a simple loop is set up, cycling from 0 to 19 to encompass all the elements. An element of the string referenced by **counter** is stored in a temporary character variable, then the element is given the value of the equivalent element in the string referenced by **counter+1**. This element is in turn given the value of the temporary variable. Once the loop has completed, all the elements have been swapped.

An alternative solution

There's another way of approaching this problem. At the moment, the program will only sort 10 words, no more, no less. Also, each word can be no longer than 20 characters in length. That's because we defined the amount of space the string array would take up at the beginning of the program, when we declared it. Declaring any variable within a function means that memory space is reserved for that variable until the function ends, at which point the memory is relinquished to the operating system. In the case of variables declared in **main**, their space remains until the program finishes executing.

It would be possible to make the program cater for more and longer words by increasing the dimensions of the array, but this would result in the program grabbing more memory than it needed if the user actually only wanted to sort a few words.

Using malloc

WHAT DOES IT MEAN? **Malloc**

What we need is a way of grabbing memory space while our program is running, if and when it needs it. There's a standard C function called **malloc** which will do just this. You call it with the quantity of memory you require, measured in units known as bytes. I'll go into more detail about bytes later, for now all you need to know is that one byte is required to store each element of a character array. **Malloc** returns as its result a pointer to the memory space given by the operating system. If no space is available, then the pointer returned has a value of NULL. Before the pointer can be used as a pointer to a string, it must first be changed into a pointer of the correct type (in our case a pointer to type **char**). This is done by a process known as "casting", whereby the pointer is preceded by parentheses containing the type it should be converted to:

EXAMPLE CODE

```
pointer_to_string=(char *)malloc(20);
```

would create space for a string of 20 elements. **Malloc** can be used as an alternative to declaring arrays at the start of the program. It is useful if your program won't know how much storage space it needs until it is actually running.

So we can create space for each string as it is needed, along with a pointer to that string, but it is still convenient to group these strings in some way so that we can process them en masse, specifically by using loop constructs rather than having to access each by its individual name.

String pointers rather than strings

This is done by storing the pointers to the strings in an array. The memory the strings themselves are held in may be scattered far and wide – **malloc** bestows chunks of memory from where it and the operating system see fit – but the pointers to these memory arrays are all stored consecutively in one array. You'd declare such an array as follows:

```
char *pointers_to_words[10];
```

This still means that an arbitrary boundary must be placed on the number of words sorted, but remember that here we're only declaring space for a group of pointers, each small in comparison to the strings they may end up pointing to, which are not themselves stored until needed. Therefore we can afford to make the limit that much higher. In the following example, I've made it 50 elements (numbered 0 to 49) by defining a constant **MAXWORDS** with the value 50 and using it in the array declaration at the beginning of **main**.

As a consequence, **input** has been modified so that it accepts as many strings as the user requires, so long as there is sufficient memory and the **MAXWORDS** limit is not exceeded. The user indicates that the last string has been entered by entering 'q'. **Input** will then return the number of words entered as an integer result. The functions **sort** and **output** have been modified to take this integer as a parameter, so that they only sort through the elements of the array of interest. I'll talk more about the program after you've typed it in...

```
#include <stdio.h>
#define MAXWORDS 50

/* declaration of three useful string functions */
int length(char *word);
void putstring(char *source, char *destination);
```

```
int stringlarger(char *first, char *second);

/* the program's primary functions */
int input(char *words[]);
void sort(char *words[],int number);
void output(char *words[],int number);

void main()
{
    char *words[MAXWORDS];
    int number_of_words;

    number_of_words=input(words);
    sort(words,number_of_words);
    output(words,number_of_words);
}

int length(char *word)
{
    /* function that returns the length of a word, not including ¬
the terminating '\0' character */
    int result=0;
    while (word[result]!='\0')
        result++;
    return result;
}

void putstring(char *source, char *destination)
{
    /* copy the contents of the first string into the contents of ¬
the second */
    int position=0;

    do {
        destination[position]=source[position];
        position++;
    } while (destination[position-1]!=0);
}
```

```
int stringlarger(char *first, char *second)
{
    /* returns a value of 1 if the first string is alphabetically ¬
after the second, 0 otherwise */

    int counter=0;

    while (first[counter]!='\0' && second[counter]!='\0' && ¬
first[counter]==second[counter])
        counter++;
    if (first[counter]=='\0' || first[counter]<second[counter]) return 0;
    return 1;
}

int input(char *words[])
{
    int counter,length_of_word;
    char entered_word[20]; /* variable for remembering most ¬
recently entered word, no longer than 19 characters plus a '\0' long */

    /* get strings until user enters an empty string */
    for (counter=0; counter<MAXWORDS; counter++) {
        scanf("%s",entered_word);
        length_of_word=length(entered_word);
        /* enter 'q' to mark end of words to be sorted */

        if ((length_of_word>1 || entered_word[0]!='q') && ¬
((words[counter]=(char *)malloc(length_of_word+1))!=NULL))

            putstring(entered_word,words[counter]);
        else return counter-1;
    }
    return counter-1;
}

void output(char *words[], int number)
{
```

```
    int counter;

    /* output elements 0 to number */
    for (counter=0; counter<=number; counter++)
        printf("%s\n",words[counter]);
}

void sort(char *words[],int number)
{
    int counter, limit;
    char *temp;

    /* work initially through elements 0 to (number-1), then 0 to ¬
(number-2), 0 to number(-3)... 0 to 0 */
    for (limit=number-1;limit>=0;limit—)

        /* work through sub-group of elements specified by outer limit */
        for (counter=0;counter<=limit;counter++)
            /* compare an element with the next in sequence */
            if (stringlarger(words[counter],words[counter+1])) {

                /* if it is greater than its successor, then swap ¬
them both */
                temp=words[counter];
                words[counter]=words[counter+1];
                words[counter+1]=temp;
            }
}
```

Further modifications

The change over from arrays of arrays to arrays of pointers has meant that we need another two string functions.

The first of these, **`length`**, returns the length of a string, not counting its final element which holds the string terminating character. In other words, it holds the element number in which the terminating character was stored. So if the user enters an empty string, **`length`** will return a value of 0 when asked to give the string's length. It works by counting element by element through the string passed it, until it encounters a terminating character. When it does, it returns the value of its counter variable.

Putstring copies the contents of one string into another. Since strings are arrays, a simple assignment won't suffice – instead, **putstring** has to copy each character in turn from one array to the other. There is no need to copy elements after a string terminator has been copied, so this happily provides the termination condition for the copying loop.

The function **input** now needs a temporary string, **entered_word**. Each of the strings entered by the user is in turn stored in this variable. **Input** then sets up a loop, counting from 0 to the maximum allowable number of words defined by **MAXWORDS**.

For each time round the loop, **scanf** is called with the array **entered_word** as an argument. The function **length** is called so that we can store **entered_word**'s length in the integer variable **length_of_word**.

The next line is the clever one. It first of all checks that the input was not a request to quit, by checking if **length_of_word** is larger than 1 or if the first character is not 'q'. It then calls **malloc** to gain the required amount of space to store the word. Notice how the second part of the **if** statement

```
&& words[counter]=(char *)malloc(length_of_word+1)
```

CODE SEGMENT

asks for the necessary amount of memory (with 1 element more than **length_of_word** being needed to take into account the string terminator) and assigns the address of this memory to the relevant pointer in the array of pointers words.

If there was insufficient space for the word, then the function would return a value of 0, meaning that the statement immediately following – the one that calls the function to copy **entered_word** into the space we've just been given – would not be executed. The failure of the **if** statement means that no more input should be expected, so the function finishes by returning the variable **counter-1**, which corresponds to the last element filled.

If the **if** statement proved true, and the entered word was copied, then the **for** loop is closed and the next word is requested from the user.

Notice that once **input** finishes, the contents of all its variables are forgotten for good. This doesn't apply to the memory obtained by **malloc**, though. This will remain throughout the program's life, and can be accessed by any part of the program that knows where it is.

The function **output** should seem straightforward, the main difference from the earlier version being that instead of checking through 10 elements, it checks through a number of elements specified by its second argument.

This also applies to **sort**. This function has one major advantage over its previous version. In that version, when two strings were to be swapped, each of their elements had to be swapped individually by means of a **for** loop. In our new version, all we do is swap the pointer values so that one element of the array points to what the other used to, and vice versa. The contents of the memory where the strings themselves are stored remains untouched, which means that this version of the program will run significantly faster.

The three string functions – **length**, **putstring** and **stringlarger** – used in this last example are primitive forms of string functions supplied with C. I've included them here so that you can see how simple string manipulation is done.

Standard library string functions

In your own programs, it's better to use the standard library functions stored in **string.h**, which can be accessed by using the include line:

```
#include <string.h>
```

The equivalent to **length** is **strlen**; the equivalent to **putstring** is **strcpy**, which returns a pointer to the original string (and works in reverse – copying the second string argument into the first); and the equivalent to **stringlarger** is **strcmp**, which is defined to return an integer less than zero if the first is less than the second string, zero if they are the same, and greater than zero otherwise.

Initialising arrays on declaration

As well as getting input from the user as a means of storing information in multi-dimensional arrays, it's also possible to initialize them with values when they are declared.

As you may remember, a simple array is declared and initialized as follows:

```
int numbers[]={5,20,7,3};
```

which would result in the array **numbers** being declared to have elements numbered 0 to 3, each with their values taken from those in the curly braces. You can initialize a multi-dimensional array as follows:

```
int numbers[][]={
    {5,20,7,3},
    {1,42,9,8},
    {7,2,1,0}};
```

would result in array with 3 elements, each consisting of 4 sub-elements. The elements of the array, as referenced by the left-most index, are often called "rows", while their sub-elements, as referenced by the right-most index, are called "columns". The terminology comes from the correspondence of a two-dimensional array with a grid. Here we've declared an array with 3 rows, each containing 4 columns. The way the array's values are laid out in the source code affirms this correspondence.

A similar initialisation can be performed for arrays of pointers. Look at the following:

```
char *future_mags[]={
    "Amiga Shopper", "Amiga Format", "Amiga Power", "some others"};
```

Space is provided for each of the strings, and then a pointer for each is stored in the array. The number of elements created is that demanded by the number of strings – in this case 4, numbered 0 to 3.

Normally, variables declared in one function can be used by that function only, and are invisible to all others. They are described as being "local" to the function. One function is normally made aware of some of the variables of another when they are passed as parameters. When this happens, copies of the variables are made, and the function receiving the parameters only modifies its own copies. The values of the original variables remain the same. The copies are local to the function to which they were passed – modifying them will not change the variables of any other function. As you have seen, pointers provide a way around this, meaning that functions can share variables so long as they have pointers that indicate where the variables are stored in memory.

When you pass a variable as a parameter, the called function simply receives a copy of the variable – it cannot modify the original. When you pass a variable pointer, however, you are telling the called function where it can find the original variable in memory – now it ***can*** *modify it.*

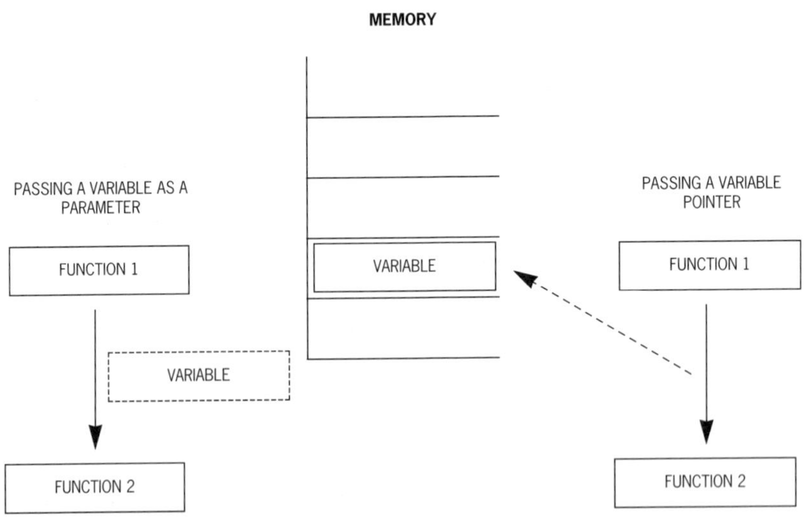

Passing pointers rather than variables

Sharing variables among functions

All of the variables we have dealt with so far are "automatic" variables. This means that space is created for them when they are defined within a function, and that when the function ends those variables are forgotten, and the memory space they used is given back to the operating system. It's a common mistake to create a variable within a function, and then pass a pointer to this variable back once the function has ended. Any other part of the program that subsequently tries to access the variable via the pointer will end up trying to access a part of memory that no longer belongs to it.

The problem doesn't occur in the above example, because the variables to be used across several functions are defined in **main**, and remain in existence until **main** ends – the end of the program. Also, memory taken for variables on the fly, via **malloc**, will remain with the program until it ends or gives the memory back by calling the function **free**.

There is another way of enabling several functions to have access to the same variable, by declaring it outside of any function definitions:

```
void main()
{ /* main program */ }
int fred;
void function1()
{ /* function definition */ }
void function2()
{ /* function definition */ }
```

In the above example, **fred** would be visible to and modifiable by both **function1** and **function2**. A further property of variables declared in this way is that, unlike automatic variables, they remain in existence throughout the life of the program.

In the above example, **fred** is invisible to **main**. Variables declared outside of functions are only visible to the functions whose definitions follow it in the source code file. Any variable type, including arrays, can be defined in this way.

If you want a variable to be 'visible' to functions, it must be declared before the functions are called. The actual variable ***definition*** *can be placed anywhere, though (but it must be defined somewhere in the code).*

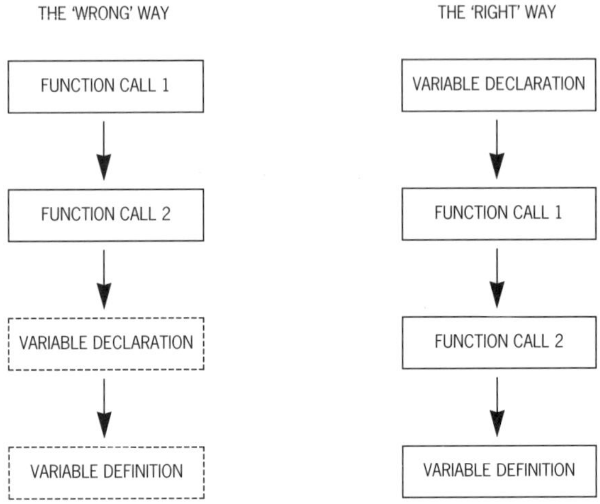

Variable 'visibility'

In this respect, the variables definitions are similar to function definitions. Any function within a source file can make use of any other function so long as the definition of the latter precedes the former. We've done things differently, in our examples we've first defined **`main`** and then defined the functions that **`main`** will call. This makes the source code easier to read, but in order that **`main`** can make use of those functions they must be declared before **`main`** is defined.

'Declaration' vs. 'definition'

The difference is between declaring and defining. A declaration simply makes the compiler aware that a function exists and aware of some of its properties. The actual definition, which contains the code that makes up the function, can follow later. So long as a function's declaration (or "prototype") appears in a source file, and a definition for it exists somewhere, then it can be called from within that source file.

The variables we've so far used have been declared and defined together. The definition causes space to be set aside for the them, and sometimes, as in the case of array initialisation, values to be assigned to them immediately. The same rule applies – a variable can only be used by code that follows its definition in the source file.

The way around the rule is the same, too – you can declare a variable without defining it until later to enable code between the declaration and the definition to use the variable.

Using extern

In the example above, **fred** is defined after the definition of **main**, so it is only visible to **function1** and **function2**. If we wanted **fred** to be visible to **main**, too, we could declare it first by use of the **extern** keyword:

```
extern int fred;
void main()
{ /* main program */ }
int fred;
void function1()
{ /* function definition */ }
void function2()
{ /* function definition */ }
```

This now means **main** is just as free as **function1** and **function2** to write to and read values from **fred**. Any variable type can be declared by **extern**. Array sizes need not be included in the declaration, so:

```
extern char sentence[];
```

is legal, although the variable must also be defined at some point in the program, too.

It is possible, and usually practical with larger works, to split several programs over several files. You might have one source file that contains your data definitions, another that holds a lot of commonly used functions, and another that contains the main processing engine, including **main**.

You may have one or more variables defined in one file that another needs to access. In this case, the second file will contain declarations of the necessary variables, each preceded by **extern**.

*The **extern** keyword lets you access variables held in other source code files.*

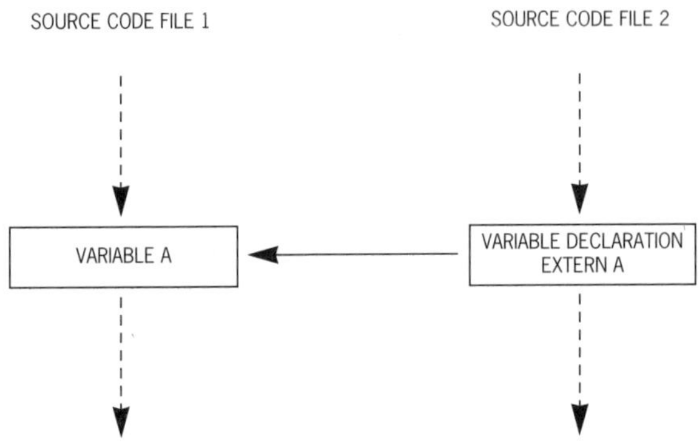

The `extern` keyword

Using static

Sometimes, it's desirable to have the opposite – a variable that is visible to all the functions in one file, but that cannot be accessed by functions in another file. One advantage of doing this is not having to worry about naming conflicts – you can name the variables in one file whatever you like without worrying about them referencing variables in another file connected with your project. This effect is achieved by preceding the variable's definition (not declaration) by the **static** keyword. For instance:

```
static int fred;

void main()
{
/* the rest of the program */
}
```

Here, **fred** would only be usable by **main** and any other functions which were defined after it in the same file. A variable called **fred** in a different file, perhaps joined with this one at compile time, would reference a different object entirely.

If you declare a variable as **static** inside a function definition, as follows:

```
int length_of_string(char *string_pointer)
{
    static int fred;
    /* rest of the function */
```

then it will only be visible inside the function – that is, no other function can access it unless they are given a pointer to it – but its contents will not be lost when the function exits. If the function is called again, then **fred** will still have the value it did when the function last exited. Similarly, if another function accesses **fred** via a pointer after the first has been called, then the value it finds there will be that left there by the first function.

WARNING

Sharing data

Pointers, declaring variables outside functions, and the **extern** keyword all enable functions to share variables. By using the **static** keyword you can ensure that this sharing is restricted to only those programs that *need* to share. The reason it's used is that by far the safest way to pass data between functions is by the use of parameters and return values. It's just so much easier to keep track of everything. If a function has access to data outside its usual scope, it's possible that a bug can be introduced that causes the function to modify that data. Such bugs can be very difficult to track down, because they can lie in any one of the functions that has access to the data. Nevertheless, it's often necessary, as you've seen, for functions to share data that cannot be passed as arguments: arguments to functions are passed as simple values – you cannot pass complex variables such as arrays – and neither can you return an array as the result of a function. So, when sharing data between functions, be careful.

Writing a spreadsheet

- The planning stage
- Designing the program
- How the program works

For this chapter we're going to create a quite ambitious program that will demonstrate some of the recently discussed topics such as arrays, pointers and strings – a spreadsheet. It won't be like the simple calculator-style programs discussed in earlier chapters, but a cell-based system capable of reasonably complex calculations.

The planning stage

When larger programs are to be written, it's often best to look at the kind of data they will use before thinking about their code structure. The most important data structure of a spreadsheet program is the spreadsheet itself – a two-dimensional grid. Clearly the best way of representing this is going to be as some sort of two-dimensional array.

For simplicity's sake, we'll limit the size of the spreadsheet to the screen area, otherwise we're going to have to get involved in screen scrolling and all sorts of tricky problems. This will give us an array of 5 by 15, with each cell taking a single line and being 10 characters wide (I'm assuming you're using an 60-column display mode).

The next question is: what kind of data is stored in the array? The most common kind is numbers, floating point numbers. But spreadsheets also need to store text messages – column headings and so forth – as well as the all-important formulae. The best way to hold text is as a string. It's possible to store numbers as strings, too, and convert each string to a number as the program needs it for calculation. This method also works well for the formulae. For now we'll restrict ourselves to simple formulae, those that include two cell references separated by a simple maths operation: `+`,`-`,`*` and `/`.

We could represent the spreadsheet as a two-dimensional array of strings – that is, a three-dimensional array of characters – but it's better to use a two-dimensional array of pointers and allocate space to each string as it is needed. That way, we only need storage for as many cells as the user wants (this advantage becomes far more important for larger spreadsheets).

Our spreadsheet is designed to occupy a single 60-column screen. Each of the 5 spreadsheet columns is 10 columns wide, each of the 15 rows is a single line. The data is held in a corresponding 15 x 5 element two-dimensional array.

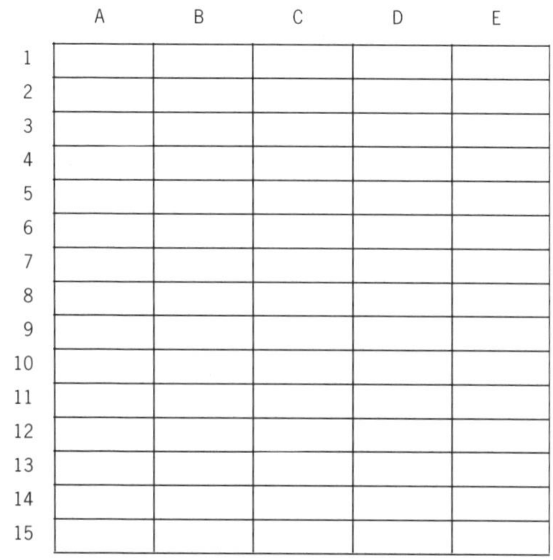

Our spreadsheet's layout

Designing the program

Given the main data structure, we can now start thinking about the program itself. The kind of data structure we've decided on immediately defines some support functions we'll need: a function to convert numbers written as strings into `float`s, and a function to interpret formulae that are represented by strings.

We'll also need a means of getting input from the user. Rather than checking the keyboard for the arrow keys and moving a cursor around the screen, we'll take the easy option. The user is asked to enter the co-ordinates of the cell of interest, and then enter the contents of that cell. If the string entered begins with an equals sign, then it is taken to represent a formula, if it begins with a numeral it is taken to be a number, otherwise it is assumed to be a text message. Every time the user enters some data, the whole spreadsheet is re-printed on the screen. If any of the cells contain formulae, then these are evaluated and their results printed out. If the user enters "`q`", then the program stops. It's simple and crude, but it demonstrates a lot of important programming points. Here it is:

```
#include <stdio.h>
#include <strings.h> /* some useful string functions */

/* declare functions for use by main */
void display_sheet();
int get_input();

void main()
{
    int quit=0; /* set to 1 if user wishes to quit */

    do {
        display_sheet(); /* call function to display spreadsheet */
        quit=get_input(); /* get user's input */
    } while (quit==0); /* loop until user asks to quit */
}

/* define array to be used by functions (not visible to main) */

char *sheet[15][5]; /* two-dimensional array of pointers to char */

/* define support functions */
float evaluate(char *cell_contents);
int find_row(char row);
int find_column(char column);
float string_to_number(char *string);
void flush_input();

void display_sheet()
{
    int row, column; /* variables used for loop control */

    printf("\n\nSpreadsheet\n\n");

    /* now print column numbers across the top */
    printf("   1         |2         |3         |4         |5         |\n");

    /* first three spaces to give space for row numbers beneath, then ¬
```

```
numbers separated by eight spaces and a bar, so that each number ¬
appears above its column */
    printf("————+————-+————-+————-+————-+\n");

    for (row=0;row<15;row++) { /* go through each row in turn */
        /* print the row number at the left of the screen */
        printf(" %c ",row+65); /* row is printed as a letter of the ¬
alphabet, with 0 being represented by "A" and so on */

        for (column=0;column<5;column++) { /* go through each column */
            if (sheet[row][column]==NULL)
                printf("         |"); /* print nine spaces and print ¬
a bar to move to the next column if this one is empty, ie its ¬
pointer points to nothing */
            else if (*sheet[row][column]=='=')
                printf("%9.2f|",evaluate(sheet[row][column])); /* if ¬
the first character is an equals sign, then the cell holds a formula ¬
which must be evaluated and then printed out */
            else /* otherwise it's contents are printed straight out */
                printf("%9.9s|",sheet[row][column]); /* the "9" in ¬
the format string indicates that strings less than 9 characters in ¬
width should be padded with spaces when printed */
        } /* now deal with next column */
        printf("\n"); /* go to the next line when all of the columns ¬
in a row have been printed */
    } /* deal with next row */
    printf("\n\n"); /* print a couple of blank lines to separate ¬
display from user input */
}

int get_input()
{
    int row,column;
    char input[10]; /* temporary string to store user's input */

    printf("Enter the coordinates of the cell to be modified (eg A1)\n");
    scanf("%3s",input); /* the "3" ensures a maximum string length of ¬
2 characters, plus a terminator */
```

```
    if (strcmp(input,"q")==0)
        return 1; /* return a value of 1 if user enters "q" */

    /* the first character of the string represents the row, and is ¬
converted to an array index by calling the find_row function */
    row=find_row(input[0]);
    /* the second character is the column number, and is converted to ¬
an array index by calling the find_column function */
    column=find_column(input[1]);

    printf("Enter the cell's new contents\n");
    scanf("%10s",input); /* ensure we get no more than 10 characters */
    flush_input(); /* get rid of any characters beyond the 10 we want */
    if (sheet[row][column]==NULL) /* check if the cell is empty */
        sheet[row][column]=(char *)malloc(10); /* if it is make ¬
storage for the string (9 characters plus a terminator) and put the ¬
pointer to it in the relevant cell of the array */
    /* either way, the contents must be copied into the area of memory ¬
pointed to by the array */
    strcpy(sheet[row][column],input);
    return 0;
}

float evaluate(char *cell_contents)
{
    /* the first character in a formula is an equals sign, and can be ¬
ignored. The next two represent the coordinates of one cell, the next ¬
the mathematical operator to be used, and the final two the coordinates ¬
of another cell. First job is to get these elements and store them in ¬
the following variables */

    int row1,row2,column1,column2;
    char operator;
    /* now define three floats - two to hold the operands, and one to ¬
hold the result of the operation */
    float operand1,operand2,result;
```

```
    /* get addresses of cells of interest */
    row1=find_row(cell_contents[1]);
    column1=find_column(cell_contents[2]);
    operator=cell_contents[3];
    row2=find_row(cell_contents[4]);
    column2=find_column(cell_contents[5]);

    /* now get numerical values stored in those cells */
    operand1=string_to_number(sheet[row1][column1]);
    operand2=string_to_number(sheet[row2][column2]);

    /* now to evaluate result, depending on the value of operator */
    switch (operator) {
        case '+': result=operand1+operand2;
            break;
        case '-': result=operand1-operand2;
            break;
        case '*': result=operand1*operand2;
            break;
        case '/': result=operand1/operand2;
            break;
        default:
/* No need for anything here, since this part of the program should ¬
never be executed */
            break;
    }
    return result;
}

int find_row(char row)
{
    /* convert from a letter between A and O to a number between 0 ¬
and 15, which is done by subtracting 65 from its ASCII code */

    return row-65;
}

int find_column(char column)
```

```
{
    /* convert to a number between 0 and 6 by subtracting 49 (the ¬
ASCII code for '1') from the letter's ASCII value */

    return column-49;
}

float string_to_number(char *string)
{
    /* convert a string into a floating point number */

    float result, divisor;
    int position;
    int sign=1; /* sign is 1 if the number is positive, -1 if it is ¬
negative */

    if (string==NULL) return 0.0;
    for (position=0;string[position]==' ';position++)
        ; /* skip leading white space */
    if (string[position]=='-') {
        sign=-1; /* turn negative if a minus sign is encountered */
        position++; /* and skip to next character */
    }
    for (result=0.0; string[position]>='0' && string[position]<='9'; ¬
position++) /* go through each numeral in turn until we come to a ¬
non-numeric character */
        result=result*10.0+string[position]-48; /* convert the ¬
character to a numerical value, and add it to the result. Before the ¬
addition is performed, result is multiplied by 10, because each ¬
successive addition means that the previous digits have a value ten ¬
times greater */
    /* now to process digits after the decimal point, if any */
    if (string[position]=='.')
        for (divisor=10.0;string[++position]>='0' && string[position]¬
<='9'; divisor *= 10.0)
            result=result+((string[position]-48)/divisor);
    result=result*sign;
    return result;
```

```
}

void flush_input()
/* Throws away unwanted characters in the input buffer, retrieved by ¬
scanf - stops when it reaches the end of the line */
{
    char c;

    while ((c=getchar())!='\n')
    ;
}
```

It's a lot longer than any of our previous examples, but if you take a close look at it you'll find it fairly easy to follow. In fact, it breaks down into easy-to-swallow chunks quite nicely. Let's go through it function by function.

How the program works

WHAT DOES IT MEAN? **Flag**

The first function, **main**, is easy. It only uses one variable, **quit**, which behaves as a "flag". Using a variable as a flag is a common programming technique – the variable is set to one value, and then when a particular condition has been met, it is set to another value. This value is subsequently tested. In **main**, **quit** is set to zero. A loop is entered. The function **display_sheet** is then called, without any arguments, to display the spreadsheet on the screen. After that the function **get_input** is called, and the value it returns is assigned to **quit**.

Normally, this will be `0`, but if the user entered "`q`" at the input stage, then it will be `1`. The program then loops, provided **quit** is still equal to `0`. If it isn't, the program terminates. Preceding **main** are declarations for the two functions it is to use – their definitions follow later.

Most programs, such as the sort examples of the last two chapters, can be broken down into three parts – input, processing and output. This one has been broken into just input and output, since the processing of the spreadsheet occurs during the output stage. The main program doesn't even have any access to the spreadsheet array – all data processing is handled by functions, so the array is declared after **main** and before the functions are needed. An alternative would have been to declare the array inside **main**, and pass each function a pointer to it. Since **main** doesn't need to know about it, though, it's better that it doesn't – besides, it saves us having to pass pointers around.

It would have been wrong to define the array in any of the remaining functions, such as **display_sheet**, since the array would be blanked as soon as the function finished executing.

Support functions

Before any more functions are defined, five support functions are declared – **evaluate**, which converts a formula expressed as a string into a floating point value and returns it; **find_row**, which converts an upper-case letter into an integer from 0 onwards; **find_column**, which converts a numeral in character form into an integer from 0 onwards; **string_to_number**, which converts a string into a floating point number; and **flush_input**, which gets rid of any unwanted characters waiting in the input buffer.

Display_sheet

The function **display_sheet** needs two local integers – **row** and **column** – which are used as the controlling variables in **for** loops to ensure each element of the two-dimensional array is checked in turn. Before doing so, the function prints out a heading and a list of column numbers. I've allowed a 3-character margin at the left of the screen for the row numbers, hence the first three spaces in the **printf**; after that, each numeral is separated by eight spaces and a vertical bar because each column is ten characters wide.

Next a loop is started that goes from the first to the last row. For each new row, its letter is printed at the left hand side of the screen, with a space before and a space after it. Adding 65 to the value of **row** gives an ASCII code between 65 and 79 – a letter between A and O.

The program then enters a loop that works through each of the row's columns in turn. The cell referenced by **row** and **column** is then checked to see if its pointer points to nothing (NULL is another way of writing 0).

If it does, nine blank spaces and a vertical bar are printed and the loop is closed so the next column can be dealt with.

If it isn't, then the string that the pointer references needs to be dealt with. It's checked to see if it begins with an equals sign, because if it does, it represents a formula. If this is the case, the **`evaluate`** function is called with the pointer to the string as argument. We can rely, at this stage, on **`evaluate`** to work out the value of the formula and return it as a float. We'll go into how it does this later.

The obtained result is then printed out. The formatting string in this **`printf`** includes yet another option. Remember that "**`%f`**" means simply "print the next argument as a **`float`**". The number **`9`** sandwiched between the two tells **`printf`** to print the **`float`** with a minimum of nine characters. If the number is shorter, space characters are added to the front. If it were longer than nine characters, then it would be printed to its full length, resulting in the formatting of the spreadsheet being spoilt. This formatting option can be used with any variable type that **`printf`** can handle.

The number following the decimal point restricts the fractional part of the number to be printed to only two digits. Remember that we're only passing the value of **`result`**, not the variable itself – this shortening of its fractional part on display doesn't affect the more precise contents of the variable.

A number following the decimal point for the formatting of a string will be used to indicate the *maximum* number of characters of the string to be printed. A formatting string of "**`%9.9s`**" would ensure that exactly nine characters of a string were printed out, with spaces being added to make up for shorter strings.

This option is the one used in the next **`printf`**. If the first character of the cell's contents isn't an equals sign, then it is assumed to be either a floating point number (but stored as a string, rather than a **`float`**) or some sort of heading text. In either case, it is printed out.

At this point the columns loop closes, and after all of the columns in a given row have been dealt with a carriage return is printed, to ensure that the next batch of output appears on a new line. Then the rows loop is closed, and that's the end of the function.

Get_input

There are two parts to the **get_input** function. The first asks the user which cell is to be operated on, and the second asks what its new contents should be. Again we need two integers, **row** and **column**, to reference a particular cell in the array. We've also defined a temporary string, **input**, to hold the user's current input.

The first **scanf** retrieves the coordinates of interest from the user. The "3" in the **scanf** formatting string behaves in a similar manner to the "9" in the **display_sheet**'s **printf**, only this time, it LIMITS the maximum length of the input string to three characters (including a terminating '\0' character).

This input is then checked to see if it equals the string "q", by calling the strings library function **strcmp**. If it is equal, then the function ends immediately, returning a value of 1 (this is the value assigned to **quit** in **main**).

If it isn't, then the function assumes it has received a pair of cell reference coordinates, the first being a letter, corresponding to a row, and the second being a numeral, in character form, corresponding to a column. It converts these into integers by calling the functions **find_row** and **find_column**, with the first and second characters respectively from the string array as arguments. Notice that there is no error-checking to ensure that the coordinates entered are in the correct range – an illegal cell address could prove disastrous.

Having pinpointed the cell of interest, the function now asks the user for its new contents. This is input as a string, with the formatting string in **scanf** ensuring we get no more than 10 characters (including a terminator) as a result.

This input – whether it be header text, number or formula – needs to be stored in an area of memory referenced by the cell's pointer. If there is already something in that cell, then it is replaced with the new string, if not, then an area of memory must first be created for it – this is done using **`malloc`**, and the line before is the one that checks if space has already been allocated for this cell's string, by seeing if the pointer points to NULL (nothing) or an address in memory.

Note that the pointers in the **`sheet[][]`** array are all initialised to NULL – this is because the array is declared outside of any function. If it were declared inside a function, as an automatic array, its contents would be undefined, and you would need to initialise each element to NULL using a simple loop.

Once memory has been allocated or simply located, the input string is copied to this memory by calling the standard strings function. Finally, the function returns a value of `0`, indicating that the user has *not* entered "`q`".

Flush_input

`Flush_input` is a very simple function that reads all the characters remaining in the input buffer until it reaches a carriage return. The reason it is necessary is that if **`scanf`** is called with a request for a string of a specific length and the user enters a longer string, then the extra characters will remain in what is called an "input buffer" – a temporary storage area managed by the standard library and used to hold a user's input. If we don't "flush" the buffer, then the remaining extra characters will be interpreted as a new input by the user when **`scanf`** is next called.

Remaining 'support' functions

The next function is **`evaluate`**. It takes a string (in other words, a pointer to a series of characters) as its argument, and produces a floating point value based on the formula it contains.

`Evaluate` assumes that the first character in the string is an equals sign, which plays no part in the evaluation, and so ignores it. Formulae take the form:

=A1*B2

so character number 1 represents the row address of the first cell. It's converted into such, and stored in the integer variable **row1**, by using it as the argument to a call to **find_row**. Similarly, character 2 represents a column address, and is converted into an integer stored in **column1**. Character 3 is the operator, and for the time being is stored in a character variable called **operator** for clarity. The row and column addresses of the next number are retrieved in the same way as those of the first.

The contents of the two cells referenced are then turned into floating point numbers. The function that does this, **string_to_number**, takes a pointer to a string as its argument. This is obtained from the sheet array given the relevant row and column co-ordinates.

Having found the two numbers, the function then goes on to process them depending on the operator that's been supplied. This is done with a **switch** decision-making construct, and is pretty much exactly the same as the calculator program introduced in chapter four. The heart of our spreadsheet program is the same. Notice that again, there is no error checking – if the user enters an unidentified operator in the formula, the result will be undefined.

Evaluate ends by returning the **float** variable **result**.

The next two functions – **find_row** and **find_column** – are hardly worth writing as functions. The body of their code – to subtract in one case **65** and the other **49** from the ASCII value of the character passed – could have replaced the function calls in the rest of the program. They've been written as functions, though, because it increases the clarity of the program, and demonstrates how functions can be written so they are useful to several other sections of your programs.

The final function, **string_to_number**, is a primitive version of a function supplied as standard with C. The real version is called **atof**, and can be used by including the header file **stdlib.h**. **String_to_number** may be primitive, but it does demonstrate the sort of processing you'll have to do to strings in your own programs.

It takes a pointer to an array of characters as its argument, and returns a **float** as its result. To do this, it makes use of two **float** variables and two integers. The first **float**, **result**, holds the value of the number as the function computes it. The second, **divisor**, is used in calculating the fractional part. The integer variable **position** is used in a **for** loop to access each of the characters of the string in turn. The final integer, **sign**, is initialized to 1. If the function discovers that the string passed it represents a negative number, it assigns a value of **-1** to **sign**. The variable result is multiplied by **sign** at the end of the function before it is returned. If **sign** has a value of -1, then this turns **result** negative.

The first check the function makes is that it hasn't been passed a NULL pointer, i.e a reference to an empty cell. If it has, it returns a value of zero (note that it is written as "0.0" to indicate it is a **float** and not an **int** value) and quits. Otherwise, the function interprets the string as holding a number.

A **for** loop then searches through the string until it comes to the first character that isn't a space. The body of the loop is empty, since no processing is required. A non-space character (more than likely the first in the string) having been found, it is checked to see if it is a minus sign. If it is, the flag variable **sign** is set to a value of -1 and **position** is incremented to point to the next character in the string.

Another **for** loop is entered. This one continues searching through the string for as long as it encounters numerical characters. The loop initializes **result** to a value of 0.0.

Each time through the loop, **result** is multiplied by 10.0 and has the numerical value of the current character added to it. This is found by subtracting 48 from the character's ASCII code. The result is an integer, but is implicitly converted to a **float** in the addition.

The reason **result** is multiplied by 10.0 before the addition is as follows. The first digit found is assumed to be a 'unit', and is added to zero. If another is found, then this reveals that the first was in fact a 'tens', and must be multiplied by 10. The second is assumed to be a 'unit', and is added to the result. If another is found, then those last two were in fact 'hundreds' and 'tens' rather than 'tens' and 'units', so they must be multiplied by `10` before having the new digit added. The process repeats until a character is found that isn't a numeral.

If this is a decimal point, then another **`for`** loop executes, searching through all of the numerical characters following it. This is where the variable **`divisor`** comes into play. Each character found is turned into its numerical equivalent and divided by the value in **`divisor`**, initially `10.0`, before being added to **`result`**. The first character found will be divided by `10`, the next by `100`, the next by `1,000`, and so on, since numbers after a decimal point represent 10ths, 100ths and 1,000ths etc.

C short-cut

`Divisor` is multiplied by `10` each time through the loop, by virtue of the last component in the loop definition, which contains a handy piece of C shorthand. You can shorten any assignment whose result depends on the variable being assigned to by putting the operator before the equals sign. Writing

```
divisor *=10.0;
```

is equivalent to writing

```
divisor = divisor*10.0;
```

Similarly,

```
divisor +=10.0;
divisor -=10.0;
divisor /=10.0;
```

mean, respectively:

```
divisor=divisor+10.0;
divisor=divisor-10.0;
divisor=divisor/10.0;
```

Back to the function. Finally, **`result`** is multiplied by **`sign`** to convert it to negative if necessary, and returned at the end of the function.

The program works, but is far from perfect. For one thing, it performs next to no checking on the user's input. This could prove fatal if the user enters the co-ordinates of a cell outside the array's bounds. You might find it a useful exercise to add various error checks to the program.

One assumption the program makes is that the cells referenced by a formula contain numbers. If they contain text or are empty, they will be taken to hold a value of `0.0`, but what if they contain a formula? Powerful spreadsheets can hold formulae whose results depend on those of other formulae. To make ours do the same, we need to make use of a technique called recursion, which forms the subject of the next chapter.

Recursion

- Mofidying our spreadsheet
- Data structures
- Recursive data structures

This sentence is the first sentence of the chapter. It's a self-referential sentence; its subject, rather than being some external object, is itself. In a similar way, it's possible for program code to refer to itself. What does this mean?

One of the most common examples is a function that contains, as part of its definition, a call to itself.

Have a look at this function:

```
int factorial (int number)
{
    return number*factorial(number-1);
}
```

You may have come across the factorial in maths, written as a number followed by a '!' sign. It works with positive integers, and produces a result by multiplying all of the numbers between one and itself together. For example, the factorial of 4 is given by:

4! = 1*2*3*4

We can re-write this as

4! = 4*3*2*1

But as you may have guessed, 3*2*1 is the same as 3!, so we could re-write the whole lot as:

4! = 4*3!

This immediately gives us the strategy for creating the function definition above. The function must take an integer as an input – the number whose factorial is to be found – and return an integer as a result.

Given that number, the function multiplies this by the factorial of one less than a number (as in the 4!=4*3! re-writing above), and the resulting value is returned as the result of the function. To perform this

You calculate the factorial of a number by multiplying it by the number-1. Then you multiply the result by (number-1)-1 and so on until you are multiplying the result by 1 – you have now calculated the factorial of your number. This can be represented as a series of steps...

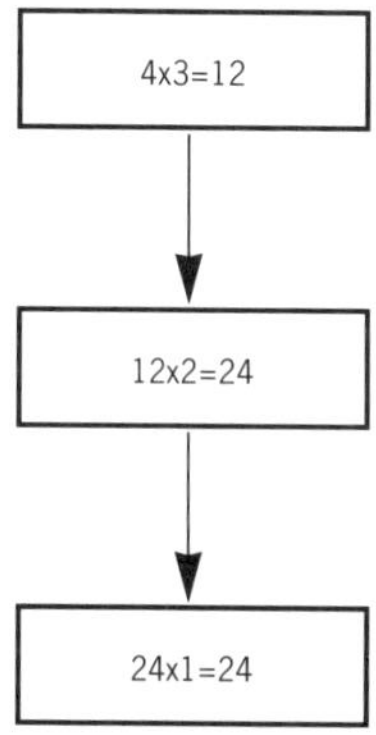

Calculating a factorial (4!)

multiplication, the function multiplies the number it has by the result returned from itself, but this second calling of **`factorial`** is with an argument one less than the number in question.

As you can see, this will result in the function successively calling itself over and over again, without returning a result. What is needed is some way of halting the function in its tracks, so that once it has been called for the correct number of times it returns a result.

The mathematical definition of factorial says that the factorial of 1 is 1. So we simply add something to our function definition so that when it is given a 1 as a parameter, it returns 1 as a result:

```
int factorial (int number)
{
    if (number==1)
        return 1;
    else
        return number*factorial(number-1);
}
```

So, given a number – say '3' – **`factorial`** will first of all check if it is a 1. It isn't, so it will attempt to return 3 multiplied by the factorial of 2. It can't return a value until the new factorial function call has been evaluated.

We can calculate factorials using a function that calls itself repeatedly, multiplying its parameter by the result of calling itself with its parameter-1 as argument, until a specific ('terminating' condition is met) – in this case, when the parameter is 1.

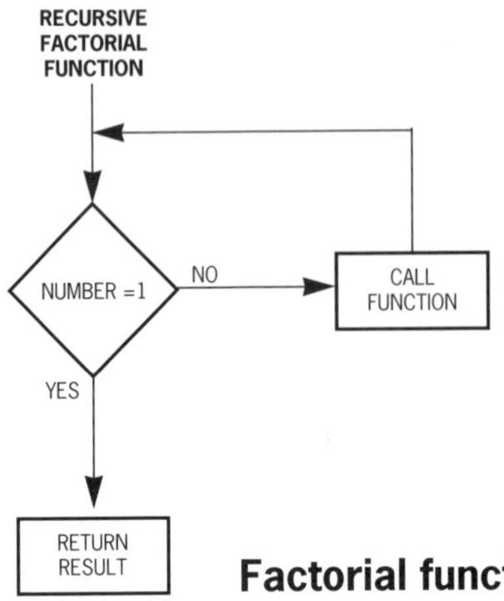

Factorial function

The second invocation of **`factorial`** is given a `2` as parameter. It checks that this isn't a `1`, and then tries to return a result of `2` multiplied by the factorial of `1`.

`Factorial` is called again. This time it has a parameter of `1`, so the first part of the **`if`** statement causes it to return a value of `1`. Control goes back to the second invocation of **`factorial`**, which multiplies this returned `1` with what it holds in its version of **`number`**, `2`. This result is then passed back to the first invocation of **`factorial`**, which multiplies it with *its* version of **`number`**, `3`. The result, `6`, is then passed back as a result to whatever called the function in the first place.

The important thing to note is that because the function's parameter is local, when it is passed as an argument in another function call (which happens to be a call to the same function) its value is copied (actually, its value minus `1` is the value that is copied) – the variable itself cannot be accessed by the new function. In other words, the variable called **`number`** accessed by **`factorial`** is not the same variable called **`number`** that is accessed by **`factorial`** when it is called again.

Recursive functions usually consist of two parts: the recursive part, that includes the code that calls the function again; and the terminating part, that decides when it's time to call a halt and return a result.

Modifying our spreadsheet

As the spreadsheet program from the last chapter stands, it can only evaluate formulae that involve defined numbers, not other formulae. We can rectify this by using recursion. Whenever **evaluate** comes across a formula reference rather than a number, it calls itself with this new formula as an argument so that it can be provided with a result for the evaluation.

It will now be possible to enter spreadsheets of the form:

	1	**2**
A	5.3	7.1
B	2.9	4.0
C	=A1+B1	=B2*C1

So that before the result for C2 can be calculated, the result for C1 must first be found. This evaluates to 8.2, giving a result for C2 of 32.8.

Here's the modified version of **evaluate**:

COMPLETE LISTING

```
float evaluate(char *cell_contents)
{
    /* the first character in a formula is an equals sign, and can be ¬
ignored. The next two represent the coordinates of one cell, the next ¬
the mathematical operator to be used, and the final two the coordinates ¬
of another cell. First job is to get those and store them in the ¬
following variables */

    int row1,row2,column1,column2;
    char operator;
    /* now define three floats - two to hold the operands, and one to ¬
hold the result of the operation */
    float operand1,operand2,result;

    /* get addresses of cells of interest */
    row1=find_row(cell_contents[1]);
    column1=find_column(cell_contents[2]);
```

```
    operator=cell_contents[3];
    row2=find_row(cell_contents[4]);
    column2=find_column(cell_contents[5]);

    /* now get numerical values stored in those cells */
    if (*sheet[row1][column1]=='=')
        operand1=evaluate(sheet[row1][column1]);
    else
        operand1=string_to_number(sheet[row1][column1]);
    if (*sheet[row2][column2]=='=')
        operand2=evaluate(sheet[row2][column2]);
    else
        operand2=string_to_number(sheet[row2][column2]);

    /* now to evaluate result, depending on the value of operator */
    switch (operator) {
        case '+': result=operand1+operand2;
            break;
        case '-': result=operand1-operand2;
            break;
        case '*': result=operand1*operand2;
            break;
        case '/': result=operand1/operand2;
            break;
        default:
    /* No need for anything here, since this part of the program should ¬
never be executed */
        break;
    }
    return result;
}
```

The only modifications are in the segment where **operand1** and **operand2** are assigned. Each of the two cells of interest are now checked to see if their contents begin with equals signs. If either does, then it is treated as a formula and supplied as an argument to a further call of **evaluate**.

Terminating conditions

Notice that in this example of recursion the terminating condition is implicit in the formula supplied by the user – the recursion ends as soon as **evaluate** comes across a formula that doesn't rely on any others.

A consequence of this is that a user may enter formulae that rely on each other in such a way as to make them impossible to evaluate. A spreadsheet such as:

	1	2
A	2.0	3.0
B	=A1+B2	=B1+A2

will send the program into an infinite loop. Try adding some form of check to ensure this doesn't happen.

The evaluation function created here is similar to, but much more primitive than the one used by your C compiler to evaluate expressions in your programs.

Recursion is a handy, if initially confusing, programming technique. Once you've got the hang of it, you'll find that it can greatly increase the underlying logic of your programs. Take the factorial example at the beginning of the chapter:

```
int factorial (int number)
{
    if (number==1)
        return 1;
    else
        return number*factorial(number-1);
}
```

It could also be re-written just as easily without the aid of recursion:

```
int factorial (int number)
{
    int result;
```

```
    for (result=1;number>1;number–)
        result=result*number;
}
```

There's not much in it, except that the iterative version needs one more variable, and the recursive version makes the underlying mathematical logic of **factorial** more obvious. In the case of our spreadsheet's **evaluate**, though, implementing an alternative to recursion would be rather more convoluted.

Data structures

It's not just functions that can contain references to themselves, but also data. The data type that permits this is called a 'structure', and we'll introduce the basic type before going on to its self-referential variety.

A structure is a variable type that you can define, and subsequently use to declare variables of that type. Structures are collections of simpler variables, and are useful for grouping related information together.

You might, for instance, be writing an address book program. It would be convenient to store a person's name as one string, each line of the address as another, and the phone number perhaps as an **int**. If you wanted to deal with 50 entries, then you could declare arrays of size 50 to hold each piece of information:

```
char *names[50]; /* pointers to 50 name strings */
char *address1[50]; /* pointers to 50 first line of addresses */
char *address2[50]; /* 50 second line of addresses */
char *address3[50]; /* 50 third line of addresses */
int phone[50]; /* 50 phone numbers */
```

The information for any given entry could then be stored or retrieved by accessing each of the arrays in turn with the same index. With a structure, though, you could group all of this information together into a single unit, making it easier to manipulate. You'd define a structure to hold the above information as follows:

```
struct entries {
    char *name; /* pointer to entry's name */
    char *address1;
    char *address2;
    char *address3;
    int phone;
};
```

Structure 'tag'

This hasn't declared any variables – no space for storage has been set aside – but defined a structure type called **entries**. **Entries** is known as a 'structure tag', allowing you to declare a variable of the tagged type as follows:

```
struct entries first;
```

This will only give us one variable, called **first**, with space to hold one name, address and telephone number, but it's easy enough to declare an array of a structure type:

```
struct entries data[50];
```

The above would provide us with an array called **data** which was capable of storing exactly the same information as the five separate arrays we started with.

It's possible to join together the defining and declaring of structures:

```
struct entries {
    char *name; /* pointer to entry's name */
    char *address1;
    char *address2;
    char *address3;
    int phone;
} data[50];
```

Notice that the syntax is similar to that used for declaring any variable type. First comes the variable type itself (which includes everything in the curly braces), and then the name of the variable to be created. If you define and declare a structure at the same time, then you needn’t include a structure tag:

```
struct {
    char *name; /* pointer to entry’s name */
    char *address1;
    char *address2;
    char *address3;
    int phone;
} data[50];
```

But using a tag means that you can easily declare another structure of the same type later on, just by using the tag name as a type rather than having to type out all of the definition in curly braces again.

Structures, like arrays, can be initialized on declaration. Here’s how it’s done:

```
struct entries {
    char *name; /* pointer to entry’s name */
    char *address1;
    char *address2;
    char *address3;
    int phone;
} data = {
    “Fred Bloggs”, “2 North Road”, “Peterlee”, “Sussex”, 123456}
```

Initialising arrays of structures is done in a similar way, with each group of data to be assigned to an element of the array being enclosed in its own curly braces:

```
struct entries {
    char *name; /* pointer to entry’s name */
    char *address1;
    char *address2;
    char *address3;
    int phone;
} data[] = {
```

```
    {"Fred Bloggs", "2 North Road", "Peterlee", "Sussex", 123456},
    {"Ben the Mad", "3 Asylum Street", "Chaos Town", "The Outer
Darkness", 666999}
};
```

As with the initialization of ordinary arrays, if the size of the structure array is left blank in the declaration it will be computed from the number of entries (in this case, 2).

When structures are made up of simple variables (**int**, **char**, **float** and so on) or strings of characters, then the interior curly braces aren't actually necessary. The above initialization could be re-written as:

```
struct entries {
    char *name; /* pointer to entry's name */
    char *address1;
    char *address2;
    char *address3;
    int phone;
} data[] = {
    "Fred Bloggs", "2 North Road", "Peterlee", "Sussex", 123456,
    "Ben the Mad", "3 Asylum Street", "Chaos Town", "The Outer Darkness",
666999};
```

Accessing structure members

Having declared a structure, how do you access each of the individual pieces of information (called 'members') within it? Let's suppose we've declared the following structure:

```
struct statistics {
    int age;
    int weight;
    int height;
} fred;
```

Members of a structure are accessed by supplying the structure's name (that is the variable name, *not* the structure tag) followed by a decimal point and the member name. To assign an age to **fred**, write:

```
    fred.age=27;
```

Similarly, to use his weight in an expression, you would write:

```
    weight_in_lift=weight_so_far+fred.weight;
```

Easy. The member names will not conflict with the names of ordinary variables, nor with the member names of a different structure type. It's best to use different names for clarity, though, except when you want to emphasise a relationship between a member in one structure and one in another.

As well as assigning values to individual members, it's possible to assign the whole of one structure to another with a single statement:

```
struct statistics {
    int age;
    int weight;
    int height;
} fred = {
    27, 10, 5.8
};

struct statistics jane;

jane=fred;
```

The program first of all declares and initializes **fred**, and then declares **jane**. The assignment statement copies the values for all of **fred**'s members into those of **jane**.

Note that although you can assign structures in this way, they must be of the same type, and you cannot compare structures in the same way that you would compare, say, **int**s.

```
if (fred==jane) {... }
```

is wrong.

Structures may be passed as arguments to functions, and returned as values by functions. Here, they are treated like simple variables rather than arrays: their values are copied into the function's private parameters, and the function cannot change the values of the original structures. The function is given a copy of the structure rather than a pointer to it, and likewise returns a structure rather than a pointer, unless you specify otherwise.

Passing structure pointers to functions

It's sometimes useful to pass structure pointers rather than structures themselves, particular if the structures are large and you don't want to waste time or memory in having them copied. You can find the address of a structure in the usual way, by preceding its name with a '**&**' sign. Similarly, you can declare a pointer to a structure by preceding the pointer name in its declaration with the type of structure it is to point to and a '*****' character:

```
struct statistics {
    int age;
    int weight;
    int height;
} fred;

struct statistics *pointer_to_fred;

pointer_to_fred=&fred;
```

Given a structure pointer, it's still possible to individually access the elements of that structure. Accessing an ordinary value held in the location referenced by a pointer is done by 'de-referencing' the pointer, by preceding it with a '*****', like so:

```
int number, *pointer_to_number; /* declares an int and a pointer to ¬
an int */
pointer_to_number=&number;
*pointer_to_number=5;
```

which will store a value of 5 in the variable **number**. De-referencing a structure pointer is done in a similar way, but with the pointer name being followed by a decimal point and the member name of interest:

```
struct statistics {
    int age;
    int weight;
    int height;
} fred, *pointer_to_fred;
pointer_to_fred=&fred;
(*pointer_to_fred).age=27;
```

The above will place a value of 27 in **fred.age**. The parentheses around '***pointer_to_fred**' are necessary because otherwise the compiler would think we were trying to access the value pointed to by a member called **age** of a structure called **pointer_to_fred**. Watch out for these conflicts – they are a consequence of 'precedence', which I'll go into next chapter. Always use parentheses if you are unsure.

Instead of this notation, C enables you to use another, equivalent form:

```
struct statistics {
    int age;
    int weight;
    int height;
} fred, *pointer_to_fred;
pointer_to_fred=&fred;
pointer_to_fred->age=27;
```

The two produce exactly the same result. Remember, though, that they are being used to access a structure member via a pointer, and not via the structure itself.

'Nesting' structures

It's possible to nest structures, so that one of the members of one structure is itself another structure. To access the members of the inner one, you could use one of the following methods:

```
struct inner {
    int age;
    int height;
};

struct outer {
    struct inner fred;
    struct inner *pointer_to_fred;
} jane, *pointer_to_jane;

pointer_to_jane=&jane;
jane.pointer_to_fred=&jane.fred;

jane.fred.age=27;
jane.pointer_to_fred->age=27;
pointer_to_jane->fred.age=27;
pointer_to_jane->pointer_to_fred->age=27;
```

Each of the last four assignments has the same effect. We've defined two structures types. The first, `inner`, contains two members, both `int`s, called `age` and `height`. The second, `outer`, contains two members also. The first member is a structure of type `inner`, and is called `fred`. The second is a pointer to a structure of type `inner`, and is called `pointer_to_fred`. We declare a variable called `jane` of the second structure type, and also declare a pointer to a structure of type `outer`, and call it `pointer_to_jane`.

The address of `jane` is assigned to `pointer_to_jane`, and the address of the member `fred` (also a structure) within `jane` is assigned to `jane`'s other member, `pointer_to_fred`. Given these two pointers, the four assignments that follow are all valid ways of accessing the member `age` of the structure `fred` which is itself a member of `jane`.

Recursive data structures

Structures containing pointers to structures are exactly what is needed to create self-referential data structures. They may sound obscure, but in fact they are used quite a lot in dealing with the operating system. Many of the objects that the operating system deals with are defined as structures, and these are often found linked together. For example, the structure that defines a viewport will, as well has holding all of the information necessary for the Amiga to set up the kind of viewport you want, hold a pointer to the next viewport in a list, thus enabling more than one screen to be displayed at the same time. This pointer to the next screen is of course a pointer to a structure of exactly the same type as the one that contains the pointer.

Let's take a simple example – the game of Animals. In it, one player thinks of an animal and the other player has to guess it. This is done by asking questions with 'yes' or 'no' answers, so narrowing down the possibilities until the correct animal has been discovered.

The program we are to write will make the guesses and find the correct animal; moreover, it will remember each new animal that it is taught, along with a question to distinguish it from the others.

The data is stored in something called a 'tree structure', after the way it looks diagrammatically. Each element of the tree, or 'node', consists of three parts – a text message, which will be either a question or the name

WHAT DOES IT MEAN?

Node

Leaving aside the dubious biological veracity of this example, it does demonstrate a simple 'tree structure', consisting either of statements or Yes/No questions leading to other statements or questions. It's built up of 'nodes' – a statement/question and two pointers. In the case of a statement, these are 'null' pointers.

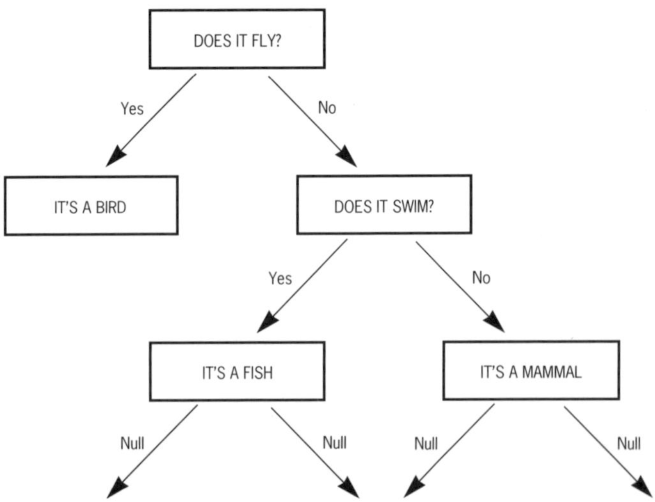

Example 'tree structure'

of an animal, and two pointers. If the text message contains the name of an animal, then the two pointers point to NULL – they are not needed. If it contains a question, then the two pointers point to two further nodes. The text and the pointers are stored together as a structure. Here's an example tree, consisting of just a few nodes:

When playing the game, the computer starts at the tree's 'root' node. It checks the pointers in that structure. If they are NULL, then it knows the string contains the name of an animal, and it makes that guess. If they point to other structures, then it knows the text asks a question meant to distinguish between the next two structures, so it asks the question. If the user enters a "`yes`", then the program goes to the structure pointed to by the left-most pointer, otherwise it goes to the structure indicated by the right-most pointer. The process then repeats.

Suppose the computer asks "`Does it fly?`" and the user responds "`yes`". The computer will then guess that the animal is a bird, and ask the user if it's correct. If it is, the game plays again, but if it isn't, the computer asks what the animal is and stores it in a new node. This new node's pointers are left as NULL. It then asks for a question to distinguish between a bird and the new animal – the answer to the question should be "yes" for the new animal. The question replaces the animal string in the old node, which is itself placed in another new node with two NULL pointers. The pointers of the old node are set so that one each points to the two new nodes. The left pointer points to the new animal, the right pointer to the old one – in this case "bird".

We'll use a structure to represent each node, and allocate space for each one as it is needed via **`malloc`**. The program initially starts knowing two animals and a question to distinguish between them. These values are given on initialisation. Here's the code:

```
#include <stdio.h>
#include <strings.h>

void getstringinto(char* result)
{
    int i=0;
```

```
    /* get first 39 characters, or up until a carriage return */
    /* put a null-terminator into last element of string array */
    while (i<40 && (*(result+i++)=getchar())!='\n')
        ;
    *(result+i-1) = '\0';
}

void main()
{
    struct node { /* define structure type "node" */
        char *text;
        struct node *left_pointer;
        struct node *right_pointer;
    };

    struct node yes = {"bird",NULL,NULL};
    struct node no = {"fish",NULL,NULL};
    struct node question = {"Does it have wings?",&yes,&no};

    struct node *current_node, *new_node1, *new_node2;
    char input[40];

    do { /* set up loop */

        printf("Think of an animal.\n");
        current_node=&question; /* start searching at the root node */
        while (current_node->left_pointer!=NULL) { /* loop through ¬
until we find a node that doesn't go any further */
            printf("%s\n",current_node->text);
            getstringinto(input);
            if (input[0]=='y')
                current_node=current_node->left_pointer; /* next ¬
node of interest becomes one pointed to by left member of current node ¬
if user replies "yes" to the question */
            else

                current_node=current_node->right_pointer; /* otherwise ¬
got to node indicated by right member */
```

```
        }
        printf("Is it a %s?\n",current_node->text);
        getstringinto(input);
        if (input[0]=='n') {
            /* if computer's guess is incorrect, it must learn about ¬
the new animal */
            printf("I give up!\n");
            printf("What is the animal you were thinking of?\n");
            getstringinto(input);
            /* create a new node to hold new animal */
            new_node1=(struct node *)malloc(sizeof(struct node));
            /* get some memory for a new node and put a pointer to it ¬
in new_node */
            new_node1->text=(char *)malloc(strlen(input+1));
            /* get memory for new node's text add one to the length ¬
to include '\0' character */
            strcpy(new_node1->text,input); /* copy name of new animal ¬
into new node */
            new_node1->left_pointer=NULL; /* both of new_node1's ¬
pointers point to NULL because it marks an end of the tree */
            new_node1->right_pointer=NULL;

            /* create another new node to hold old animal */
            new_node2=(struct node *)malloc(sizeof(struct node));
            /* get memory for it and address */
            new_node2->text=current_node->text;
            /* this new node's text becomes the animal from the ¬
current node */
            new_node2->left_pointer=NULL;
            new_node2->right_pointer=NULL; /* this node is also an ¬
end to the tree */

            /* now to change current_node so that it contains a ¬
question instead of an animal guess */
            printf("Give me a question with the answer 'yes'\n");
            printf("for a %s and 'no' for a %s.\n",¬
new_node1->text,new_node2->text);
            getstringinto(input);
```

```
            current_node->text=(char *)malloc(strlen(input+1));
            /* grab memory to store new text and make current_node's ¬
text pointer point to it*/
            strcpy(current_node->text,input); /* copy the input ¬
string into the new memory space */
            /* new_node1 gets pointed to by current_node's left ¬
pointer, and new_node2 gets pointed to by current_node's right pointer */
            current_node->left_pointer=new_node1;
            current_node->right_pointer=new_node2;
        } /* finished creating the new nodes */
        printf("Would you like another game?\n");
        getstringinto(input);
    } while (input[0]=='y');
}
```

The program first of all defines the structure type **node**, and then creates three variables of this type. These are to hold the question and the two animals that it distinguishes. The node that holds the question also holds two pointers, one to each of the other nodes.

The program enters a **do... while** loop, terminated at the program's end when the user enters anything other than a 'y' after being asked for another game.

Another loop is entered, searching from the root node until it comes to a node without further connections. In the meantime, it asks the question supplied in each node it searches. It decides which node to search next by picking one of the current node's two pointers, depending on the user's answer to the question.

When the loop terminates, a node has been found that contains a guess. The computer makes the guess, and if, according to the user's response, it is correct, the end of the outer loop is reached and the computer asks the user for another game.

If the guess is incorrect, the program adds two new nodes to the tree structure. The new animal is placed in one of these, and its two pointers are initialized to NULL to show that the node represents a guess, not a question. The second new **node** is given over to containing the guess held in the first. Since the **node**s hold pointers to **string**s, and not the **string**s themselves, the new **node** is simply given the address of the current **node**'s **string** – the **string** contents do not have to be moved. The second new **node**'s pointers are also initialized to NULL, because it too represents a guess.

A question to distinguish between the two guesses is obtained from the user. Memory to store this is got via **malloc**, and the user's input is placed there. The string pointer in the current **node** is modified so that it points to this new area of memory. Its structure pointers are given the addresses of the two new **node**s. They are assigned so that an answer "yes" to the current node's question will send the program searching in the **node** indicated by the left member for a guess.

Notice that in the creation of **new_node1**, **malloc** is used twice. The first time is to get space for the structure itself. This doesn't actually contain the animal **string**, just a **pointer** to it, so space for the **string** must be **malloc**ed separately.

The first call to **malloc** makes use of a new function called **sizeof**. Strictly speaking, it's not a function, but an instruction to the compiler to insert a number corresponding to the amount of memory the variable type in its parentheses will require. You can put any variable type in there, and **sizeof** will return the amount of space it requires. It's used here to ensure enough space is got to store the structure pointed to by **new_node1**.

MAKE A NOTE!

C shorthand

Using complex structures in this way can lead to confusion. C provides a way of defining a shorthand version of a structure's type. Then, whenever we want to use a structure type declaration, we can use the shorthand we've defined rather than the long-winded version. You haven't created a new type, just a shorthand notation for an already existing one, which can help to make things clearer.

In the above example, we could define a type that represents the complex **node** structure:

```
struct node { /* define structure type "node" */
    char *text;
    struct node *left_pointer;
    struct node *right_pointer;
};
```

If we defined a type for this structure called **animal_node**, like so:

```
typedef struct node { /* define structure tag "node", and give it type
definition of "animal_node" */
    char *text;
    struct node *left_pointer;
    struct node *right_pointer;
} animal_node;
```

Then you could declare structures of the required type with this syntax:

```
animal_node yes = {"bird",NULL,NULL}; /* declare three nodes */
animal_node no = {"fish",NULL,NULL};
animal_node question = {"Does it have wings?",&yes,&no};
```

Similarly, you could make a **typedef** for the **pointer** type that is to point to the structure:

```
typedef struct node *animal_node_pointer;
```

You could then declare your **pointer**s to the structure with:

```
animal_node_pointer current_node;
```

The use of **typedef** causes the compiler to perform a text substitution. Where it sees "**animal_node_pointer**" in the above line, it interprets it as meaning "**struct node ***", and so a variable of the required type (i.e. a **pointer** to a **node** structure) is declared.

Having declared these two types, then you can make the call to **malloc**, which occurs when you need to get more space for a new **node**, more explicit. Previously, it looked like this:

```
            new_node1=(struct node *)malloc(sizeof(struct node));
            /* get some memory for a new node and put a pointer to it ¬
in new_node */
```

But with the two **typedef**s it becomes:

```
            new_node1=(animal_node_pointer)malloc(sizeof(animal_node));
            /* get some memory for new node and put a pointer to ¬
it in new_node */
```

Unions

A **union** is a form of variable declared with the same sort of syntax as a structure. A **union** holds several different data types but, unlike a structure, holds only one type at a time. Basically, you're defining a single variable that can be used at different times to hold different types of data.

To declare a **union** called **fred**, with the **union** tag **details_tag**, that could be used to hold either the age or surname of **fred** – an **int** or a pointer to a string of **char** – you would use the following syntax:

```
union details_tag {
    int age;
    char *surname;
} fred;
```

At any one time you could access either **fred**'s age, by using **fred.age**, or its surname, by using **fred.surname**, which would yield a **pointer to char.**

If you're accessing **fred** by a **pointer** to it, rather than by the **union** itself, then accessing its elements is done in the same way as it would be for accessing a structure's elements by **pointer**s:

```
a=pointer_to_fred->age;
```

would interpret the value of **fred** as an integer and put it in **a**.

The compiler ensures that a **union** variable is large enough to contain the biggest of its possibilities. It's possible to construct a **union** consisting of more than just two variable types, but it is up to you to ensure that you access the **union** as the correct type of variable as and when you need it.

Linked Lists

- How lists work
- Lists of any type
- Pointers to functions

The tree data structure used for the animal game in the previous chapter is a specialised variant of the data structure known as the linked list.

List

A list is an ordered grouping of data. It is particularly useful when, as in the animal game, you don't know how many items of data will need to be stored in the list. Space for each list element can be obtained from the operating system – usually by a call such as **`malloc()`** – as and when it is needed.

Each item in a linked list consists of two parts: the first is the data being stored; the second is a "link" to the next item in the list. The link performs two functions – because each element of the list is **`malloc`**ed separately, they may each lie in completely different areas of memory, so links are needed so that your program can access whichever list item it wants to; secondly, the items in a list are ordered, and the ordering is defined by the links.

Heads and tails

The first item in a list is called the "head". It consists of an item of data and a pointer to the next item in the list. The remainder of the list is known as the "tail". The tail can be thought of as a list in its own right, complete with a head (actually the second item in the initial list) and its own tail. The final item in the list holds only data, its link is a pointer to NULL, indicating that there are no further items.

A simple list

The first step in implementing a list is to design the data structure used for each element. For the sake of simplicity, let's start with a list designed to hold integers. Each element then must be capable of holding an integer and a pointer to another element. We define the item as a structure. The pointer it contains is not a pointer to **`int`**, but a pointer to a structure of the same type that it is itself a part of. Here's the structure definition:

```
typedef struct liststruct *list;

struct liststruct {int datum;
    list next;};
```

The elements in a list consist of two parts: the data (the information stored in the list) and the link, which indicates the next list element.

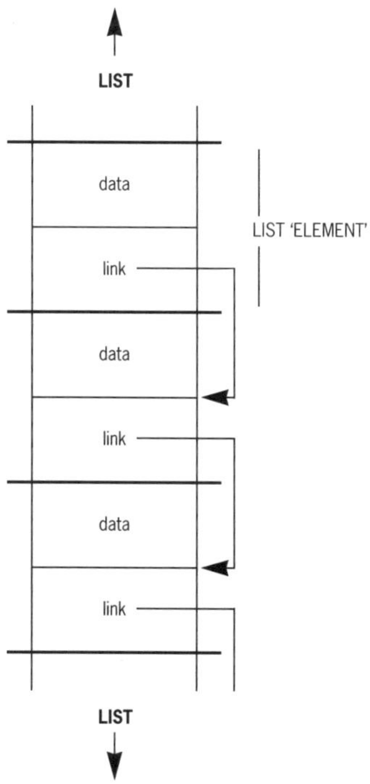

How a list works

The first line has defined the type `list` as being equivalent to a pointer to a structure of type `liststruct`. The second line then defines this structure. It consists first of an integer element called `datum`, and then next, a pointer of type `list`.

List functions

Given this kind of list, we now need to think about the sort of functions we will need to manipulate it. Certain functions are common to all lists. Once we have these functions, we can tuck them away in our own library file and we need never worry about how they work again. By linking our own programs with this file we can make use of the list and call its corresponding functions if we ever need to.

Heads and tails

Lists consist of two parts: the 'head' and the 'tail'. The head is the first element in the list while the tail is the remainder of the list. If you remove the first element, or head, the first element of the tail becomes the new head.

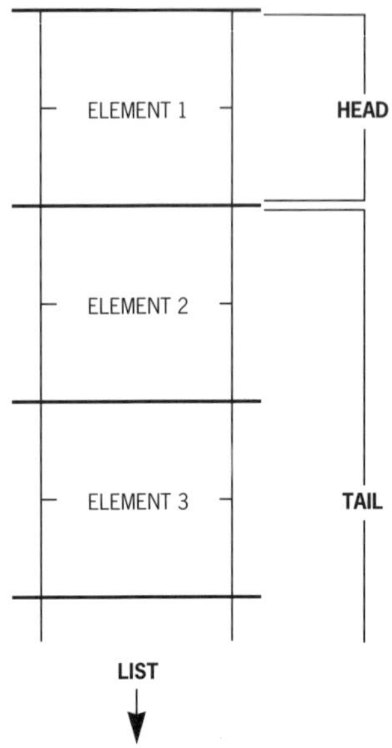

'Heads' and 'tails'

We will need a function to create an empty list. It takes no parameters, and simply returns a pointer to list, with its value initialized to NULL.

Another useful function will be **cons**, which enables us to construct lists. **Cons** takes an integer and a pointer to list, and returns a new list with the integer at its head and the old list as its tail. With **cons** and **empty** it's now possible to create lists of any length. Suppose you wanted to create a list with three elements – with values 5, 10 and 15 – you could do it with **cons** and **empty** as follows:

```
list l;

l=cons(5,cons(10,cons(15,empty())));
```

The innermost call to **cons** creates a list with 15 at its head and nothing as its tail. The preceding **cons** then takes this as a tail and adds 10 to the head. The outermost **cons** then takes the resulting list, which now consists of the elements 10 and 15, and adds 5 to its head.

We need a function to check whether or not a list is empty. The function called **isempty** will take a list pointer and return a non-zero value if it points to a list item, and zero if it points to NULL.

The function **head** will return the first item of data in the list – an integer – while the function **tail** returns a pointer to the list without its first item. Both expect a list as their parameter.

The function **length**, given a list as parameter, will return the number of elements in a list, expressed as an integer. It is defined such that **length(empty())** equals zero.

In the listings that follow we've made use of a function called **WriteList**. This will take a list as a parameter and write each of its elements in turn out to the screen. It takes three further parameters – strings called **opener**, **separator** and **closer** respectively. **Opener** contains the character with which you wish to precede the list when it is output, **separator** contains the characters you with to separate each item printed, and **closer** contains the characters used to delimit the list when it is printed. Typically they will contain an open bracket, a command and a close bracket respectively so that, given the list created above using **cons**, printing it out with the following call:

```
WriteList(l, "[",",","]");
```

EXAMPLE CODE

would produce the output shown below:

```
[5,10,15]
```

Those are the most basic functions necessary for manipulating our list of integers. In the code that follows, you'll find two more: **reverse** and **append**. **Reverse** takes a list and returns another list with the same elements as the first, but in reverse order. **Append** takes two lists and returns a list consisting of the first list passed followed by the second.

Summary of functions

Name	Purpose
`empty`	creates a new, empty list
`cons`	adds a new head to the list
`isempty`	checks whether a list is empty
`head`	returns the first data item in the list
`tail`	returns a pointer to the list's tail
`length`	returns the number of elements in the list
`writelist`	displays the list elements on the screen
`reverse`	reverses the order of elements in the list
`append`	adds one list to the end of another

Data & function declarations

Here are the data and function declarations for the integer list. Type them in using **dme** and save them as a file called **list.h**. You can then use this file as an ordinary C header file, to be included with **#include** whenever you want to use an integer list. Here's the code:

```
/************************************************************************/
/*      LIST.H              */
/************************************************************************/

/* Integer lists */
/* M. Harman, University of North London, 1993.      */

#define TRUE 1
#define true 1
#define FALSE 0
#define false 0
#define boolean int

typedef struct liststruct *list;

struct liststruct {int datum;
            list next;} ;
```

```
list empty();
/* a list with nothing in it. */

boolean isempty(list l) ;
/* isempty(empty()) = true */
/* isempty(cons(x,l)) = false */

int head(list l) ;
/* the first element of the list.*/

list tail(list l) ;
/* the list obtained by removingthe first element. */

list cons(int d, list l) ;
/* the list which has d at its head and l as its tail.
    head(cons(x,l)) = x
    tail(cons(x,l)) = l
*/

int length(list l) ;
/* The empty list has length zero. */

void WriteList(list l,

    char *opener,
    char *separator,
    char *closer) ;

/* Prints the elements of the list l */
/* The elements are delimitted by opener and closer and separated by
   separator.                    */

list reverse(list l) ;
/* returns the list obtained by reversing the order of elements in l */

list append(list l1, list l2) ;
/* concatenates L1 onto the front of L2 */
```

Notice the **#defines** at the top of the listing. These define the type **boolean** to be equivalent to **int**, and **true** and **false** values too. Using these makes the rest of the code easier to follow.

Function definitions

As well as the include file, of course, you'll also need the code that actually defines the functions. Once this is written, you can compile it into an object file. This object file can then be used as a library. Type the following in and save it as a file called **list.c**:

```
#include "list.h"
#include<stdio.h>

list empty()
{ return NULL; }

boolean isempty( list l )
{ return NULL==l; }

int head( list l )
{ return l->datum; }

list tail( list l )
{ return l->next; }

list cons( int d, list l )
{ list r;

    r = (list) malloc(sizeof(struct liststruct)) ;
    r->datum = d ;
    r->next = l;
    return r;
}

int length( list l )
{ if (isempty(l)) return 0;
    else return 1+length(tail(l));
}
```

```
void WriteList( list l,
        char* opener,
        char* separator,
        char* closer)
{
    printf("%s",opener);
    while(!isempty(l))
        {printf("%d",head(l)) ;
        l=tail(l);
        if (!isempty(l)) printf("%s",separator) ;
    }
    printf("%s",closer);
}

list accreverse( list l, list accl )
{
    if (isempty(l))
        return accl ;
    else return accreverse( tail(l), cons(head(l),accl) ) ;
}

list reverse( list l )
{ return accreverse(l,empty()) ; }

list append( list l1, list l2 )
{
    if (isempty(l1))
        return l2;
    else return cons(head(l1),append(tail(l1),l2)) ;
}
```

The implementation of all of the functions we've discussed is fairly straightforward. Read through the code to be sure you understand what is going on. Notice in particular the recursive calls in **length**, **append** and **accreverse**, the function called by **reverse**.

This second file must be compiled. We don't want DICE to try and link it and create an executable, though, because there is no **main()** function. To get DICE to compile and not link, use the **-c** option. Typing the following will create a library file called **list.o**:

```
dcc -c list.c
```

Checking our code

Now we need to write a simple program to call on the services of our library and check that its functions work. Type the following into dme and save it as a file called **main.c**:

```
#include <stdio.h>
#include <list.h>

void main()
{
    list l,k;
    l=cons(1,cons(2,cons(3,empty())));
    k=reverse(l);

    WriteList(append(k,l),"{",",","}");
}
```

Notice how the **list** header file is included in exactly the same way as **stdio.h**. If we want to compile this and link it with the **list.o** library file, we need to tell DICE explicitly. It has the intelligence to work out that any standard libraries need linking, but not our own. You can compile and link with the following command:

```
dcc main.c list.o -o main
```

Now, if you type **main** you will get the following output:

```
{3,2,1,1,2,3}
```

Lists of any type

A list of integers is all very well, but perhaps of limited use. It's surprisingly easy, however, to alter our list library so that it can cope with lists of any type.

Pointers not data

Again, each item in the list consists of two elements: a pointer to the next list item, and a data element. In this case, though, the data element is not a simple variable type such as integer, but a pointer. This pointer is used to indicate the area in memory whether the real data that the list item contains is stored. In other words, the data itself is stored entirely separately from the list. Here's the new structure definition and definition of **list**, the pointer to it:

CODE SEGMENT

```
typedef struct liststruct *list;

struct liststruct {void *datum;
    list next;);
```

The only difference is in the declaration of **datum**, which is now a pointer to **void**.

WHAT DOES IT MEAN

Pointer to void

So far we have only used **void** to indicate that a function returns no result. It can also be used, as it is in the structure definition, to indicate that a pointer can point to any kind of data. Normally, we declare a pointer to point to a specific data type, such as an **int**. If we use the pointer to access anything else, such as a string, then the compiler will generate an error. Misuse of pointers can lead to horrible crashes, so we should be thankful of this limited form of type-checking.

If we declare a pointer to point to type **void**, though, the compiler doesn't check what kind of data we're using it to access, so we can use it to point to different things throughout the program, but the onus is on us to make sure nothing goes wrong. We need a pointer to **void** with our modified list program because the kind of data the list holds, and therefore the type that **datum** is used to point to, varies.

You are not restricted to storing data In lists – you can also store pointers to data, making it much easier to handle different types and sizes of data.

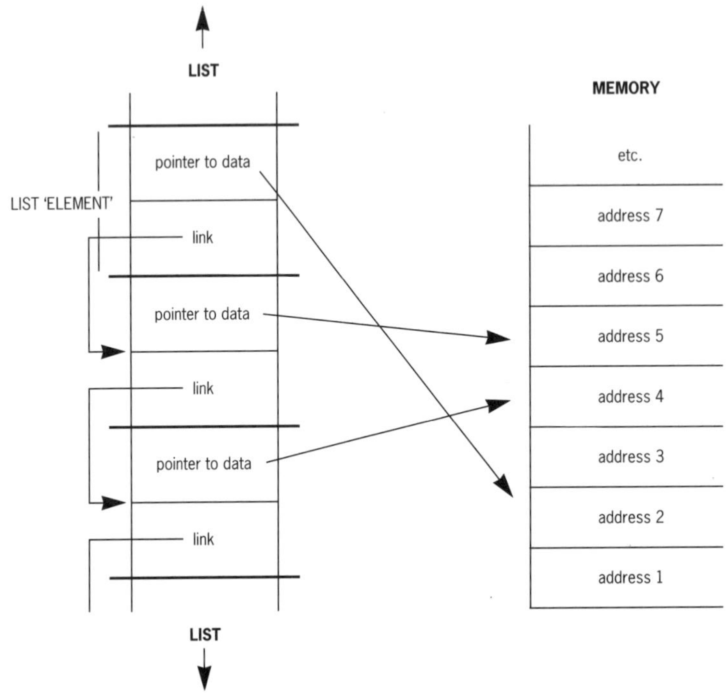

Using lists for pointers, not data

Our new header file

Shown below is the new header file for our list library. Type it into dme and save it with the name **`list2.h`**.

```
/***********************************************************************/
/*       LIST.H              */
/***********************************************************************/


/* Polymorphic lists. */
/* or rather - untyped lists, implemented using pointer to void for */
/* the elements of the list, and pointers to functions for the output */
/* of elements of the list */
/* M. Harman, University of North London, 1993 */
```

```
#define TRUE 1
#define true 1
#define FALSE 0
#define false 0
#define boolean int

typedef struct liststruct *list;

struct liststruct {void *datum;
            list next;} ;

list empty();
/* a list with nothing in it. */

boolean isempty(list l) ;
/* isempty(empty()) = true */
/* isempty(cons(x,l)) = false */

void *head(list l) ;
/* the first element of the list.*/

list tail(list l) ;
/* the list obtained by removingthe first element. */

list cons(void *d, list l) ;
/* the list which has d at its head and l as its tail.
    head(cons(x,l)) = x
    tail(cons(x,l)) = l
*/

int length(list l) ;
/* The empty list has length zero. */

void WriteList(list l,
        void (*printer)(void*),
        char *opener,
        char *separator,
```

```
        char *closer) ;

/* Prints the elements of the list l, using the print function ¬
"printer". */
/* The elements are delimitted by opener and closer and separated by */
/* separator */

list reverse(list l) ;
/* returns the list obtained by reversing the order of elements in l */

list append(list l1, list l2) ;
/* concatenates L1 onto the front of L2 */
```

You might be surprised at how similar the function declarations are to those for the integer list library. The main difference, of course, is that where a function previously took an integer as a parameter it now takes a pointer to **void**, and functions that returned integers now return pointers to **void** (aside from **length**, which naturally still returns the number of elements in a list as an integer).

If you look at the declaration – or "prototype" as it is also known – for **WriteList**, you'll notice that it now takes an extra parameter:

```
void (*printer)(void*)
```

CODE SEGMENT

What does this mean?

Pointers to functions

As you may gather from the heading, we're defining a parameter of the type pointer to function.

The reason it's necessary is that **WriteList** will need to output different list types in different ways. When our list was made of integers, **WriteList** simply had to call **printf** with the **%d** option. Writing out a list of screen structures, though, will require far more complex processing. By defining the actual function that prints out a list item elsewhere, and passing a pointer to it to **WriteList**, **WriteList** can

You can use pointers to functions in just the same way that you can use pointers to variables. This kind of structure is far more efficient than complex 'if' structures since the function pointer is passed to the 'writelist' function as an argument.

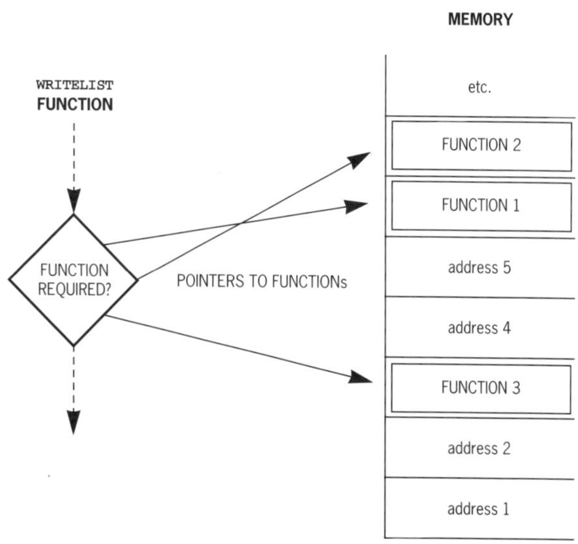

Using pointers to functions

call the relevant function by its address, depending on the kind of list it is processing.

In the definition above, the first **`void`** indicates that the function to which the parameter points returns no result. The first part in parentheses indicates that the parameter name is **`printer`**, and that, because it is preceded by an asterisk, it is a pointer type. The code in the second set of parentheses ensures that the compiler interprets the pointer as pointing to a function and not, as would otherwise be the case, a pointer to **`void`**. The code within the second set of parentheses declares the parameter that the function pointed to takes – a pointer to **`void`** in our case.

Function definitions

Now let's take a look at the function definitions. Type the following in and save it as a file called **`list2.c`**:

COMPLETE LISTING

```
#include "list2.h"
#include<stdio.h>
```

```
list empty()
{ return NULL; }

boolean isempty( list l )
{ return NULL==l; }

void* head( list l )
{ return l->datum; }

list tail( list l )
{ return l->next; }

list cons( void* d, list l )
{ list r;
    r = (list) malloc(sizeof(struct liststruct)) ;
    r->datum = d ;
    r->next = l;
    return r;
}

int length( list l )
{ if (isempty(l)) return 0;
    else return 1+length(tail(l));
}

void WriteList( list l,
        void (*printer)(void*),
        char* opener,
        char* separator,
        char* closer)
{
    printf("%s",opener);
    while(!isempty(l)) {
        (*printer)(head(l)) ;
            l=tail(l);
            if (!isempty(l)) printf("%s",separator) ;
    }
    printf("%s",closer);
```

```
}

list accreverse( list l, list accl )
{
    if (isempty(l))
        return accl ;
    else return accreverse( tail(l), cons(head(l),accl) ) ;
}

list reverse( list l )
{ return accreverse(l,empty()) ; }

list append( list l1, list l2 )
{
    if (isempty(l1))
        return l2;
    else return cons(head(l1),append(tail(l1),l2)) ;
}
```

The majority of the function definitions are the same as they were in the integer example, barring the fact that they deal with pointers to **void** rather than integers.

With **cons**, we are only using **malloc** to gain space for the actual **liststruct** structure. This contains a pointer to the next item and a pointer to the actual data. It is up to the calling program to find space for the data itself. We'll look at how this is done later.

The function **WriteList** has been altered so that it accepts a pointer to a function as one of its parameters, and so that it uses this function to output each element.

The definition of the parameter is the same as in the header file:

```
void (*printer)(void*);
```

a variable called **printer** which is a pointer to a function returning no result and accepting one parameter, a pointer to **void**.

The function pointed to is called by preceding the pointer name with an asterisk – just as the value pointed to by an ordinary pointer is accessed. Immediately following it is the parameter to be passed to the function, enclosed in parentheses:

```
(*printer)(head(l));
```

Compile **list2.c** into an object file like so:

```
dcc -c list2.c
```

Using our new library file

We now need to write a program to make use of our new library file. Save this next listing as a file called **main1.c**:

```
#include <stdio.h>
#include <list2.h>

int *MakeIntPtr(int i)
{
    int *r;

    r = (int*) malloc(sizeof(int)) ;
    *r = i ;
    return r;
}

int GetInt(int*i)
{ return *i; }

void PrintInt(int*i)
{
    printf("%d",GetInt(i)) ;
}

void main()
{
    list l,k;
```

```
    l=cons(MakeIntPtr(1),cons(MakeIntPtr(2),¬
cons(MakeIntPtr(3),empty())));
    k=reverse(l);
    WriteList(append(k,l),(void(*)(void*))PrintInt,"{",",","}") ;
}
```

This code uses the **list2** library to create a list of integers – exactly the same as the first version, for the sake of comparison.

Extra functions

Notice that now, though, we've had to define three extra functions before we can make use of our lists. For one thing, we need to define a function that creates space for, and stores, the data for a list item. This is performed by **MakeIntPtr**. It takes an integer as its parameter, and returns a pointer to integer as its result.

As you can see by looking at the code, it **malloc**s space for an **int**, stores the integer passed to it in this space, and then returns a pointer to the space.

The second function, **GetInt**, is used to obtain the data stored in a list item. All it does is return the integer pointed to by the parameter it's passed. Its use isn't strictly necessary, since the pointer de-reference can easily be made in the main code that calls it, but it helps to clarify everything. If you are using lists of more complex items than integers, then the function equivalents of **GetInt** will prove their worth.

The third function defined is that used to print out a list item. It is a pointer to this function that is passed to **WriteList**. We've called the function **PrintInt**. It returns a **void** and takes a pointer to an integer as its parameter. The body of the function extracts the data pointed to by its parameter, then passes this to **printf** with the **%d** option to print it out.

The main function

The main function is much the same as before. In our calls to **cons**, however, we cannot simply pass an integer value as the head of the list. Instead, we must pass a pointer to **int**, as created by a call to **MakeIntPtr**, which creates space for the argument passed to it.

The call to **WriteList** includes one extra argument – the **pointer** to the print function to be used. This is the parameter written as:

```
,(void(*)(void*))PrintInt,
```

CODE SEGMENT

The first part casts **PrintInt** to be of type "pointer to a function returning nothing and accepting a pointer to void as a parameter." The second part gives the function whose address is to be passed. Notice that the **&** operator is not necessary to take the function's address. The compiler takes it automatically, as it does when arrays are passed.

You can compile the whole lot into an executable file called **main1** by typing the following:

```
dcc main1.c list2.o -o main1
```

CODE SEGMENT

If you run the resulting program, you'll get exactly the same output as that produced by the previous example.

Using the extra power

To demonstrate the extra power afforded by the polymorphic list library, let's write another program that makes use of more complex lists.

The following file, which you should save with the name **main2.c**, makes use of lists of complex numbers. Complex numbers, used extensively in mathematics and engineering, consist of two separate parts: a "real" and an "imaginary" part. With the complex number (5,2i), the 5 indicates the real part and 2i the imaginary. The character 'i' represents the square root of -1, so the complex number can be represented by 5+2*squareroot(-1). There is no real value for the square root of -1, though, hence the necessity for imaginary numbers.

If you're not familiar with complex numbers, don't worry. Just think of the real and imaginary parts as representing coordinates on a two-dimensional graph. Here's the code:

```
#include <stdio.h>
#include <list2.h>

struct ComplexStruct {
    float real;
    float imaginary;
    };

typedef struct ComplexStruct *complex;

complex MakeComplex(float i, float j)
{
    complex result;

    result = (complex) malloc(sizeof(struct ComplexStruct)) ;
    result->real = i ;
    result->imaginary=j;
    return result;
}

float GetReal(complex c)
{ return c->real; }

float GetImaginary(complex c)
{ return c->imaginary; }

void PrintComplex(complex c)
{ printf("(%f+%fi)",GetReal(c),GetImaginary(c)) ;
}

void main()
{
    list l,k;
    l=cons(MakeComplex(1.2,5.3),cons(MakeComplex(2.7,4.51),¬
cons(MakeComplex(3.92,3.38),empty())));
    k=reverse(l);
    WriteList(append(k,l),(void(*)(void*))PrintComplex,"{",",","}") ;
}
```

You can compile this and link it with the polymorphic list library by typing:

```
dcc main2.c list2.o -lm -o main2
```

(The **-lm** option is needed to link with the maths library.) Here we've defined a structure of type **ComplexStruct**, and a pointer to it with the **typedef** shorthand of **complex**.

Revised functions

Next comes **MakeComplex**, the equivalent of the **MakeIntPtr** function in the previous example. **MakeComplex** takes two **float**s as parameters. It **malloc**s enough space for a **ComplexStruct** structure, stores the two **float**s within it, and returns a pointer to it.

GetReal and **GetImaginary** are the equivalents of the earlier **GetInt** – they retrieve the real and imaginary data respectively stored in the structure whose pointer is passed to them.

The printing function we've defined is called **PrintComplex**. It takes a pointer to a **ComplexStruct** structure as its parameter, and returns no result. Given a structure, it prints its two elements out (obtained by calls to **GetReal** and **GetImaginary**) as **float**s with a call to **printf** with the **%f** option. The item is surrounded by parentheses when printed, the two elements are separated with a plus sign, and the imaginary part is followed with the character "i" – this is the standard form for printing out complex numbers.

Our **main** function works pretty much as before. When it calls **cons**, it first calls **MakeComplex** to create the complex number data needed for the list head. When **WriteList** is called, it is this time passed a **pointer** to the **PrintComplex** structure. If you run the program, you should get the following output:

```
{(3.920000+3.380000i),(2.700000+4.510000i),(1.200000
+5.300000i),(1.200000+5.300000i),(2.700000+4.510000i
),(3.920000+3.380000i)}
```

Try writing your own programs to create and use different kinds of lists. You may also want to try using the other functions declared in the **`list2.h`** header file, and seeing what uses you can put them to.

Additional concepts

- More variable types
- Pre-processing
- Octal and Hexadecimal
- Bitwise operators
- Precedence
- Automatic variables

Before going any further, it's as well to round up all of those aspects of C that we haven't had cause to discuss so far. There are a couple of variable types that we've missed, a few things to be mentioned about the C pre-processor, a note about number systems and some new operators, and we need to talk about precedence.

More variable types

Word

As you may recall from chapter 1, a single address in memory can only store an integer number in the range 0 to 255. This is known as a byte. Two bytes may be joined together to form what's called a 'word'. In this case, the second byte is interpreted as being 256 times more valuable than the first, enabling the word to hold numbers in the range 0 to 256*255 + 255 or 65,535. The number in the higher byte acts just like a number in the 'tens' column of an ordinary number written on paper.

Longword

It's also possible to combine two words together to create a 'longword', which can hold numbers between 0 and 255*256*256*256 + 255*256*256 + 255*256 + 255 or 42,798,677,295. Each byte is 256 times more valuable than its less significant brother.

Byte size

The integers we've been using in our C programs are clearly larger than one byte. In fact, the size of an **int** depends on the C compiler in question. For DICE, it is four bytes. The upper numbers given above are not strictly true, because C interprets half of those numbers as being negative. So in fact the range for an ordinary **int** in DICE is from -2,147,483,648 to 2,147,483,647. It comes about because of the peculiar way in which the machine stores negative numbers.

Unsigned

Sometimes, you'll want the contents of an **int** to be positive no matter what. This immediately means you can use it to store a number twice as large. You do this by using the **unsigned** keyword before the variable's type specifier in its declaration:

```
unsigned int positive_number;
```

Unsigned can also be applied to **char** variables. When **unsigned** they contain an integer between 0 and 255, corresponding to an ASCII code.

'Bytes' take up one memory address and are capable of storing a number in the range 0-255. 'Words' take up two memory addresses, while 'longwords' take up four.

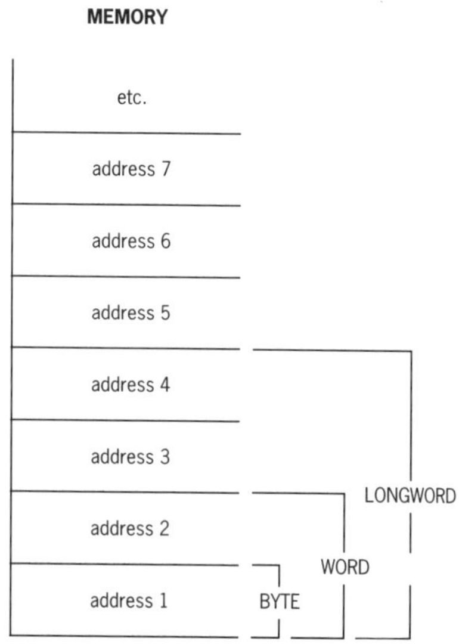

Bytes, words and longwords

You can also declare **ints** and **chars** as **signed**:

```
signed char letter;
```

Signed

A **signed char** will vary in value between -128 and 127. It's unnecessary to use a **signed** keyword with **int**s, as they are automatically assumed to be **signed** unless an **unsigned** keyword is present. **Char**s are automatically **signed** or **unsigned** depending on the C compiler you're using; with DICE they are **signed**.

Short and long ints

There are two more specifiers you can use with **int** – **short** and **long**. The definition of C states that a **long int** must use more bytes than a **short int**. With DICE, **short int**s take two bytes and have a range of -32,768 to 32,767, while **long int**s take four bytes and have a range of -2,147,483,648 to 2,147,483,547. **Int**s which are declared neither **short** or **long** are automatically given four bytes. You'd declare a **long int** with the following:

```
long int big__number;
```

Chars can be either signed or unsigned. Signed chars can have either positive or negative values.

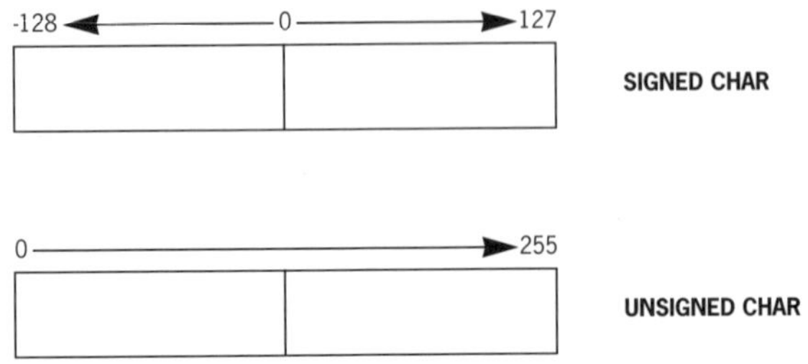

Signed and unsigned chars

and an **unsigned** one with this:

```
unsigned long int big_positive_number;
```

Double variable

You can also use a longer version of a **float**, so that your fractional numbers are stored with more precision. The variable type is **double**, meaning "double precision", and you declare a variable of the type as follows:

```
double big_fractional_number;
```

You can also precede **double** with the keyword **long**, to specify an even more precise **float**:

```
long double very_big_fractional_number;
```

A **float** uses 4 bytes, a **double** 8, and a **long double** 16.

Long, **short**, **signed**, **unsigned**, and the keywords **extern** and **static** from chapter 8, are known as 'storage class' specifiers. They precede an ordinary variable type in a declaration to give the programmer more precise control over the kind of variables used.

Another storage class specifier is '**register**'. You may remember from chapter 1 the distinction that was drawn between a computer's memory and registers: registers are memory locations, few in number, held within

Register

the central processing unit itself, while ordinary memory is contained in separate silicon chips. As a consequence, the computer can access and alter the values in its registers much quicker than it can values in memory. If you precede a variable declaration with the **`register`** specifier, it means you want that variable to be stored in one of the processor's registers, usually because you want accesses to it to be extra quick.

Registers are not always available, so DICE will treat the specifier as a piece of advice, rather than as an order. It will put the variable in question in a register if it can. In fact, DICE attempts to put variables into registers anyway, to increase the overall speed of your programs. If you declare a variable with the **`register`** keyword it will increase that variable's priority when DICE comes to decide which ones ought to be stored in registers.

Pre-processing

The C pre-processor is a part of the compiler. It performs a 'first pass' on your source code, getting it into shape ready for the compiler proper to translate it into machine code. One of its many functions is to strip out the comments in a program, since these play no part in the translation but are there for the convenience of human beings.

#include and #define

It's possible to write instructions to the pre-processor. These instructions are different to ordinary C instructions: they don't get converted into machine code, but instead guide the pre-processor in its job. We've already made extensive use of two pre-processor instructions: **`#include`** and **`#define`**. The first instructs the compiler to load in a separate file, called a 'header file', whose contents are to be considered part of the overall program. The contents of the header file are then compiled along with the programmer's code.

Header files

Header files contain pre-written C source code, more often than not code that declares functions (remember that a function must be declared if it is to be called in a source code file that does not contain its definition) and variables to be used in other programs. DICE comes with a number of

You can greatly simplify your programs using the #include and #define commands.

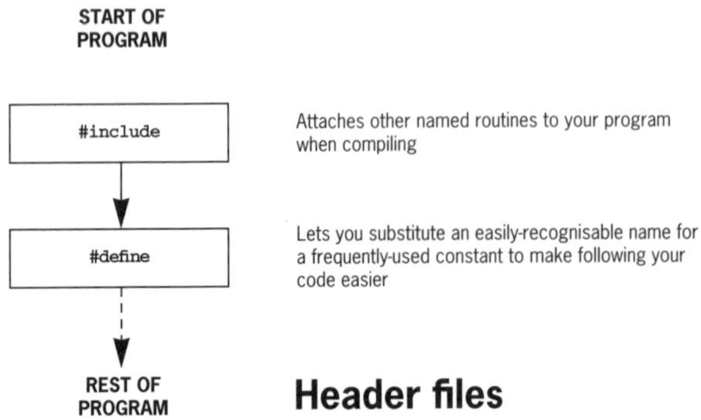

Header files

them, including **stdio.h**, which contains various input and output functions, and **strings.h**, which contains useful functions for manipulating strings. You can create your own header files, and it is often useful to do so if you're writing a large program that consists of several different source code files. By including header files in each of these source code segments you can ensure that each has access to all the function and variable declarations it needs. These declarations can be safely hidden away in the header file, preventing the others from becoming too cluttered.

Defining constants

Also commonly found in header files are **#define** statements. These enable you to create constants, which aid the readability of your programs. Suppose your program involves lots of string manipulation, and you want the maximum length of string processed to be 20 characters. You could set up a constant like so:

```
#define MAX_STR_LENGTH 20
```

and use this constant throughout the program. It would produce code much more comprehensible than that which merely contained lots of references to the number 20. In addition, if you decided at a later date that you wanted the program to handle strings 30 characters in length, you need only change this one **#define** line rather than every occurrence of 20 within the program.

The use of **#define** forces the pre-processor to perform a substitution. Wherever it sees the keyword (**MAX_STR_LENGTH** in the above example) in the source code, it replaces it with the text following it in the **#define** statement. The keyword must be separated from the substitution text by a space. The substitution text is whatever follows on the same line. If you want to substitute with some text that won't fit on a single line, you can use the '\' character to cause the pre-processor to include the text on the following line as well. For example:

```
#define LONG_STRING A very long text string that in a working \
program would be unlikely to be of any practical use, but \
which nevertheless illustrates a point.
```

The substitution will only be made in the source code if the keyword so defined appears as a separate word. For instance, no substitution would be made for the word **A_VERY_LONG_STRING**. Neither are substitutions made for keywords appearing within quotes. **Printf("LONG_STRING")** would result in the output

```
LONG_STRING
```

not

```
A very long text string that in a working program
would be unlikely to be of any practical use, but
which nevertheless illustrates a point.
```

Macros & parameters

These substitutions are termed 'macros'. You can create macros with parameters, too. Look at the following:

```
#define SUM(A,B) A+B

printf("%d\n,SUM(7,5));
```

After the C pre-processor worked through this code, it would produce the following:

```
printf("%d\n",7+5);
```

which, when the final stage of compilation was complete and the program run, would of course produce the output '12'. Notice also that the macro **SUM** would work equally well for characters or **float**s, as well as **int**s. Because a textual substitution is taking place, rather than a call to a function, the parameters defined with the macro can be used to represent any data-type.

Removing definitions

It is sometimes useful to be able to remove a definition. Suppose you were writing a program where at one point you wished to use the macro definition above, of **SUM(A,B)**, but at another point you wanted your program to call a function of the same name. Preceding the call with the statement

```
#undef SUM
```

would ensure that the following piece of code would call a function and not be substituted with the macro text.

It is also possible to perform conditional tests with the pre-processor. This could be useful if you were writing code that needed to be compiled differently depending on the kind of system it was to be run on. For instance, you might want to include one set of headers for machines running Workbench 1.3, and another for those running 2.0 or higher. The four statements in question are:

```
#if
#elif
#else
#endif
```

#if must be followed by a constant expression (i.e. one not dependent on variables) that evaluates to an integer result. If the evaluated result is non-zero, then the statement(s) immediately following the **#if** are executed; otherwise, control jumps to the next **#elif** (similar to C's **else if** statement) or **#else** if there is one, or to the closing **#endif**. Suppose a previous **#define** had set up a constant called **VERSION**, containing either the text `1.3` or `2.0+`. You could then use the following code to include the relevant header file:

```
#if VERSION==1.3
    #include <version1.3.h>
#else
    #include <version2.h>
#endif
```

Often it is useful to be able to test to see whether a macro has already been defined. You can do this with the specialised forms of **#if**: **#ifdef** and **#ifndef**. The first, when followed by a macro name, is true if the macro has already been defined, while the second is true if it hasn't.

Another form of constant

The **#define** statement, in its most common form, enables the programmer to set up a number of constant values and refer to them by meaningful names. This means that programs are easier to read, and sweeping changes can often be made by the simple procedure of modifying the values of the constants.

Enumeration constant

C provides another way of defining constants, called the 'enumeration constant'. Use of the **enum** statement enables you to define a series of constants, each with related values. As a bonus, you can get the compiler to generate the values for you. Here's an example:

```
enum numbers {ZERO,ONE,TWO};
```

enum automatically gives the first constant – **ZERO** in this case – a value of 0. The next is given a value of 1, the next and a value of 2, and so on. You can change the start value that **enum** chooses by use of the **=** sign:

```
enum numbers {SEVEN=7,EIGHT,NINE};
```

starts the sequence off at the value 7. You can use a second equals sign to give a new start value to one of the constants in the series. In the absence of any equals signs in the following constants, their values are derived by successive adding one to the value of the last constant assigned:

```
enum numbers {SEVEN=7,EIGHT,TWENTY=20,TWENTYONE};
```

EXAMPLE CODE

More on binary

When we count, we do so in a number system known as 'base ten', which has evolved because we have ten fingers. This way of counting has become so ingrained that it takes a little time to look at it and realise that it's possible to count in other ways.

WHAT DOES IT MEAN?

Base 10 and binary

In base ten arithmetic, each digit can have one of ten possible values, ranging from 0 to 9, and each digit, working from right to left, is worth 10 times more than the digit to its right. It's possible to work in other number bases, though, and sometimes convenient. At their lowest level, computers operate in a base two system. This means that each digit can only have one of two values, either 0 or 1, and that each digit is twice as valuable as the neighbour to its right.

For example, the base two (or 'binary') number:

1111

has a value, expressed in everyday base ten, as 15. The right-most digit can be taken literally, as representing a value of 1. The next digit along has a value of 2, the one after that a value of 4 and the one after that the value of 8. Each digit is directly analogous to the thousands, hundreds, tens and units of primary school mathematics. Let's look at another example:

1001

WHAT DOES IT MEAN?

Bits and bytes

This has a value of 9. Each digit of a binary number is known as a 'bit' (short for 'binary digit'). Binary numbers usually consist of 8 bits. The most significant bit of such a number has a value of 128. If you add up 128+64+32+16+8+4+2+1, you get the value of 255. A memory location consists of eight binary bits, which explains why if can hold a value of between 0 and 255. Adding two locations, or 'bytes', together to create a word gives us a number with 16 digits, capable of holding a number between 0 and 65,535. Two words, can be combined to form a **longword**, with a resolution of 32 bits.

'Bitwise' logical operators

It's useful to be able to manipulate numbers in binary form rather than as base ten, because of the way computers are designed. Each digit inside a byte can often be used as a separate 'switch', perhaps controlling a piece of hardware. For instance, an address in memory that represents the controls to the Amiga's display hardware contains a bit that, if 0, puts the screen in normal mode, or in interlace mode if it contains a 1.

The following operators can be applied to **char**, **short**, **int** and **long** variables. The first is called 'bitwise AND', and is written as **&**. The logical AND, as used in conditional expressions, only returns a true result if both its operands are true. If either or both are false, then so is the overall result. A bitwise AND will compare each bit in an operand with the corresponding bit in the other operand. If both are 1, then the result will be 1, otherwise it will be 0. Here's an example:

```
result=a&b;
```

If **a** contains the binary number 11001100, and **b** the binary number 10101010, then the value assigned to **result** will be 10001000.

Similarly, the 'bitwise OR' (written as |) will set a bit to 1 if either of the corresponding bits in its two operands are 1. The assignment

```
result=a|b;
```

will put a value of 11101110 into **result**, if **a** and **b** contain the same as stated above. The 'one's complement' or 'bitwise NOT' operator (written ~) will turn every bit in a number whose value is 1 into 0, and every 0 into a 1. Note that, unlike the others, it operates on one variable only:

```
result=~a;
```

will put a value of 00110011 into the variable **result**.

Each binary digit inside a byte can be manipulated with logical operators.

Bitwise AND

`result=a&b;`

1	1	0	0	1	1	0	0	a
1	0	1	0	1	0	1	0	b
1	0	0	0	1	0	0	0	result

Bitwise OR

`result=a|b;`

1	1	0	0	1	1	0	0	a
1	0	1	0	1	0	1	0	b
1	1	1	0	1	1	1	0	result

Bitwise NOT

`result=~a;`

1	1	0	0	1	1	0	0	a
0	0	1	1	0	0	1	1	result

Bitwise exclusive OR

`result=a^b;`

1	1	0	0	1	1	0	0	a
1	0	1	0	1	0	1	0	b
0	1	1	0	0	1	1	0	result

Bitwise shift

`result=a<<3;`

			1	1	0	0	1	1	0	0	a
1	1	0	0	1	1	0	0	0	0	0	result

`result=a>>4;`

1	1	0	0	1	1	0	0	a
				1	1	0	0	result

Bitwise logical operators

There's an operator similar to bitwise OR, called 'bitwise exclusive OR', written as **^**. When a bitwise exclusive OR is performed on two numbers, it will give a result of `1` if either of the corresponding bits in the numbers are `1`, or a result of `0` if both are `0` or both are `1`. Here's an example:

```
result=a^b;
```

This would put a binary value of `01100110` into **result**.

The final two bitwise operators are called 'shift' operators. They will shift the binary digits in a number either to the left or two the right according to a number of places specified by the second operand. Imagine an ordinary base 10 number, say 567. If you were to shift the digits of this one place to the left, and put a zero in the right-most column, you'd end up with the result 5670. Effectively you would have multiplied the number by 10. If you had shifted the digits by 2 places, you would have effectively multiplied it by 100, giving the result 56700. Similarly, if you had shifted the digits right by one place, losing the right-most digit, you would have ended up with the result 567. It would be equivalent to dividing the number by 10. Shifting right two places would divide by 100; three places would be dividing by 1000; and so on.

The bitwise shift operators perform the same function, except on binary digits rather than base ten digits. This means that numbers are multiplied or divided by 2, or powers of 2 (4, 8, 16, 32 and so forth) instead of 10 or powers of 10 (100, 1000, 10000 etc). You shift a number to the left in an expression by following it with the **<<** symbol and a number representing the number of places to shift. Shifting to the right is performed by the **>>** symbol.

If **a** contains the binary number `11001100`, then

```
result=a<<3;
```

would put the value `11001100000` into **result**. The operation

```
result=a>>4;
```

would put the value `1100` into **`result`**. (Leading digits would be filled with zeros.)

Even though you may have written the values of these variables into your source code as ordinary base ten numbers, the bitwise operators will perform their operations on them as if they were in binary form. If you like, you can think of them first translating the numbers from base ten to binary, performing their operations, and then translating them back into base ten again. In fact, this translation does not occur – all numbers are stored inside the computer as binary numbers.

There is no convention in C for writing numerical constants in binary form. However, dealing with individual bits when you are working in base ten can be awkward – it involves a lot of mental translation on the part of the programmer, because the two ways of representing the numbers are so dissimilar. Happily, C enables us to write our numbers in two other bases, both more akin to the binary format.

The first is known as 'octal'. Octal numbers are in base eight format. Each of their digits lies between 0 and 7, and each digit in the number has a value eight times greater than that of the digit to its right.

Hexadecimal numbers

The second format, 'hexadecimal', works in base 16. Each digit in isolation has a value between 0 and 15. When computing the overall quantity of a hexadecimal number, each digit is 16 times more significant than the one to its right. In this case, though, there's a slight complication. If each digit can have a value between 0 and 15, then the digits 10 and above are going to cause confusion when the number is written down – these digits seem to be comprised of two digits, rather than the single one that they represent. How do we distinguish between 12 as representing two digits, one sixteen times the value of the other (giving a base ten value of 1*16+2=18) or just one hexadecimal digit, representing the base ten value of twelve?

The answer is that hexadecimal digits 10 to 15 are instead represented as the letters a to f. Hence the hexadecimal number ce is the same as the base ten number 13*16+14=222.

You can express a hexadecimal constant in C by placing the characters '0x' – that's the number 0 and the letter x – before it. Expressing a number in octal is done by preceding it with just the number '0'. Given this, the following assignments to result are all equivalent:

```
result=29; /* number in base 10 */

result=035; /* number in base 8, octal */

result=0x1d; /* number in base 16, hexadecimal */
```

Decimal/binary/octal/hexadecimal equivalents

Base 10	Binary	Octal	Hexadecimal
0	0	0	0
1	1	1	1
2	10	2	2
3	11	3	3
4	100	4	4
5	101	5	5
6	110	6	6
7	111	7	7
8	1000	10	8
9	1001	11	9
10	1010	12	a
11	1011	13	b
12	1100	14	c
13	1101	15	d
14	1110	16	e
15	1111	17	f
16	10000	20	10
17	10001	21	11
18	10010	22	12
19	10011	23	13
20	10100	24	14
21	10101	25	15
22	10110	26	16
23	10111	27	17

24	11000	30	18
25	11001	31	19
26	11010	32	1a
27	11011	33	1b
28	11100	34	1c
29	11101	35	1d
30	11110	36	1e
31	11111	37	1f
32	100000	40	20
33	100001	41	21

As you can see from the table, three digits of a binary number are represented by one digit of an octal number. Four digits of a binary number correspond to one digit of a hexadecimal number. There is no simple correspondence between binary and base ten digits.

Octal and hexadecimal format numerical constants (written with '**0**' and '**0x**' before them respectively) can appear in your C programs wherever you would an ordinary constant – on the right-hand side of expressions, including simple assignments, in relational comparisons and so on.

ASCII characters

They can also be used to represent character constants. Normally, a character constant is written as the character in question surround by single quotes:

```
char letter='a';
```

EXAMPLE CODE

MAKE A NOTE!

ASCII codes

the variable **letter** can be treated like a **char** variable, but also as holding an integer number. This is because characters are stored internally as a number between 0 and 255. These corresponding numbers are known as the ASCII code – you'll find a list of them, and the characters they represent – in the back of your Amiga manual. In the above example, the variable **letter** could be treated as holding the value 97.

Some character constants can't be written in this way. For example, the character that represents a 'newline'. Typing this into your source code would simply result in the editor skipping to a newline. Instead, C uses the following convention:

```
char letter='\n';
```

with which you should be by now familiar. The backslash character inside a string constant indicates that it and the character following it are to be treated as a special control sequence. The two characters are replaced by the compiler with the ASCII code for a carriage return. In other words, the variable letter DOES NOT hold the two characters ‘\’ and ‘n’ – these are used only as a convention to tell the programmer that you mean the single character that corresponds to a carriage return. There are similar control sequences for other things – ‘**\t**’ means a tab, ‘\'’ means a single quote, and ‘\\’ means a backslash – the variable to which this is assigned will end up containing the backslash character itself.

Non-ASCII characters

The notation enables character values to be represented in your program that are not easily entered from the keyboard. The notation can be extended to any character by representing the required character in either octal or hexadecimal notation. This is done by following the backslash by one to three octal digits, or by the letter ‘**x**’ and one or two hexadecimal digits. The following three assignments to **result** are equivalent:

```
char result='a';

char result='\121'

char result='\x61';
```

Defining 'bit-fields'

With C you can access the individual bits within a word without having to make use of the bitwise operators. You do so by defining ‘bit-fields’. What this does, essentially, is give names to each of the bits, or collections of bits, within a word. The individual bits can then be accessed via the names, rather than having to be isolated via bit-wise ANDs, ORs and NOTs. The syntax for declaring bit-fields is similar to that for declaring a structure:

```
struct {
    unsigned int bold : 1;
    unsigned int italic : 1;
} text;
```

This has declared a variable **text** with two defined bit-fields, each a single bit big. The bit-fields must be of type unsigned **int**; the number of bits that comprise them is given after the colon. Access to the bit-fields is as follows:

```
text.bold=1;
if (text.italc==0) { /* do something if italic is not selected */ }
```

As you can see, bit-fields are often used as 'switches', or 'flags', indicating that certain conditions apply. In the above example, both bit-fields are only one bit large, and so both can only have a value of **0** or **1**. It's possible to define a field with more than 1 bit in it. In this example:

```
struct {
    unsigned int bold : 1;
    unsigned int italic : 1;
    unsigned int colour : 2;
} colour_text;
```

the field **colour_text.colour** can have a value between 0 and 3 (the range of values expressible in two binary digits).

Precedence

Precedence is a subject that so far we've skirted around. This is because programs that rely on precedence tend to be more difficult to understand than those that don't. Precedence, basically, defines the order in which operations are carried out within an expression. You may remember when we first dealt with arithmetic, and noted that 3+4*5 would give the result 23, not 35. Rules of precedence are needed to resolve ambiguities like these. One of the rules is that the multiplication operator, '*****', has a higher precedence that the addition operator, '**+**'. This means that a multiplication operation occurs *before* an addition. In the above example, the numbers 4 and 5 are multiplied together before the result is added to 3. As far as possible in this book so far, I've overridden the rules of precedence by making use of parentheses. Parentheses force any operation that they contain to be evaluated before the result is then used in any containing expression. For instance, the parentheses in (3+4)*5 force C into evaluating first 3+4, to give a result of 7, before multiplying it by 5 to give the answer 35.

Parentheses

Rules of precedence are applied not only to arithmetic operators, but all operators, and also in the declaration and defining of some variables. Remember that use of parentheses can always force a change of precedence so that expressions are evaluated in the order you want them to be.

Table of precedence

<table>
<tr><th>Operators</th><th>Associativity</th></tr>
<tr><td>() [] -> .</td><td>left to right</td></tr>
<tr><td>! ~ ++ -- + - * & (type) sizeof</td><td>right to left</td></tr>
<tr><td>* / %</td><td>left to right</td></tr>
<tr><td>+ -</td><td>left to right</td></tr>
<tr><td><< >></td><td>left to right</td></tr>
<tr><td>< <= > >=</td><td>left to right</td></tr>
<tr><td>== !=</td><td>left to right</td></tr>
<tr><td>&</td><td>left to right</td></tr>
<tr><td>^</td><td>left to right</td></tr>
<tr><td>|</td><td>left to right</td></tr>
<tr><td>&&</td><td>left to right</td></tr>
<tr><td>||</td><td>left to right</td></tr>
<tr><td>?:</td><td>right to left</td></tr>
<tr><td>= += -= *= /= %= ^= |= <<= >>=</td><td>right to left</td></tr>
<tr><td>,</td><td>left to right</td></tr>
</table>

Those operators higher in the table have the higher precedence. Notice that the operators +, - and * have a higher precedence when they apply to only one operand (performing the functions of giving the value of the operand, negate (i.e. returning the value of the operand multiplied by 'minus one') and access the value or function held at an address indicated by a pointer, respectively) than when in their more usual form, of adding, subtracting and multiplying two accompanying operands. Therefore they are given two entries in the table.

Associativity

The associativity of each operator, which can be either left to right or right to left, defines how collections of the same operator in an expression are evaluated. With left-to-right associativity, the left-most operator is evaluated first, with evaluation progressing to the right. For example:

```
a=b+c+d+e;
```

is evaluated as if it contained the following parentheses:

```
a=((b+c)+d)+e;
```

The reverse is true for operators with right-to-left associativity. Here:

```
a=b=c=d=e=1;
```

is the same as the longer version:

```
a=(b=(c=(d=(e=1))));
```

A few of the operators listed in the table could do with further explanation.

The operators **+=**, ***=** and so on have been discussed before. They are shorthand notations for assignment, where the variable to be assigned is also part of the expression to be evaluated to yield its new value. For example:

```
a+=5;
```

adds five to the value of **a**, and is equivalent to:

```
a=a+5;
```

The same applies for the modulo operator '`%`', which finds the remainder from an integer division.

The bitwise operators discussed earlier in this chapter can also be used with this assignment shorthand. For instance:

```
a<<=2;
```

would shift the bits of the variable `a` two places to the left – or multiply `a` by 4.

The operator `?:` is the ternary operator, used to perform simple `if... else` type assignment decisions, as discussed in an earlier chapter.

(Type) – the cast operator

The entry written '`(type)`' is the cast operator, as mentioned briefly in chapter 8. It forces the operand following it to be interpreted as an object of the type specified within the parentheses. This type is the same keyword used when defining a variable of that type. Casting is useful for assigning integers to floats and vice versa:

```
int a;
float b;

a=7;
b=(float)a;

b=9.3;
a=(int)b;
```

We have used it in the past to cast a pointer to the required type. `Malloc` returns the address of an area of free memory requested from the operating system. The the type of pointer that should be used to store the address depends on the kind of data to be put there. Previously, we used it to store strings, so the value returned by `malloc` was cast to be of type 'pointer to `char`' by use of the `(char *)` operator. (Note that the asterisk is necessary to turn the address into a pointer; otherwise it would be interpreted merely as a character itself.)

The final operator of interest is the comma operator, ',', which so far we haven't mentioned.

The comma operator can be used to separate two expressions. When it does so, the first expression is evaluated before the second. The overall value of these two expressions separated by the comma is the same as that of the right-most expression. Commas are most often used within the defining clause of a **for** loop, where they can be used to alter the value of more than one indexing variable:

```
for (i=0,j=20;i<10;i++,j*=2);
```

In the above case, **i** counts from 0 to 9, while **j** begins with a value of 20, and has its value doubled each time through the loop.

As you may have gathered, assignments themselves can be treated as expressions, with their value being that of the value assigned. The assignment **j*=2** in the above for loop is also an expression.

A consequence of this is that you can perform multiple assignments:

```
int a,b,c;
a=b=c=5;
```

will assign the value five to all three variables. The assignment operator, '=', associates right to left, meaning that the right-most expression is evaluated first. So the first thing to be done is assign the value 5 to the variable **c**. This assignment is treated as an expression with a value of 5. This number becomes an operand in the expression to the left, '**b=**', so **b** is also assigned the value 5. This assignment is also treated as an expression with a value of 5, which is the value used in the final assignment, that made to **a**.

Automatic variables

We've already talked about how variables declared within a function (and this goes for **main()**, too) are 'automatic' and 'local'. They are local because they can only be used within that function, unless passed explicitly to another. They are 'automatic' because they are created when their function is called, and destroyed when the function ends. Use of the keywords **extern** and **static**, or defining variables outside of any function, alters these rules slightly, as discussed earlier.

Not only can you declare automatic variables inside functions, but also inside smaller statement blocks, normally inside the body of a loop enclosed in curly braces:

```
for (i=0;i<26;i++) {
    char letter;
    letter=i+97; /* add ASCII code for the letter 'a' */
    printf("%c\n",letter);
}
```

would print out the letters of the alphabet in lower case. The variable **letter** ceases to exist as soon as the loop has finished.

Interfacing with the machine

- Handling files
- C and the Shell
- Useful pre-defined functions

All of the examples so far have been designed to run from the CLI or Shell. The functions from **`stdio.h`** that we've been using – **`scanf`** and **`printf`** – have been used to take their input from the keyboard and put their output in the console window – that is, the Shell window.

The functions are said to be connected to data streams. As a default **`scanf`** is connected to a data stream known as '**`stdin`**', while **`printf`** is connected to '**`stdout`**'. On the Amiga, these are defined to be the keyboard and console window respectively. It's possible to change the data streams so that the functions take and receive data from different sources – most importantly, files.

Files are almost universally used in real-world applications. Just about any application you have used is likely to have an option to save results to disk, and retrieve results from disk.

Handling files

You can perform basic file-handling operations in C fairly simply. You need a pointer to a file, and a number of file functions to manipulate files. These functions are supplied with the pointer as one of their arguments, so that they can manipulate the file required by the programmer.

The pointer must be declared to be of type FILE (a data-type defined by **`stdio.h`**). You can then give it a value by assigning it the result of a call to the function **`fopen`**. This opens a file. Before you can perform any operations on a file, it must first be opened in this way. Once you have finished with it, it is important to then close the file with the **`fclose`** function, which ensures that the file's new contents are saved to disk.

The function **`fopen`** expects two arguments – a pointer to a **`string`** which represents the file's name as it is stored on disk (and possibly a path too, if it is in a different directory to the program), and the 'mode' in which the file should be opened. The mode is a pointer to another **`string`**, containing a set of characters which define what the programmer wants to do with the file. The table below shows the most common modes used when opening a file:

Table of file modes

Mode code	Function
r	Open an ASCII file for reading
w	Create an ASCII file to be written to
a	Open an ASCII file for new information to be added to the end ('append'). Create a new file if none exists
rb	Open a binary file for reading
wb	Create a binary file for writing
ab	Open a binary file for appending.
r+	Open an ASCII file for reading and writing
w+	Create a new ASCII file for reading and writing

Error checking

Opening a file for writing creates a new file with the specified name. If such a file already exists, then it is replaced with the new one. Naturally, opening a file for reading pre-supposes that one with the supplied name exists. If it doesn't, or if the specified file can't be opened for any other reason, then the pointer value returned by **fopen** is NULL. Your programs should by no means expect all file handling operations to go without error – not enough room on a disk is just one possible error condition they are liable to encounter – so you should always check the file pointer (or 'handle') to ensure it isn't NULL before carrying out further operations.

Within **stdio.h** there are the function declarations – or prototypes – of a number of functions designed for file manipulation. Two – **fscanf** and **fprintf** – correspond directly to their more common equivalents, **scanf** and **printf**. The difference is that the file versions expect a file pointer as their first argument.

The following will create a short text file on your RAM disk:

```
#include <stdio.h>

void main()
{
    FILE *fred_pointer;
```

```
    if (fred_pointer=fopen("ram:fred","w")) {
        fprintf(fred_pointer,"Hello from planet C\n");
        fclose(fred_pointer);
    }
}
```

You can examine its contents with the

```
type ram:fred
```

AmigaDOS command. Two file pointers are defined in **stdio.h** – **stdin** and **stdout**. Using these, you can direct input from the keyboard and output to the console window. The statements:

```
fprintf(stdout,"Hello from planet C\n");
```

EXAMPLE CODE

and

```
printf("Hello from planet C\n");
```

EXAMPLE CODE

are equivalent. As you can see, **printf** and **scanf** are specialised cases of the file versions, where their data streams are always linked to **stdout** and **stdin** respectively.

Two more useful functions in this context are **fgetc** and **fputc** – which retrieve characters from and put characters to the specified file. The first, **fgetc**, takes just one parameter – the file handle – and returns a character result that can be assigned to a variable. The second, **fputc**, takes two parameters – the first a character to be 'put', and the second the file handle of where it is to go.

Here's a program to print out the contents of a text file – a simple version of the AmigaDOS '**type**' command:

COMPLETE LISTING

```
#include<stdio.h>
#define FILE_NAME_MAX 50

void main()
```

```
{
    FILE *file_handle;
    char filename[FILE_NAME_MAX];
    char letter;

/* get path and filename from user - no longer than 49 characters */

    printf("Enter the name and path of file to print out\n");
    scanf("%49s",filename);

/* open file */
    if (file_handle=fopen(filename,"r")) {
        while ((letter=fgetc(file_handle))!=EOF)
            fputc(letter,stdout);
        fclose(file_handle);
    }
}
```

Notice that the file is only read from and closed if the program first succeeded in opening it. The assignment in the definition of the **while** loop ensures that the next character in the file is placed in the variable **letter**. The value of this overall expression is the character retrieved, which is then compared with the character **EOF** by the logical operator '**!=**', or 'not equal' to create the conditional expression needed by **while**. **EOF** is a symbolic constant, defined in **stdio.h**. It means End Of File, and is the character used to represent just that. The **while** loop continues, printing out each character at a time to the file whose handle is **stdout** (in other words, the console window) until the end of file is reached, at which time the file is closed.

Arguments with the Shell

Unlike the vast majority of AmigaDOS commands useable from the Shell – themselves written in C – the programs we've so far written are unable to take arguments typed in on the same Shell command line as the name of the program to be run. Also, our usage of the **main()** function so far has always been without it taking any parameters. Could these two facts be related?

Well yes, they are, but not in the way you might immediately think. It's useful for a C program to be able to take a variable number of command-line parameters, depending on the kind of things the user wants the program to do. The AmigaDOS command '**type**' is a good example of this. The problem is that C functions can only take a set number of parameters (with the notable exceptions of **printf** and **scanf**, but how these functions were written is beyond the scope of this book), but if we write **main()** so that it expects a fixed number of parameters, an error will occur if the user enters too few or too many.

argc and argv

The problem is solved by writing **main** so that it expects just two parameters (assuming you *want* command-line arguments, of course – if not, you carry on as before, without any parameters). The first of these is an integer, containing the number of command line arguments that have been passed. It's conventional to name this variable **argc**, short for argument count. The second parameter is a pointer to an array of strings – that is, a pointer to an array of pointers, each in turn pointing to a string of **char**. Its conventional name is **argv** – argument vector. Address arithmetic and the interchangeability of pointers and array names enable us to access each string in turn by supplying **argv** with an array index – e.g. **argv[2]** will give us the third string.

Each string in the array pointed to by **argv** contains one of the command line arguments, initialized automatically when your program is run. The first string, the one pointed to by **argv[0]**, is the name by which the program was run, which means that **argc** will have a value of 1 if no other arguments are passed. The last pointer in the array contains a NULL value. This appears after the pointers for each of the strings, which take up elements from **argv[0]** to **argv[argc-1]**. The NULL pointer is therefore stored in **argv[argc]**. As you can see, the strings containing the actual arguments supplied by the user for the program are pointed to by elements **argv[1]** to **argv[argc-1]**.

Using argc and argv

The simplest example of **argc** and **argv** in use is to show them being used to implement an 'echo' command. We'll write it so that it takes each of its arguments in turn and prints them out to the screen, each on a new

Using two variables (usually called argc and argv) you can pass your main function any number of AmigaDOS arguments while only using two parameters.

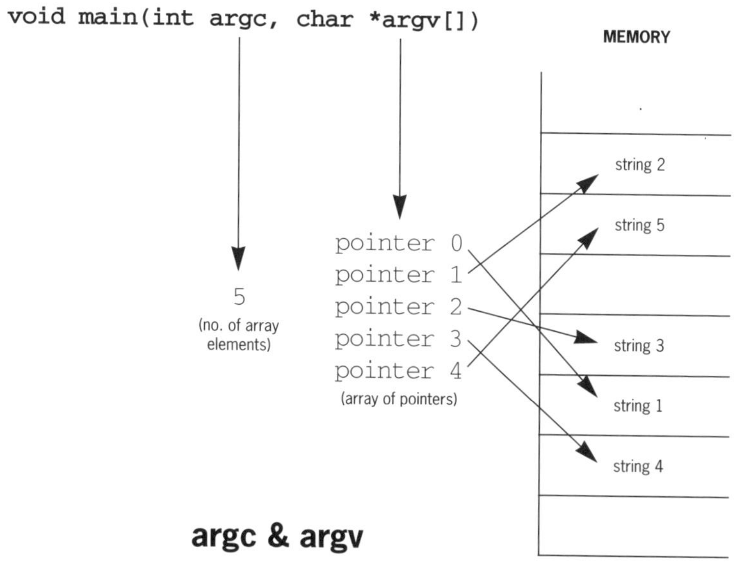

argc & argv

line. Remember when you compile it to give it a different name from the actual AmigaDOS command '**echo**'. Here's the code:

```
#include <stdio.h>

void main(int argc, char *argv[])
{
    int count;

    for (count=1;count<argc; count++)
        printf("%s\n",argv[count]);
}
```

The code should be pretty straightforward by now. We're not interested in the first element of the **argv** array, because it points to the name by which the program was called, so we initialize **count** to a value of `1`. Then the loop just counts from `1` to `argc-1`. Each value of **count** in turn will access a different element in the array **argv**. Each of these is a pointer to a string of **char**, remember, and so can be passed directly to **printf** so that the string is printed out.

Another example

As another example, let's convert the previous function, which typed out the contents of a file specified by the user, so that, instead of asking the user for the file name, it accepts it as a command line argument. Here's the new version:

COMPLETE LISTING

```
#include <stdio.h>

void main(int argc, char *argv[])
{
    FILE *file_handle;
    char letter;

/* if a filename has been specified (argc>1) then attempt to open file */
    if (argc>1)
        if (file_handle=fopen(argv[1],"r")) {
            /* if the file is successfully opened, print it out */
            while ((letter=fgetc(file_handle))!=EOF)
                fputc(letter,stdout);
            fclose(file_handle);
        }
}
```

Useful pre-defined functions

So far we've avoided as much as possible using the pre-defined functions in C's standard library. This has been for the purposes of demonstration – it's useful to be able to see how such functions might be written.

In real life, however, it would be much better to call on those functions already supplied with C. Why re-invent the wheel? Here's a list of some of the more useful functions, along with what they do and the kind of arguments they expect. Functions are listed under the header names by which they must be included. Note the functions themselves are written as prototype declarations, so you can easily see the types of their arguments and return values.

ctype.h

Contains functions useful for manipulating characters.

int isalpha(char c) returns a non-zero value if **c** is alphabetic, 0 otherwise

int isupper(char c) returns a non-zero value if **c** is upper case, 0 otherwise

int islower(char c) returns a non-zero value if **c** is lower case, 0 otherwise

int isdigit(char c) returns a non-zero value if **c** is a digit, 0 otherwise

int isalnum(char c) returns a non-zero value if **c** is alphabetic or numeric, 0 otherwise

int isspace(char c) returns a non zero value if **c** is a space, tab, newline, carriage return, formfeed or vertical tab, 0 otherwise

int toupper(char c) returns the upper case equivalent of **c**

int tolower(char c) returns the lower case equivalent of **c**

string.h

Functions for manipulating strings.

char *strcat(char *s,char *t) Concatenates **t** on to the end of string **s**, and returns string **s**

char *strncat(char *s,char *t) Concatenates **n** characters of **t** on to the end of **s**, and return **s**

int strcmp(char *s,char *t) Returns a negative integer if **s** is less than **t** (compares ASCII values of each character in turn), 0 if they are both the same, or a positive integer otherwise

int strncmp(char *s,char *t,int n) As above, but only comparing the first **n** characters of each string

char *strcpy(char *s,char *t) Copies the string **t** to **s**, including the string terminator '\0', and returns **s**

char *strncpy(char *s,char *t,int n) As above, but only the first **n** characters of **t**

int strlen(char *s) Returns the length of string **s** as an integer

char *strchr(char *s,char c) Returns a pointer to the first character with value **c** in **s**, NULL if there is none

char *strrchr(char *s,char c) Returns a pointer to the last character with value **c** in **s**, NULL if there is none

stdlib.h

An assortment of useful things

double atof(char *s) Returns the numerical equivalent of a non-integer numbered expressed as an ASCII text string

int atoi(char *s) Returns the integer equivalent of a number expressed as a string

int rand (void) Returns a pseudo-random integer

void srand(unsigned int seed) Sets the random number generator with a seed of value **seed**. A different seed produces a different set of pseudo-random numbers

void *calloc(size_t n, size_t size) Returns a pointer to an array of objects (a pointer to void can be used to point to any type of data) with **n** elements, each of size **size**. A NULL pointer is returned if no space can be found. If space is found, it is all initialized to 0. (Don't worry about the **size_t** type in the definition – it's the unsigned integer type returned by the special function sizeof.)

void *malloc(size_t size) Returns a pointer (again a pointer to **void**, so the space can be used for any type of variable) to an area of memory **size** bytes big. NULL is returned if the operating system will not give up the space. If space is granted, be aware that it is not initialized – it will contain garbage data

void free(void *pointer) Expects a pointer to an area of memory previously obtained by **calloc** or **malloc**. A call to free with this pointer will return the memory to the operating system and free it for use by something else. Freeing an area of memory not owned by the program can result in serious crashes.

void exit(int status) Causes program execution to stop. The integer value status is passed back to the operating system. This is the return value that can be used by AmigaDOS scripts.

int system(char *s) Executes the AmigaDOS command contained in the string **s**.

math.h

Contains floating point mathematical functions. Note that with DICE you must use the `-lm` option when compiling if you want to use floating point numbers. This makes sure it links with the maths library. Angles in the following functions should be expressed in radians, not degrees.

`double sin(double x)` Returns sine of angle `x`

`double cos(double x)` Returns cosine of `x`

`double tan(double x)` Returns tangent of `x`

`double asin(double x)` Returns arcsine of `x`, where `x` is in the range `-1` to `1`

`double acos(double x)` Returns arcosine of `x`

`double atan(double x)` Returns arctangent of `x`

`double sinh(double x)` Returns hyperbolic sine of `x`

`double cosh(double x)` Returns hyperbolic cosine of `x`

`double tanh(double x)` Returns hyperbolic tangent of `x`

`double exp(double x)` Returns exponential of `x - e` to the power of `x`

`double log(double x)` Returns natural logarithm of `x`

`double log10(double x)` Returns base 10 logarithm of `x`

`double pow(double x, double y)` Returns `x` to the power of `y`

`double sqrt(double x)` Returns the square root of `x`

This list of functions is by no means complete, but it should suffice to get you started. By all means experiment with them to see exactly how they can be used. Several functions listed here can be used instead of our versions in the example programs we've already written, making them shorter and more efficient. Try going back to some of them and modifying them accordingly.

Eliminating Errors

- Errors of language
- Errors of meaning
- Three debugging tips

It's a sad fact of a programmer's life that it is next to impossible to create a program of any size that contains no errors. Just about every application you can buy will have some sort of bug obscurely nestled within it. Obviously, though, it's important to eliminate as many errors as possible from your program. This process is known as 'debugging' a program.

You've probably already had to do some debugging of your own. The chances are that you've incorrectly typed at least one of the examples so far, in which case you would have introduced an error. This error may have either meant that the program failed to compile, or that it behaved strangely when it did compile and you ran it. Hopefully, you managed to track down the error and correct it.

There are a few established methods in C that help you debug, but before we go on to them it's as well to distinguish between the different types of error you can expect to find.

Errors of language

WHAT DOES IT MEAN?

Syntax error

These are known as syntax errors, in which some of what you have written fails to adhere to the rules of C's grammar, or its syntax. These kinds of errors can occur from simple typing mistakes. Equally, if you're relatively inexperienced, you might use the wrong form of syntax by mistake. You might, for example, include the body of a `while` loop inside ordinary parentheses instead of curly braces.

These sorts of errors are usually spotted by the compiler when it tries to translate your code. It will give you some sort of message – usually they're fairly obscure, until you get the hang of them – and the number of the line on which the error occurred. These errors are generally easy to correct. You load your source file into the editor and look at the line in question. The error usually lies on that line but can, as a result of the way compilers work, actually be in a previous line. Once you get the hang of C's syntax, you'll find yourself making fewer of these errors.

The compiler picks up most of them, but not all. There are times when you may have made an error, whether through mis-typing or being unsure of the correct syntax, which results in a statement which doesn't do what you meant it to do, but which still obeys C's rules of syntax. This brings us on to the second class of error:

Errors of meaning

Errors of meaning, or semantic errors, are the kind where your program is syntactically correct – it will compile and, to some extent, run – but doesn't produce the desired result. The meaning expressed by the collection of C statements doesn't express the meaning of your design. Or, in cases where the C program corresponds exactly to what you intended, your design itself was not a correct solution to the problem.

Errors of meaning can cause your program to halt unexpectedly, to produce strange results, or even to bring on the dreaded Guru message. The latter is unlikely with the kind of programs we've been writing so far, but you'll become more than used to it once you start using operating system calls.

Here are some common causes of this type of error:

Confusion of precedence

You may write:

```
a=b+c*d;
```

when what you actually intended was

```
a=(b+c)*d;
```

Both are legal syntax, but only one produces the result you intended. Another common mix-up with precedence is between the declarations of pointers to functions, and of functions that return pointers. Here's the first:

```
int (* func_pointer)(int);
```

this declares a variable, **func_pointer**, that can hold the address of a function taking an **int** as an argument and returning an **int** as a result.

Here's the second:

```
int *func_pointer(int);
```

which declares a function called **func_pointer** that takes an **int** as an argument and returns a pointer to an **int**.

If the first meaning is desired, the parentheses are necessary to specify the required precedence.

Array accessing

Remember that the first element of an array is number 0, with the last element being the element numbered the size of the array minus one. When you declare your array, you declare the number of elements, which is one more than the actual number by which the final element is accessed.

Loop bounds

Check the logic of your loops carefully. It is easy to mis-use increment and decrement operators, and relational operators to use your indexing variable one too many or one too few times. For instance, the statement

```
for (i=0;i<=100;i++) { /* body of loop */ }
```

would cycle **i** from 0 to 100 inclusive, i.e. the loop is executed 101 times. If you wanted 100 iterations, you would need to change the loop to read:

```
for (i=0;i<100;i++) { /* body of loop */ }
```

Increment and decrement

On a related note, be aware that putting ++ or – before a variable means that the variable will be incremented or decremented *before* its value is used in the expression that contains it. In other words, the modified value is used.

If ++ or -- comes after the variable name, then its old value is used in the expression, and *then* it is incremented or decremented. Errors of this kind are common within loops, and when accessing arrays.

In many cases, such as the loop example above, it's immaterial whether the increment or decrement operator precedes or follows the variable name. But if you're using them in an expression, be careful that you've got them the right way round. It would be possible to take the previous loop example and compact the increment operation into the comparative part of the loop, like so:

```
for (i=0;++i<100;) { /* body of loop */ }
```

Here the variable **i** is incremented once before the loop begins. In other words, its value loops from `1` to `99`. Once it is incremented to `100`, the loop terminates. Using post-increment on **i**, as shown below, would modify the loop so that it counted from `1` to `100`:

```
for (i=0;i++<100;) { /* body of loop */ }
```

Recursion

Remember that if you make use of recursion, each function call requires a certain amount of memory. If a function recursively calls itself many times, it's possible that it will run out of memory. You can make this happen inadvertently if you have failed to put in a condition to terminate the recursion, or if the condition you are checking for somehow never occurs. Look at the part of your recursive function that returns a result, from here you should be able to track down the error.

But a recursive routine can be fine, and still run out of memory. You can increase the amount of memory a program has to use by use of the AmigaDOS **stack** function. Execute this with the number of bytes you require before running your program.

Poor error-handling

You should always check any input that your program takes from the user. It's all too easy to write programs that will perform a certain task depending on what the user enters, and assume that the user will always enter a correct option. Always write your programs so that they will take into account an invalid user entry.

Your programs need to be able to handle errors generated not just by the user, but by the operating system, too. We'll go into operating system calls in more detail next chapter, but we've already used a couple of calls – **malloc**, for one, and the file handling functions too. **Malloc** asks the operating system for some memory. It's quite conceivable, if memory is tight, that the operating system is unable to give your program the memory it asks for. If this happens, and your program fails to check for it (the pointer returned by **malloc** will be NULL if no memory was given) then it will cause a crash as soon as it attempts to access the memory it thinks it has. A common check for a successful **malloc** is shown below:

```
char *s;

if ((s=(char *)malloc(50))!=NULL) { /* do something if s points to an
area of memory */ }
```

This attempts to grab 50 bytes to store a **string**, accessed by **s**. Notice that the pointer returned by **malloc** is cast to a pointer to **char** before being assigned to **s**. The result of this expression is the new value of **s**, which is compared to NULL in the **if**'s relational expression. If it is not equal, the body of the loop executes. A more common shorthand, frequently used when accessing **malloc** and other system resources, is:

```
if (!(s=(char *)malloc(50))) { /* do something if s points to an area of
memory */ }
```

Assignment and equality

One of the most common errors is caused by people confusing = and ==. The first assigns a value to a variable, the second compares its two operands, returning 0 if they are dissimilar, or a non-zero value if they are the same. If an assignment is used as part of an expression, then the result it yields is the value assigned. Look at this:

```
if (a=1) { /* do something */ }
```

The programmer probably intended the `something` to be done only if `a` held the value `1`. Unfortunately, the assignment gives `a` the value `1` no matter what. This assignment is then treated as a logical expression. Its result is `1` – non-zero – so the logical expression is true and the `something` is done, no matter what the original value of `a`. The correct form is this:

```
if (a==1) { /* do something if a contains 1 */ }
```

Similarly, it's also easy to confuse the logical operators `&&` and `||` with the similar bitwise operators `&` and `|`. Be careful.

Nested `ifs`

Nesting `if` statements inside one another can be a great way to confuse yourself. If you're unsure which `else` or `end if` belongs to which `if`, make use of curly braces to emphasise the logic. Also, be sure to indent your code with tabs – the indents again make the logic more apparent.

Pointers

WARNING

Pointers

Pointers, by their very nature, are dangerous things. The compiler can't keep its eye on pointers for you as it can with ordinary variables. You can only access variables that you have properly declared, but with pointers you can access just about anything. Accessing memory that your program does not own is a sure fire way to a crash. For this reason, you should be doubly careful about checking pointers for NULL values, and that your pointer arithmetic doesn't produce any unexpected results.

The use of pointers is especially prevalent in programs that interface with the operating system. Because the use of the functions that do this can seem quite overwhelming to newcomers, it's no surprise that confusion leads to pointer misuse. Be on your guard.

Global variables

Variables that can be accessed globally – i.e. by more than one function – can sometimes cause problems. If the value of a local variable is not what you expected, you can track the offending code down to somewhere within the function that defines it. With a global variable, the error could be in any number of functions that access it.

Be sure to only use global variables when you need to. Each time a parameter is passed to a function, time is spent copying the argument value to the parameter, and memory used in creating space for the parameter. When your programs are using certain system structures (screens or windows, for example) it's impractical to pass them in this way. So global variables are a necessary evil. Try to make sure that only those functions that need to can modify your global variables.

Three debugging tips

Comments

Always comment your code. It will help no end in the debugging of your program. It's impossible to over-emphasise how valuable the proper labelling of obscure bits of code can be. You can be sure that a couple of months after you've written a routine, you won't be able to remember exactly why it was written as it was. You should use comments to bring out the logic of your program design.

Write modular code

If you write your program as a series of modules, you can test each module individually to ensure that it works before adding it to the overall project. One of the most important skills in debugging is being able to trace a fault to a particular area in your program. You want to have to search through as few lines as possible for the error. Writing your programs as a set of modules means that tracing a fault will be so much easier.

A common way to write modular code is to first write your **main** routine, which usually provides the containing structure. From here, various other functions are called. Initially, just write these functions as dummy functions – just the bare bones of their definitions, with no content other than, perhaps, a statement to print a message to the screen letting you know the function has been called. Your **main** program can then be tested until you know it works.

Once it does, you can begin writing the functions, one by one. As you write each one, you can test it by calling it from **main**. If an error appears, you can be fairly sure that it's going to be in the piece of code you've just written. If you sit down and write your whole program in one sitting before running it, well, your problem could be anywhere.

Taking modular code one step further – once your programs get to be of an appreciable size, you'll find it useful to section parts off, according to the functions they perform, into different source code files. At this stage you'll find header files useful. For one thing, a header file can contain all the **#includes** that your other modules depend on. You can also use it to declare functions (themselves defined in a separate source file) to be used by the other modules. (Remember that functions need to be declared before they can be called in source code.)

Diagnostics

Get your troublesome programs to give status reports. A few **printf**s placed here and there will help you see what is going on while a program is running. As mentioned above, you can put a **printf** in a function to let you know it has been called. It's sometimes a good idea to put another message at the end of the function to let you know when it has exited:

```
int find_biggest(int a, int b)
{
    printf("** Entered find_biggest\n");
    /* body of function */
    printf("** Leaving find_biggest\n");
    return (result);
}
```

You might also want to print out the values of key variables at certain parts of your program. Printing out the index of a loop that isn't working properly is a common example:

```
for (i=0;i<limit;i++) {
    printf("Value of i is %d\n",i);
    /* body of loop */
}
```

You'll develop more of your own debugging tricks as you progress. Debugging is a fact of programming life. With large projects, it can sometimes take longer to debug them than to write them in the first place.

Using Amiga libraries

- Amiga-specific C
- Exec
- Using libraries – examples

By now you should be familiar with, or at the very least have had a passing acquaintance with, all the major aspects of the C language. Given your knowledge, you can create programs of any complexity you choose, and they will compile and run on any computer system that has a C compiler.

The key to the portability of all previous programs is the simple, text-based interface they have relied on. This interface has been built around C's standard library, **stdio**. Every C compiler on every system comes with **stdio**, which contains the same functions. The exact way in which these functions are written, and the methods by which they perform their tasks on the computer in question, may be quite different; but from the C programmer's point of view they are identical on all systems: they have the same names, they take the same arguments and they carry out the same tasks.

Amiga-specific programming

Libraries

We're now going to deal with how to write programs especially for the Amiga, making use of its special features. Programs such as these rely on a set of Amiga-specific libraries. Although computers such as the Macintosh and PC have similar features to the Amiga, these features are accessed by completely different libraries – any programs you write that take advantage of the Amiga's facilities will have to be re-written before they can be compiled and run on a different type of machine. However, if you make careful use of the Amiga libraries, you can be pretty sure that your programs will run on any model of Amiga, memory permitting.

Unlike ordinary libraries, which the linker connects to your program at the final compilation stage, the Amiga-specific libraries are stored either in the computer's ROM, or on disk, ready to be loaded as they are needed. When you come to compile a program that makes use of these libraries, DICE links in an **amiga.lib** file (the exact name varies depending on the version of the operating system you are using) which contains, not the functions themselves, but entry points to the functions in ROM. You must, in your own programs, also **#include** various header files that contain function prototypes and associated data-type definitions.

It's beyond the scope of this book to discuss in detail the many, many Amiga library functions available to you. There are some very substantial official Commodore manuals that do just that. If you're serious about programming the Amiga, you'll need them. They are: *Amiga ROM Kernel Autodocs*, *Amiga ROM Kernel Devices* and *Amiga ROM Kernel Libraries*, and all are published by Addison-Wesley.

A practical demonstration

To demonstrate the use of the Amiga's facilities, I'm going to show you how to write a simple game: Four In A Row. The game is played on an eight-by-eight grid, with two players, each using different coloured pieces. Players take it in turn placing pieces on the board, with the object of getting four of their own pieces in a row, horizontally, vertically or diagonally. The pieces, though, are "dropped" into the board, so they always fall to the lowest free row of whichever column you choose.

Before we get involved with a discussion of how to get the computer to play the game – in itself an interesting problem – we'll go into the mechanics of creating a display on which the game can be played.

Exec

The Amiga's operating system is organised into a number of different parts, each dealing with a specific area. For instance, the part of the operating system dealing with the Workbench windows environment is known as Intuition. The most fundamental part of the operating system is **`Exec`**. **`Exec`** controls all other programs running on the Amiga, it is the part that enables multi-tasking to occur – it divides the system's time between different programs, and passes messages between them.

Each of these areas of the operating system can be utilised by a programmer by calling on their corresponding library functions. But before this can be done, the library that contains the functions must be "opened". Each area of the operating system has a corresponding library.

When you open a library, you inform **`Exec`** that your program wishes to make use of that library. If the library is on disk, rather than in ROM, **`Exec`** will load it into memory for you. The opening of a library is performed by calling an **`Exec`** function called **`OpenLibrary`**. You can use **`OpenLibrary`**, even though it is itself a function of the **`Exec`**

Our 'Four-in-a-Row' game consists of 8 vertical columns into which each player in turn drops counters. The winner is the first player to make a horizontal, vertical or diagonal line of four counters.

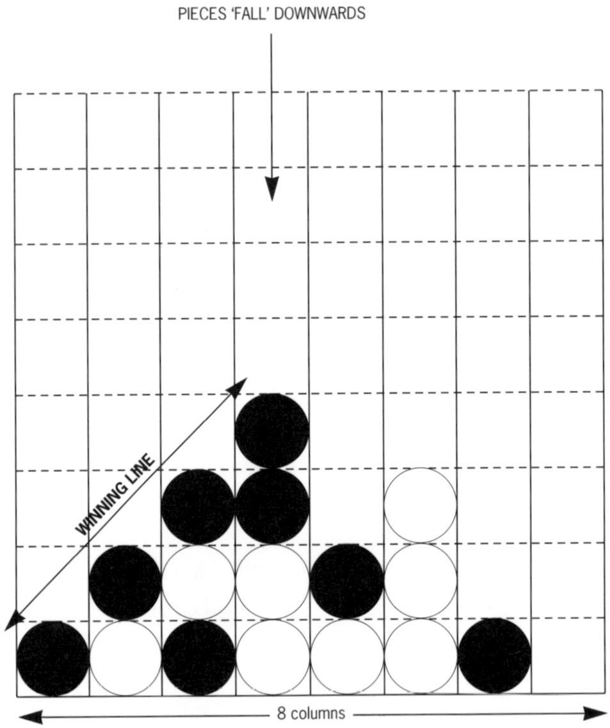

'Four-in-a-Row'

library, because **Exec** is "opened" automatically when your program runs.

When you call **OpenLibrary**, you pass it two arguments. The first is a string, or more correctly a pointer to a string, that names the library you require. The second is the version number of the library. If, for example, you are writing a program that relies on a function only provided with Workbench 2, then you will want to be sure that it is a Workbench 2 library you are opening. If you supply a version number of zero, the library will be opened no matter which version it is. All of the examples in this book will work with Workbench 1.3 and above.

The function **OpenLibrary** returns a result: a pointer to a structure. The exact type of this structure depends on the library you have tried to open

– the declarations are contained within the relevant header files, which must be `#include`d in your program.

This result must be stored in a pointer variable of the correct type. Furthermore, the name of the variable is fixed, depending on the library opened, and it must be global. This is because the various operating system functions will need to use it. The structure indicated by your pointer contains information on how each of the library's functions can be found and called. You need not worry about this; once you have the library base pointer you can call on the functions by their names, as you would any other C function, and the compiler will sort out the rest.

It's possible for your call to `OpenLibrary` to fail. It may be that `Exec` has been unable to find a library version as recent as the one you specified, or that there is insufficient room in memory to load the library, or that you have asked for a non-existent library. In these cases, the value returned will be NULL. It is up to your program to check for this – calling the functions of an un-opened library will result in a crash.

WARNING

Closing libraries

Also, when your program finishes it must close down each of the libraries opened. This is done by a call to `CloseLibrary` with your library pointer as argument. Your program must also relinquish its hold on any other resources it may have obtained from the operating system, usually windows and screens. We'll come on to how to do this in due course.

Using two libraries

The two libraries we'll be needing are Intuition and the graphics library, called "`intuition.library`" and "`graphics.library`". Their base pointers must be assigned to global variables called `IntuitionBase` and `GfxBase` respectively. Upper and lower case is important. The first of these is declared as being of type pointer to `struct Library` – the standard declaration for library pointers. `GfxBase` is something of an exception, and it must be declared as being a pointer to `struct GfxBase`. Notice also that the `GfxBase` pointer must be cast to be of type pointer to `struct Library` when the library is closed.

Here's how we would attempt to open them and then close them again:

```
/* include operating system header files */

#include <exec/types.h> /* contains type definitions useful to ¬
system libraries */
#include <intuition/intuition.h> /* contains data types used by ¬
Intuition */
#include <intuition/intuitionbase.h> /* contains definition of ¬
IntuitionBase structure type */

/* declare pointers to graphics and intuition libraries */

struct GfxBase *GfxBase;
struct Library *IntuitionBase;

/* define the function that opens the libraries */

void setup()
{
    /* open graphics library and get a pointer to it */
    GfxBase=(struct GfxBase *)OpenLibrary("graphics.library",0);

    /* leave program if failed to open library */
    if (GfxBase==NULL) exit(100);

    /* open intuition library and get pointer to it */
    IntuitionBase=(struct Library *) OpenLibrary("intuition.library",0);
    /* if failed to open, close graphics library and stop */
    if (IntuitionBase==NULL) {
    CloseLibrary(GfxBase);
    exit(200);
    }
}
void closedown()
{

    /* close down libraries */
```

```
    CloseLibrary(IntuitionBase);
    CloseLibrary((struct Lbrary *)GfxBase); /* cast GfxBase to be of ¬
type pointer to library */
}

void main()
{
    /* call function to open libraries */

    setup();
    /* call function to close them */
    closedown();
}
```

Notice how **IntuitionBase** and **GfxBase** are declared as global variables. The result returned by **OpenLibrary** is cast to be of a pointer to the structure required at each call. Also, notice that after the attempt to open each library, the pointer is checked to see if the call was successful. If it wasn't, the program can proceed no further so it quits. But in the case of it failing to open Intuition, it first closes the graphics library, which it must have successfully already opened. It is important to ensure that your program closes *everything* that it opened, no matter how it finishes.

If both libraries were opened successfully, the program calls another function that closes them again. In general there's no need to worry about calls to **CloseLibrary** failing. You must remember, though, to pass it a valid pointer.

Now that we can open the libraries, lets look at how we can use their functions.

Opening a screen

Our first task is to open a screen. This is achieved with a call to the **OpenScreen** function. This function returns a pointer to a **Screen** structure which the function creates for us in memory. We can then use this pointer for all further operations on the screen.

We pass as an argument to the function a pointer to a **NewScreen** structure. This shouldn't be confused with a **Screen** structure. A **NewScreen** structure contains the definitions for the kind of screen we want, and is initialized by our program. A **Screen** structure contains information supplied by the call to **OpenScreen**.

A **NewScreen** structure is declared and initialized like this:

```
struct NewScreen InitScreen = {
    0,0, /* the top left coordinate of the screen */
    640,200, /* the bottom right coordinate */
    3, /* the number of bitplanes - 3 gives us eight colours */
    0,1, /* detail and block pens - define colours of title strip */
    HIRES, /* the view mode we want */
    CUSTOMSCREEN,
    NULL, /* use default font for title */
    "Our custom screen", /* the screen's title */
    NULL /* no gadgets */
};
```

And it's opened like this

```
struct Screen *CurrentScreen;
/* CurrentScreen is a global variable pointing to a Screen structure */

CurrentScreen=(struct Screen *)OpenScreen(&InitScreen);
```

Notice how the address operator is used to take the address of our **InitScreen** structure. Notice also that the pointer returned is cast to be of type pointer to **Screen structure**.

In practice, you must always check that the pointer returned is not NULL, that the screen has been opened successfully. Once you have finished with the screen, you close it by passing your screen pointer to **CloseScreen**:

```
CloseScreen(CurrentScreen);
```

Creating a window

Windows are created in a similar way. First we initialize a **NewWindow** structure:

```
    struct NewWindow InitWindow = {
        0,11, /* position of top-left of window relative to the ¬
top-left of the screen */
        640,189, /* the width and height of the window */
        0,1, /* use the same detail and block pens as window's screen */
        MOUSEBUTTONS|CLOSEWINDOW,
        /* these flags indicate the messages our window wants to ¬
receive from Intuition */
        ACTIVATE|WINDOWCLOSE,
        /* further window flags */
        NULL, /* no gadgets */
        NULL, /* no user checkmark */
        "Four in a row", /* the window title*/
        NULL, /* pointer to the window's screen - assigned later in
program */
        NULL, /* pointer to a superbitmap */
        0,0,640,189, /* the minimum and maximum widths of the window -
ignored because we have not selected the sizable flag */
        CUSTOMSCREEN /* type of screen to be used */
    };
```

You'd open the window like this:

```
struct Window *CurrentWindow;
/* CurrentWindow is a global variable pointing to a Window structure */

/* having opened a screen, we must put a pointer to it in the ¬
NewWindow structure InitWindow */
InitWindow.Screen=CurrentScreen;

CurrentWindow=(struct Window *)OpenWindow(&InitWindow);
```

Notice how in **InitWindow**'s declaration NULL is assigned to the pointer used to attach the window to a screen. This gap is filled once we've successfully opened a screen, by assigning a pointer to the screen to the **.Screen** part of the **NewWindow** structure. Having done this, the window can be opened in much the same way as a screen can.

It's customary, having opened a window, to take something from its structure known as a "rast port" pointer. It points to a **RastPort** structure, and it is used in all drawing operations. We won't be needing it just for now, but here's how it is declared and assigned:

```
struct RastPort *rp;

rp=CurrentWindow->RPort;
```

Here, **CurrentWindow** is a pointer to a **Window** structure, not a **Window** structure itself, so it must first be de-referenced with the **->** operator before we can get at the **RPort** pointer.

Using Intuition

In the structure definition for **InitWindow** above, there were two lines of "Intuition flag" assignments. These flags tell Intuition about the sort of window we want. The first line deals with the IDCMP, or Intuition Direct Communications Message Port. This is the means by which Intuition gives your program messages relating to the window. In our case, we've elected to receive messages if the user clicks the mouse button or (the vertical bar is a logical OR, remember) if the user clicks on the close window gadget. These and other flags are defined in the Intuition header files.

The second line informs Intuition that we want the window to be made active when it is opened (that is, all user input is directed there until another window is selected by them) and that we will be closing the window ourselves.

In order to receive messages from Intuition (which is to say, to get user input), we need to reference something called an **IntuiMessage**. This is a structure, which we access by a pointer, that contains the information Intuition communicates to us. You can declare a pointer of the required type with:

```
struct IntuiMessage *message;
```

And you can retrieve a message from Intuition by making a call to **GetMsg**. The result it returns is a pointer to an **IntuiMessage** structure. If no message was waiting, the function returns NULL. Here's how you call it:

```
message=(struct IntuiMessage *)GetMsg(CurrentWindow->UserPort);
```

The **UserPort** element of the **Window** structure is devoted to receiving Intuition messages.

Intuition messages

The **IntuiMessage** structure takes the following form:

```
struct IntuiMessage {
    struct Message ExecMessage;
    ULONG Class;
    USHORT Code;
    USHORT Qualifier;
    APTR IAddress;
    SHORT MouseX,MouseY;
    ULONG Seconds, Micros;
    struct Window *IDCMPWindow;
    struct IntuiMessage *SpecialLink;
}
```

The types in capitals are **#define**d shorthands: **ULONG** is equivalent to **unsigned long int**, **USHORT unsigned short int**, **APTR** a pointer to an arbitrary address.

Many of these fields are of use only to the system. The **Class** field, however, contains information about the type of message you've got. You can compare this field directly with the flags you supplied in the **NewWindow** structure to specify which kinds of messages you wanted to receive. You must retrieve the information from the **IntuiMessage** structure as follows:

```
unsigned long int class;

class=message->Class;
```

The **IntuiMessage** also contains the position of the mouse when it was sent, and the system time, held in **MouseX**, **MouseY**, **Seconds** and **Micros** respectively. **IAddress** contains the address in memory of the structure that caused the message. This might be a gadget that you have created for your window – we won't be using it. **IDCMPWindow** is a **pointer** to the window that received the message, while the **Code** and **Qualifier** fields depend on the kind of message received. We will not be needing them.

Once you have retrieved all the information you need from the message, you must reply to it. This tells Intuition that you have received and understood the message, and enables it to use the space the message took up for something else. You reply to a message like this:

```
ReplyMsg(message);
```

The program

With all that under our belts, we're ready to write a program to open the graphics and Intuition libraries, open a screen and a window on it, and wait until the user clicks on the window's close gadget. When this happens, we must close the window, then the screen, and finally the libraries. Here's the code:

```
/* include operating system header files */

#include <exec/types.h>
#include <intuition/intuition.h>
#include <intuition/intuitionbase.h>

/* include prototypes for library functions */
#include <clib/intuition_protos.h>
#include <clib/exec_protos.h>
#include <clib/graphics_protos.h>
```

```
/* declare pointers to graphics and intuition libraries */
struct GfxBase *GfxBase;
struct Library *IntuitionBase;

/* define a pointer to a rastport structure */

struct RastPort *rp;

/* define the text to be used in the screen title */

struct TextAttr TextFont = {
    "topaz.font",
    8,0,0
};

/* declare pointers to the Window, Screen and Intuition Message data
structures */

struct Window *CurrentWindow;
struct Screen *CurrentScreen;
struct IntuiMessage *message;

/* define the parameters of our new screen */

    struct NewScreen InitScreen = {
    0,0,
    640,200,
    3,
    0,1,
    HIRES,
    CUSTOMSCREEN,
    &TextFont,"Our custom screen",NULL
    };

/* define the parameters of our new window */

    struct NewWindow InitWindow = {
```

```
    0,11,
    640,189,
    0,1,
    MOUSEBUTTONS|CLOSEWINDOW,
    ACTIVATE|WINDOWCLOSE,
    NULL,
    NULL,
    "Four in a row",
    NULL,
    NULL,
    0,0,640,189,
    CUSTOMSCREEN
    };

/* define the function that opens the libraries, screen and window */

void setupdisplay()
{
    /* open graphics library and get a pointer to it */
    GfxBase=(struct GfxBase *)OpenLibrary("graphics.library",0);

    /* leave program if failed to open library */
    if (GfxBase==NULL) exit(100);

    /* open intuition library and get pointer to it */
    IntuitionBase=(struct Library *) OpenLibrary("intuition.library",0);
    /* if failed to open, close graphics library and stop */
    if (IntuitionBase==NULL) {
        CloseLibrary((struct Library *)GfxBase);
        exit(200);
    }
    /* open a new screen according to the parameters in InitScreen */
    /* put a pointer to the new screen in CurrentScreen */
    CurrentScreen=(struct Screen*)OpenScreen(&InitScreen);

    /* if OpenScreen failed, close the Intuition and Graphics ¬
libraries */
    if (CurrentScreen==NULL) {
```

```
        CloseLibrary(IntuitionBase);
        CloseLibrary((struct Library *)GfxBase);
        exit(300);
    }

    /* Make our new window belong to the new screen */
    InitWindow.Screen=CurrentScreen;
    /* Open a new window with the parameters in InitWindow, and put */
    /* a pointer to it in CurrentWindow */
    CurrentWindow=(struct Window *)OpenWindow(&InitWindow);
    /* if failed to open window, close screen and libraries */
    if (CurrentWindow==NULL) {
        CloseScreen(CurrentScreen);
        CloseLibrary(IntuitionBase);
        CloseLibrary((struct Library *)GfxBase);
        exit(400);
    }
    /* get the opened windows rastport, and store it in rp */
    rp=CurrentWindow->RPort;
}

void closedown()
{
    /* close down window, screen and libraries */
    CloseWindow(CurrentWindow);
    CloseScreen(CurrentScreen);
    CloseLibrary(IntuitionBase);
    CloseLibrary((struct Library *)GfxBase);
}

void main()
{
    unsigned long int class; /* class of message received */

    /* call function to open screen and window */
    setupdisplay();
    /* wait until user clicks the close gadget */
    do {
```

```
        while((message=(struct IntuiMessage *)GetMsg¬
(CurrentWindow->UserPort))==NULL)
        ; /* wait for message */
        class=message->Class;

        ReplyMsg(message);
    } while (class!=CLOSEWINDOW); /* repeat until user asks to ¬
close the window */

    /* relinquish all system resources */
    closedown();
}
```

Rather than using the default font for its screen, the program specifies it wants a particular one by putting a pointer to a **TextAttr** structure in the **NewScreen** structure. The **TextAttr** structure is declared immediately above, and is asking the system to use Topaz 8.

Notice that immediately after the program attempts to open each system resources, it checks for success. If it meets with failure, then it closes down every previously opened resource before exiting. The C function **exit** forces a program to terminate immediately; the argument it is passed gets returned to AmigaDOS as an error code.

In the function **main**, the program goes into a loop that is only ended when the user clicks on the window's close gadget. This can be checked by comparing the message type assigned to the variable **class** with the flag **CLOSEWINDOW**. When the two are equal, the loop ends and the system resources are relinquished with a call to **closedown**.

Wait function

It's not generally a good idea to put your programs into loops like this. Because your program is running in a multi-tasking environment, it's wasting valuable processing time just waiting for the user to do something. This time would be better spent on other programs that are trying to do some work.

You can resolve this problem by calling a function named **Wait**. This will send your program "to sleep". **Exec** will only wake it up again when it has received one of the messages from **Intuition** that it specified an interest in, which was done by setting the **IDCMP** flags in the **NewWindow** structure. You can get your program to wait quietly for input with the following line:

```
Wait(1L<<CurrentWindow->UserPort->mp_SigBit);
```

EXAMPLE CODE

The **mp_SigBit** field is made active when a message has been sent. Immediately after this line, you can place the assignment to message from the call to **GetMsg**, as it will only be executed once a message is waiting. We'll make use of this better method in our final version of the game.

'Four-in-a-Row'

- Planning a game
- Programming a computer opponent
- The game code

It's time to look at how we are going to write the part of the program that actually plays the game. When we've done that, we'll go on to how to draw the board and pieces in our window, and then present the finished program.

With more complex programs, you'll often find that the best way to start is to think about the sort of data they will be handling, and how this data is best to be stored. Four In A Row is played on an eight-by-eight board, which is its fundamental data-type.

Planning the structure

We need to be able to indicate whether each position is empty, or contains one of two types of pieces. We can store these as single characters, and therefore represent the board as a two-dimensional array of **`char`**. Although the game is only played on an eight-by-eight grid, our task will be easier if we define a bigger array. Part of the strategy for finding the computer's move will involve searching from one board position to up to three positions away in each direction. Rather than having to check that we are not searching beyond the bounds of the board, we can declare a bigger array, and define the gaps around the eight-by-eight area's edge as being permanently empty. To this end, they are initially filled with the null character, '`\0`', while the places in the eight-by-eight area are filled with spaces. Characters representing the Human and Computer pieces are defined to be '`X`' and '`O`' respectively.

The overall structure of the program breaks down as follows: open the libraries, screen and window; draw the board; get a move from the player; update the board; make a move for the computer; update the board; get another move from the player until the window is closed.

The computer's move

The part of interest is the part that generates the computer's move. This uses an algorithm known as "**`Mini-max`**", common to many strategy games. It consists of two parts. The first part generates the moves it is possible to make at a given point in the game, and then proceeds to make each of them in turn. The second part evaluates a given board position. It can give a result with respect to either player. Its result is a number; the

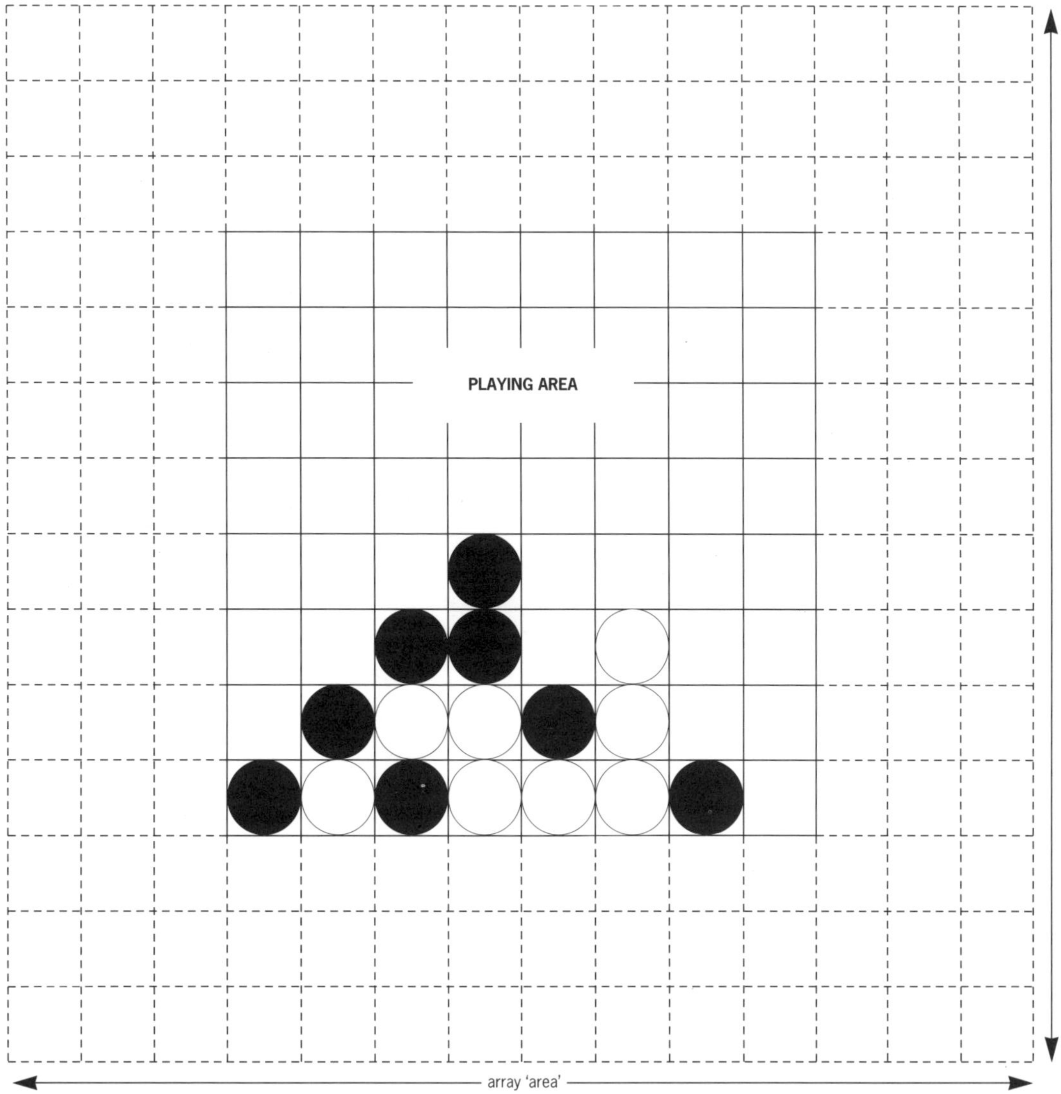

Our 'oversized' array

By using an oversized array (3 squares around the board in the example illustrated above) it's possible to extrapolate possible moves without having to worry about continually checking the playing area boundaries.

Here's a flowchart to illustrate the basic structure of our 'Four-in-a-Row' game. Simplifying the structure like this makes it easier to plan the individual functions necessary and when they should be called.

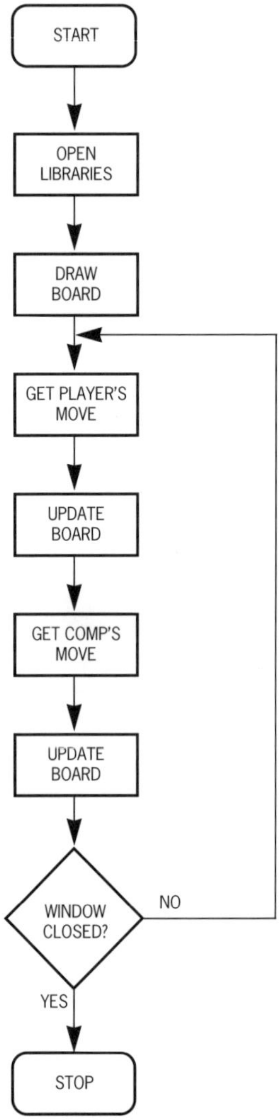

'Four-in-a-Row' flowchart

higher it is, the stronger the given player's position on the board. It is usually positive if the player is winning, negative otherwise. Given the evaluation function, the move generator can make one of its moves, get a score for it, then take the move back before trying the next one. It then knows that the move that obtained the highest score is the one to take.

MAKE A NOTE!
Recursion

Using that method would produce a very basic game. **`Mini-max`**'s approach is a little more complicated, relying as it does on recursion. With it the computer is able to "look ahead" and make moves that will yield results later on in the game. It does this by making moves both for itself and then responses on the human's behalf. After it has chosen what it thinks is the human's best response, it goes on to make its best response to that move, and then pretends to be the human again, and so on... The algorithm used to determine how the human will move is the same as that used by the computer to decide on its moves.

The move generator takes as one of its arguments the player who is making the move. When it is initially called, this will be Computer, as it is the computer making the move.

The move generator then goes through each of the possible moves in turn – there are a maximum of eight, the number going down as each of the columns is filled to the top. After making a move, the move generator then calls itself, but with the other player as an argument. If the move generator was called with Computer as its argument it will call itself again with Human as argument, and vice versa.

When called again, it continues as before, making each legal move in turn on behalf of the human player. After making each move, it calls itself again, and again switching its Player argument to that of the opponent.

WHAT DOES IT MEAN?
'Look-ahead' or 'ply'

The recursion repeats for a pre-set number of levels, known as the "look-ahead" or "ply" of the search. The bigger this number, the better the computer plays, but the longer it takes. With 1-ply it checks eight possible moves, with 2-ply this becomes 8*8 or 64, 64*8 for 3-ply, and so on. The version we are going to write will use 5-ply, the minimum necessary for it to play a decent game. Unfortunately, it does mean you'll be waiting a few minutes for the computer to move if you're using a 68000-based Amiga.

When the move generator has been called for the fifth time, control is passed to a different part of the function. Here it again generates each of the possible moves, and makes them in turn. Rather than calling itself again, though, it instead calls the **evaluate** function to find a score for the board position it has arrived at. It then takes back the move it has just made, so as to leave the board as it found it.

The score for the move is made up of two components. The first is the opponent's score, given by the evaluate function before any of the move generator's final set of eight moves have been made. The second component is the score from the current player's point of view, given by the **evaluate** function after the move generator has made a move. The score for any one of these eight final moves is found by subtracting the first component from the evaluation after the move. As each move is tried in turn, its score is compared against a current maximum. If it exceeds the maximum, then the maximum is set to this new score and the column in which the move was made is stored in a variable. After all the moves have been checked, the function is left with a record of the highest scoring move. It then returns the column of the best move as an integer and alters, with the aid of a pointer, the variable **ScoreForMove**.

When the function returns, the recursion backs down one level and control continues immediately after the line in the move generator that called itself. This is in the position of having just tried a move, remember. It now takes that move back, and reverses the sign (makes a positive number negative, or vice versa) of the score returned by the recursive call. After it has made all of its moves at this level of recursion, it chooses the move that yielded the highest score, returns the column number of the move that made it, and alters the variable **ScoreForMove** via a pointer, in much the same way as the part of the function that deals with the bottom level of recursion.

Why is the score for each move made negative? After the move generator has been recursively called, what it returns is a score for the *opponent's* best move, not the player whose moves it has been making on the recursive level that calls it. By negating all of the scores and choosing the largest, it is effectively choosing the smallest. In other words, it is choosing the move for the player that produces the weakest response from the opponent, even though the opponent is assumed to be making the best move possible in the circumstances presented by the player.

That's the most complicated part of **`Mini-Max`** over with. You can use pretty much the same best move generator in many sorts of board games, such as noughts and crosses or even chess.

Calculating your game position's 'score'

The evaluation function used depends on the type of game you are writing. The more subtle your evaluation function, the better your program will play. Here, the function, which is called **`PlayersScore`**, takes two parameters – the board, and the player whose position is to be evaluated. It returns a score whose value depends on the strength of the given player's position.

It arrives at this score by looking at each of the positions on the board in turn. **`Playersscore`** is only interested in those positions that contain the player's pieces.

When it finds such a position, it calls the function **`TryADirection`** four times. What this does is to look along the board in a specified direction

In order to work out the desirability of any one move, the computer has to have some way of working out its value. It does this by using a 'points-scoring' system based on the values of specific counter arrangements. Obviously, four in a row (the winning move) has the highest value, while other layouts are of decreasing value.

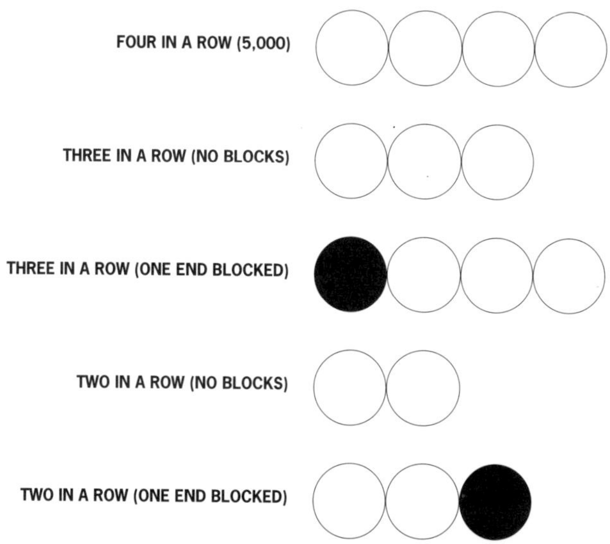

Calculating the 'score' of your board position

and see whether or not it can establish a line of pieces owned by the player. The values for different situations are scored according to a set of **#define**s at the beginning of the program. Four in a row (**#define Worth4 5000**), a winning situation, is scored the highest at 5000 points. Next comes the value of three pieces in a row with no blocks, followed by three pieces in a row blocked on one side, then two pieces in a row with no blocks, and finally two pieces in a row with one side blocked. Any other configurations have no score.

The pieces are checked from the top left corner of the board moving across and to the right, so we only need to call **TryADirection** with the following directions: diagonally up and right, horizontally across, diagonally down and right, and vertically down. The scores for each of the directions are summed, and these scores are summed for each of the player's pieces. This final sum is the result returned by **Playersscore**.

The program itself

Here is the source code to the final program:

```
/* four_row.c */

/* — Include ANSI C headers — */

#include <stdio.h>
#include <stdlib.h>

/* include operating system header files */

#include <exec/types.h>
#include <intuition/intuition.h>
#include <intuition/intuitionbase.h>

#include <clib/intuition_protos.h>
#include <clib/exec_protos.h>
#include <clib/graphics_protos.h>

/* declare pointers to graphics and intuition libraries */
```

```
struct GfxBase *GfxBase;
struct Library *IntuitionBase;

/* define a pointer to a rastport structure */

struct RastPort *rp;

/* define the text to be used in the screen title */

struct TextAttr TextFont = {
    "topaz.font",
    8,0,0
};

/* declare pointers to the Window, Screen and Intuition Message ¬
data structures */

struct Window *CurrentWindow;
struct Screen *CurrentScreen;
struct IntuiMessage *message;

/* define the parameters of our new screen */

    struct NewScreen InitScreen = {
    0,0,
    640,200,
    3,
    0,1,
    HIRES,
    CUSTOMSCREEN,
    &TextFont,"Our custom screen",NULL
    };

/* define the parameters of our new window */

    struct NewWindow InitWindow = {
    0,11,
```

```
    640,189,
    0,1,
    MOUSEBUTTONS|CLOSEWINDOW,
    ACTIVATE|WINDOWCLOSE,
    NULL,
    NULL,
    "Four in a row",
    NULL,
    NULL,
    0,0,640,189,
    CUSTOMSCREEN
    };

#define boolean int
#define true 1
#define false 0

/* CONSTANTS */
#define InitialLookAhead 6 /* anything less than 5 is pathetic */

/* Values associated with each line */
/* changing these will change the importance the computer */
/* places upon different board positions */
#define Worth4                5000 /* the value of 4 in a row */
#define WorthUnBlocked3       1000 /* the value of three in a row */
#define Worth3BlockedOneSide 150 /* the value of 3 in a row with block */
#define WorthUnBlocked2       15
#define Worth2BlockedOneSide 1

#define Human    'X'
#define Computer 'O'

/* all have 5 added to position of column to try first in best move ¬
search.  The order makes the computer try columns starting in the ¬
middle and working outwards */
#define try1 8
#define try2 9
#define try3 7
```

```
#define try4  10
#define try5  6
#define try6  11
#define try7  5
#define try8  12

/* TYPES */
typedef char Board[19][19] ;
/* A board has blank space arround it to allow checking for 4,3,2 */
/* in-a-row to be carried out at any position, regardless of how near */
/* the edge we are, using the same algorithm */

typedef int NextFreeType[19] ;
/* this tells us the row position at which the next counter will */
/* placed for each column of the board */
typedef int TryOrderType[9] ;
/* tell the computer in which order to check columns */

/* GLOBAL VARIABLES */
int LookAhead ;
NextFreeType NextFree ;
Board TheBoard ;

int ComputersScore ;
TryOrderType TryOrder ;

/* — Prototypes for Functions — */

voidsetupdisplay(void);
voiddrawboard(void);
voidReleaseResources(void);
voidInitialise(void);
voidPlayGame(void);
voidAlterBoard(Board ABoard, char Player, int Move );
voidUnAlterBoard( Board ABoard, int Move );

/* graphics-related function definitions */
/* define the function that opens the libraries, screen and window */
```

```
void setupdisplay(void)
{
    /* open graphics library and get a pointer to it */
    GfxBase=(struct GfxBase *)OpenLibrary("graphics.library", 0);

    /* leave program if failed to open library */
    if (GfxBase==NULL) exit(100);

    /* open intuition library and get pointer to it */
    IntuitionBase=(struct Library *) OpenLibrary("intuition.library",0);
    /* if failed to open, close graphics library and stop */
        if (IntuitionBase==NULL) {
        CloseLibrary((struct Library *)GfxBase);
        exit(200);
    }
    /* open a new screen according to the parameters in InitScreen */
    /* put a pointer to the new screen in CurrentScreen */
    CurrentScreen=(struct Screen*)OpenScreen(&InitScreen);

    /* if failed, close the Intuition and Graphics libraries */
    if (CurrentScreen==NULL) {
        CloseLibrary(IntuitionBase);
        CloseLibrary((struct Library *)GfxBase);
        exit(300);
    }

    /* Make our new window belong to the new screen */
    InitWindow.Screen=CurrentScreen;
    /* Open a new window with the parameters in InitWindow, and put */
    /* a pointer to it in CurrentWindow */
    CurrentWindow=(struct Window *)OpenWindow(&InitWindow);
    /* if failed to open window, close screen and libraries */
    if (CurrentWindow==NULL) {
        CloseScreen(CurrentScreen);
        CloseLibrary(IntuitionBase);
        CloseLibrary((struct Library *)GfxBase);
        exit(400);
```

```
    }
    /* get the opened windows rastport, and store it in rp */
    rp=CurrentWindow->RPort;
}

/* define the function to draw the board */
void drawboard(void)
{
    /* draw the four-in-a-row board - an eight by eight grid */
    int i;
    /* set pen colour */
    SetAPen(rp,3);

    /* draw horizontal lines */
    for (i=20;i<191;i+=19) {
        Move(rp,20,i);
        Draw(rp,619,i);
    }
    /* draw vertical lines */
    for (i=20;i<639;i+=75) {
        Move(rp,i,20);
        Draw(rp,i,171);
    }

    /* Now label each column with text */
    SetAPen(rp,4); /* different pen colour */
    Move(rp,53,183);
    Text(rp,"1",1);
    Move(rp,128,183);
    Text(rp,"2",1);
    Move(rp,203,183);
    Text(rp,"3",1);
    Move(rp,278,183);
    Text(rp,"4",1);
    Move(rp,353,183);
    Text(rp,"5",1);
    Move(rp,428,183);
    Text(rp,"6",1);
```

```
    Move(rp,503,183);
    Text(rp,"7",1);
    Move(rp,578,183);
    Text(rp,"8",1);
}

/* function that places a piece at a specific coordinate */
void drawpiece(char player, int x, int y)
{
    /* declare data structures for filled ellipse drawing */
    UWORD areabuffer[1000]; /* buffer is used to hold maximum of ¬
400 fill vectors */
    struct TmpRas tempraster;
    struct AreaInfo myareainfo;
    PLANEPTR templane;

    /* initialise myareainfo */
    InitArea(&myareainfo,areabuffer,400);
    rp->AreaInfo=&myareainfo;
    /* Get space for a temporary rastport, which must be at least as ¬
big as largest object to be drawn */
    templane=(PLANEPTR)AllocRaster(65,20);

    rp->TmpRas=(struct TmpRas*)InitTmpRas(&tempraster,¬
templane,RASSIZE(65,20));

    /* choose colour depending on variable palyer */
    if (player==Computer)
        SetAPen(rp,5);
    else
        SetAPen(rp,6);
    /* set up ellipse in myareainfo vector list */

    AreaEllipse(rp,(x-5)*75+57,(y-5)*19+30,20,8);   /* x and y ¬
coordinates passed vary between 5 and 12 - convert these to between ¬
0 and 7 before using them to compute screen coordinates */
    /* draw and fill area */
    AreaEnd(rp);
```

```
    /* free temporary raster */
    FreeRaster(templane,65,20);  /* must free exactly the same size ¬
area as was allocated with AllocRaster */
    rp->TmpRas=NULL; /* remove references to temp raster and area info */
    rp->AreaInfo=NULL;
}

int getmove(unsigned long int class, struct IntuiMessage *message)
/* get move from player */
{
    int x,y; /* position of mouse */

    if (class & MOUSEBUTTONS) {
        x=message->MouseX;
        y=message->MouseY;
        if (y>20 && x>20 && x<619) /* user has clicked in board area */
            return (x-20)/75+5; /* convert x coordinate of mouse to a ¬
number between 5 and 12 */
        else return -1; /* clicked outside board - no move made */
    } else return -1; /* no mouse click received */
}

void ReleaseResources(void)
{
    /* close down window, screen and libraries */
    CloseWindow(CurrentWindow);
    CloseScreen(CurrentScreen);
    CloseLibrary(IntuitionBase);
    CloseLibrary((struct Library *)GfxBase);
}

void Initialise(void)
{
    int Row ;
    int Col ;

    LookAhead = InitialLookAhead ;
```

```
    /* Mark each square on the board as empty */
    for(Row=0; Row<=18; Row++)
    {
        for(Col=0; Col<=18; Col++)
            {
            TheBoard[Row][Col] = '\0';
        }
    }

    /* Now mark each square on the playable area of the board ¬
as containing a space */
    for(Row=5; Row<=12; Row++)
    {
        for(Col=5; Col<=12; Col++)
            {
            TheBoard[Row][Col] = ' ';
        }
    }

    /* the next free row for each column is initially 12, the ¬
deepest playable row */
    for(Col=0;Col<=18;Col++) NextFree[Col] = 12 ;

    /* defines the order in which the move algorithm tries the columns */
    TryOrder[1] = try1 ;
    TryOrder[2] = try2 ;
    TryOrder[3] = try3 ;
    TryOrder[4] = try4 ;
    TryOrder[5] = try5 ;
    TryOrder[6] = try6 ;
    TryOrder[7] = try7 ;
    TryOrder[8] = try8 ;
}

/* function makes a move by putting a piece of type Player into the ¬
board  in the column specified by Move, and the row speficied ¬
by NextFree[Move] */
```

```
void AlterBoard(Board ABoard, char Player, int Move )
{

    ABoard[NextFree[Move]][Move] = Player ;
    NextFree[Move]– ;
}

/* removes a piece previously made by Alter Board */

void UnAlterBoard( Board ABoard, int Move )
{

    NextFree[Move]++ ;
    ABoard[NextFree[Move]][Move] = ' ' ;
}

int TryADirection( Board ABoard,
            int Row,
            int Col,
            int RowChange,
            int ColChange,
            char Player )
{
    int Score ;

    Row += RowChange ;
    Col += ColChange ;
    if (ABoard[Row][Col] == Player) {
        Row += RowChange ;
        Col += ColChange ;
        if (ABoard[Row][Col] == Player) {
            Row += RowChange ;
            Col += ColChange ;
            if (ABoard[Row][Col] == Player)  Score = Worth4;
            else {
                if (ABoard[Row+RowChange][Col+ColChange] == ' ') {
                   if (ABoard[Row-4*RowChange][Col-4*ColChange] == ¬
' ') Score=WorthUnBlocked3;
```

```
                else Score = Worth3BlockedOneSide;
            }
            else {
                if (ABoard[Row-4*RowChange][Col-4*ColChange] == ¬
' ') Score=Worth3BlockedOneSide;

                else Score = 0 ;
            }
        }
    }
    else if (ABoard[Row+RowChange][Col+ColChange] == ' ') {
        if (ABoard[Row-3*RowChange][Col-3*ColChange] == ¬
' ') Score=WorthUnBlocked2;

        else Score =  Worth2BlockedOneSide ;
    }
    else Score = 0;
  }
  else Score = 0 ;
  return(Score);
}

int PlayersScore( Board ABoard, char Player )
{
  int Score ;
  int Row, Col ;

  Score = 0 ;
  for(Row=5;Row<=12;Row++)
    for(Col=5;Col<=12;Col++) {
      if (ABoard[Row][Col] == Player) Score += ¬
(TryADirection(ABoard,Row,Col,-1,1,Player)+
          TryADirection(ABoard,Row,Col,0,1,Player)+
          TryADirection(ABoard,Row,Col,1,1,Player)+
          TryADirection(ABoard,Row,Col,1,0,Player));
    }
  return (Score) ;
```

```
}

/* given a Player, this function returns the opponent - ¬
Computer for Human and vice versa */
char OtherPlayer( char Player )
{ if (Player==Human) return(Computer); else return(Human) ;
}

/* the rows numbered 0 to 4 are outside the playable area, ¬
so this function returns false if NextFree indicates such a row ¬
for a given column */
boolean LegalMove( Board ABoard, int Move )
{ return( NextFree[Move] > 4 ) ; }

int BestMove( Board ABoard,
        char Player,
        int Level,
        int *ScoreForMove )
{
    int TheMove, Col, MaxScore, DummyMove, MoveValue, ¬
OtherPlayersScore, try ;

    MaxScore = -999999 ;
    TheMove = -1 ;
    if (Level > 1) {
        try = 1 ;
        while(try < 9) {
            Col = TryOrder[try] ;
            if (LegalMove(ABoard,Col)) {
                AlterBoard(ABoard,Player,Col) ;
                DummyMove = BestMove(ABoard, OtherPlayer(Player), ¬
Level - 1, &MoveValue);
                UnAlterBoard(ABoard,Col) ;
                MoveValue = -MoveValue ;
            }
            else
                MoveValue = -999999 ;
```

```
            if (MoveValue > MaxScore) { MaxScore = MoveValue; ¬
TheMove = Col;}
            try++;
        }
    }
    else { /* Level = 1 */
        OtherPlayersScore = PlayersScore(ABoard,OtherPlayer(Player)) ;
        for(try=1;try<=8;try++) {
            Col = TryOrder[try] ;
            if (LegalMove(ABoard,Col)) {
                AlterBoard(ABoard,Player,Col) ;
                MoveValue = PlayersScore(ABoard,Player) - ¬
OtherPlayersScore;
                UnAlterBoard(ABoard,Col) ;
            if (MoveValue > MaxScore)
                { MaxScore = MoveValue; TheMove = Col; }
            }
        }
    }
    *ScoreForMove = MaxScore ;
    return(TheMove) ;
}

void PlayGame(void)
{
    boolean TimeToQuit = false ;
    int HumansMove,ComputersMove;
    unsigned long int class; /* class of Intuition message received */

    Initialise() ; /* set up the board */
    setupdisplay(); /* open screen and window */
    drawboard(); /* draw the empty board */

    do {
        do {
            /* Put up message telling player it's their turn */

            SetAPen(rp,4); /* pen colour */
```

```
            Move(rp,283,18);
            Text(rp,"Your move",9);

            Wait(1L<< CurrentWindow->UserPort->mp_SigBit);  /* wait ¬
until we receive a message */
            /* find out the kind of message received */
            message=(struct IntuiMessage *)GetMsg(¬
CurrentWindow->UserPort);

            class=message->Class;
            HumansMove=getmove(class,message);
            ReplyMsg(message);
            if (class!=CLOSEWINDOW) {
                /* if user hasn't closed the window, then wait for ¬
and get next message */
                /* This absorbs the Mouse button release message ¬
Intuition gives after the user clicks the mouse */
                Wait(1L<< CurrentWindow->UserPort->mp_SigBit); /* wait ¬
for message */
                message=(struct IntuiMessage *)GetMsg(¬
CurrentWindow->UserPort);

                ReplyMsg(message);
            }
        } while (class!=CLOSEWINDOW && HumansMove<0); /* repeat until ¬
user selects close or enters a valid move */
        if (class==CLOSEWINDOW)
            TimeToQuit=true;
        else {
            drawpiece(Human,HumansMove,NextFree[HumansMove]);
            AlterBoard(TheBoard,Human,HumansMove);

            /* let player know computer is thinking */
            SetAPen(rp,4); /* set pen colour */
            Move(rp,283,18);
            Text(rp,"My move  ",9);

            ComputersMove = BestMove(TheBoard,Computer,¬
```

```
LookAhead,&ComputersScore);
              drawpiece(Computer,ComputersMove,NextFree[ComputersMove]);
              AlterBoard(TheBoard,Computer,ComputersMove) ;
         }
     } while (TimeToQuit==false); /* repeat until user asks to ¬
close the window */
}

void main(void)
{
     PlayGame();
     ReleaseResources();
}
```

Once you've typed it in and saved it, you can compile it with a simple **dcc** command:

```
dcc four_row.c
```

How it works

The first part of the code includes our system header files and defines the data structures we'll need for our graphics. Then come some definitions for the game.

We've defined **boolean** to be an **int**, and the values **true** and **false** as 1 and 0 respectively. This makes clear the process of calling a function which returns a **true** or **false** value which we want to act on, for example the **LegalMove** function which returns **true** if there is a row free in a given column.

The constant **InitialLookAhead** is used to determine the depth of the **Mini-max** recursion, while the **Worth** constants are used by **TryADirection** to evaluate lines of a player's pieces. The two character constants **Human** and **Computer** are used both to mark positions taken on the board, and to mark the player being dealt with in the **Mini-Max** algorithm.

At any level of recursion, there are only eight possible moves. The following set of **defines** – **try1**, **try2** etc. – are used to determine the order in which the columns are tested. They do so in such a way as to favour testing central columns first, as these are the more powerful board positions.

Next some **typedef**s are used to aid the clarity of the program. **Board** is set up to represent an array of **char** with 19 by 19 elements, and **NextFreeType** is set up to be an array of ints with 19 elements. **TryOrderType** is likewise set up. Global variables of these types are created, called **TheBoard**, **NextFree** and **TryOrder** respectively. A global variable called **LookAhead**, representing the number of moves ahead **Mini-max** will search, is also declared, as is **ComputersScore**, which is a global variable used by **Mini-max**.

After the preliminaries come the definitions for all the functions our program will use. The first is **setupdisplay**, which opens the graphics and Intuition libraries, and then opens the screen and window the game is to be played on. Refer to the last chapter for details of this function.

The next function, **drawboard**, is also graphics related. Its purpose is to draw an empty board in the window. It's only called once, at the beginning of the program. **Drawboard** makes use of a number of graphics functions that we haven't dealt with yet.

The function **SetAPen** will set the colour of the pen used for drawing operations. It takes two parameters – the first is the **rastport** pointer, obtained from the **Window** structure, and the second is the required colour. We've opened an eight colour screen, so this value has to be between 0 and 7. The "**A**" pen is the foreground or primary pen. You can also set the background colour, useful sometimes for printing text or patterns, with the equivalent call **SetBPen**.

We draw a line in two parts. First we move an imaginary cursor to a position in the window. The position is defined by two co-ordinates, across and then down (known as "x" and "y"), relative to the very top left-hand corner of the Window. This is performed by a call to the **Move** function, which needs a **RastPort** pointer and integers for the x and y co-ordinates.

A call to the function **Draw**, again with the **RastPort** pointer and two more co-ordinates will draw a line from the position specified with **Move** to the new position.

In **drawboard** we've used a couple of **for** loops to break the playing area into an eight-by-eight grid. Then we've called the function **Text** to label each of the columns. **Text** takes a **RastPort** pointer, a string of text and an integer representing the length of the text (not including a delimiting '\0') as its parameters. The text is placed at the current cursor position, which we've defined for each column here by a call to **Move**.

The function **drawpiece** is used to draw a piece in a particular grid position. It takes as its parameters the player in question, and the position in the board array of the piece, represented as two integers. It uses the variable **player** to determine the colour for the ellipse used for a piece.

MAKE A NOTE!

AreaEllipse function

A complete discussion of the **AreaEllipse** function call is beyond the scope of this book, but, broadly, this is what happens. The ellipse is drawn in two stages, first a series of vectors are defined, which create an outline for the shape, then the space enclosed by the vectors is filled. To this end, you need to declare some space for the vectors to be stored. This is the function of the **areabuffer** array of **unsigned words**. Five bytes are required for each vector, so this gives us space for 400 vectors. By declaring it as an array of **words**, rather than bytes, we ensure that it begins on even address boundary, which is a requirement of the functions that use it.

We first of all set this vector storage with a call to **InitArea**. This takes as its parameters a pointer to a system structure of type **AreaInfo**, a pointer to the space for your vectors, and the maximum number of vectors you will need. I've chosen 400 here, just to be on the safe side.

We then modify the **RastPort** we are using, by de-referencing our **RastPort** pointer, so that its **AreaInfo** element now points to the **AreaInfo** structure **InitArea** has just initialized for us.
The fill operation is not performed directly in the window, but in a

temporary, invisible area. Once it is complete, the system places it on to the screen for us. To this end, we need to create a temporary raster where the drawing and filling can take place. The call to **AllocRaster** achieves this. It is passed the size of the raster we need, which need be no bigger than the largest object to be drawn. We've asked for a raster of 65 pixels across by 20 down. **AllocRaster** returns a pointer to the temporary raster, which is stored in the variable **templane**. **Templane** has previously been declared of type **PLANEPTR**, a system-defined pointer type.

We then initialize our **tempraster** structure, declared earlier, by calling the function **InitTmpRas**. It takes the address of the structure, the address of the temporary raster we've just been allocated, and the size of the raster (obtained with the system-defined macro **RASSIZE**). It returns a pointer to the initialized **tempraster** structure, which is assigned to the **TmpRas** field of our window's raster.

Having set all this up, we can now call **AreaEllipse**. Its parameters are: a pointer to the **RastPort**, the x coordinate of the ellipse's centre, the y coordinate of the ellipse's centre, the horizontal radius and the vertical radius. A call to **AreaEnd**, with the **RastPort** pointer as argument, will complete the drawing, causing the vectors to be drawn, the area to be filled, and the result placed in the window.

Before the function closes, it first calls **FreeRaster**, which returns the space taken by our temporary raster back to the operating system. It takes a pointer to the temporary raster and its horizontal and vertical dimensions. These must be *exactly* the same as the size specified when the raster was allocated with **AllocRaster**. The function also sets the **AreaInfo** and **TmpRas** fields of our **RastPort** to NULL, indicating that the corresponding structures are no longer attached to it.

With all of that out of the way, the function **getmove** now looks easy. It takes both the **class** of an **IntuiMessage** and a pointer to the same message as its parameters. It assumes that the message has already been received.

It then checks to see if the left-hand mouse button has been pressed, and if so it reads the mouse's x and y coordinates from the message structure. If the mouse lies within the area of the board, then its x coordinate is used to indicate one of the eight columns. This is done by subtracting the position of the left-most column from x, then dividing the result by `75`, the width of each column. A value of `5` is added to the result so that the function returns a number between `5` and `12`, indicating one of the legal board positions in the larger **`TheBoard`** array. If the mouse is outside the board area, or the mouse button was not pressed, then **`getmove`** returns a value of `-1`.

The function **`ReleaseResources`** should look familiar – just like **`closedown`** in the last chapter, it closes the window, screen and libraries we have previously opened, prior to the program quitting.

Other functions

Now that all of our interface-related code has been defined, it's time to define the functions necessary for the mechanics of the game.

`Initialize` is used to set up the starting position. It sets the variable **`LookAhead`** to the constant defined at the beginning of the program. If you've got a faster Amiga, make this value higher than `5` for a more challenging game.

The function then marks every location in the array as being "off limits" by putting a `'\0'` character in them. Afterwards it puts empty spaces (' ') into those which represent valid board positions – those elements numbered `5` to `12` in both directions.

The array **`NextFree`** has all its elements initialized to `12`. These values represent the next free row for each column. Given a column, you can easily find where your piece will land by using the column as an index to this array.

The array **`TryOrder`** is initialized with the constants defined earlier on. It is this that is used to define the order in which **`BestMove`** considers the possibilities. It will only become of significance if the program includes some sort of "pruning", a method by which **`BestMove`** ceases to consider certain moves and their consequences after having found a move which it already knows must prove to be better. The version of Four In A Row shown here doesn't include pruning, but you might like to think about how you'd implement it yourself.

The function **`AlterBoard`** takes as its parameters a pointer to a **`Board`** called **`ABoard`**, a player called **`Player`**, and a column number called **`Move`**. It places the player's piece in the next available row in the column **`Move`**. The corresponding element in **`NextFree`** is then reduced by one, since another piece played in the same column must fall on top of this one.

The mirror function **`UnAlterBoard`** takes just two parameters – **`ABoard`** and a column number called **`Move`** – and takes back a previously made move. The value of **`NextFree`**'s corresponding element is increased accordingly.

The function **`TryADirection`** is used to help evaluate a board position. It is given as its parameters the board, the row and column of a particular piece, the vertical and horizontal directions in which it is to search, and the player whose pieces it is dealing with. It then looks at the pieces in the specified direction and returns a score, depending on the number of the player's pieces in a line, and whether or not future expansion in that line is blocked.

The function **`PlayersScore`** is the core of the evaluation algorithm. It takes a board and a player as its parameters. It looks at each valid position on the board in turn, and if it finds a piece belonging to the player there, it obtains scores for it in each of four directions. These scores are summed, and then summed again with the scores for any other pieces on the board. The overall result is returned.

The function **`OtherPlayer`** takes a player as its parameter and simply returns the player's opponent as a **`char`** value.

`LegalMove`, given a board and a column number, returns a **`true`** value if there is space in that column for another piece (remember only rows numbered 5 and above are in the playing area), and **`false`** otherwise.

BestMove is the move generating function, as discussed earlier. Its parameters are as follows: **Board**, the board array; **Player**, the player whose moves it is checking; **Level**, the depth of recursion it is at (the function is initially called with the number of moves we want to look ahead, obtained from the variable **LookAhead**); and **ScoreForMove**, a pointer to an integer where a score for the best move in this level of recursion can be stored.

The integer **MaxScore** is set to a very small value, so that a move of any value will usurp it. The associated variable **TheMove** holds the column number that produces the best move. It is initially set to `-1`.

The path the function takes then depends on the level of recursion, as determined by the **Level** variable. If this is greater than one, then the function loops through each of the eight columns available to it. The variable **try** counts from `1` to `8`, and is used to access the next column to try from the **TryOrder** array. The function **LegalMove** is called with this column, and is used to determine whether or not there is room for any more pieces there. If there is, **BestMove** makes the move by calling **AlterBoard**. After that it recursively calls itself, reducing the recursion level by one, and giving a pointer to its local variable **MoveValue** so that the called function can give back the score of the best move. The column in which this particular move is to be made is returned by the call. We don't need it at this stage, so it is assigned to **DummyMove** and forgotten about.

The move is then taken back with **UnAlterBoard**, and the value of the move is negated.

If there was no more space in the column under inspection, then the value for that move is assigned to be very low.

The particular move's value is then compared with the best so far, as held in **MaxScore**. If it is higher, then **MaxScore** is given its value and **TheMove** is given the number of the column that was being tested. After this the loop closes until all of the possible moves have been checked. At this point, execution continues after the **else** clause, which we'll deal with first.

This clause gets executed when the function discovers that it has reached the end of its recursion, indicated by the parameter **Level** having a value of 1. It is the function's "base case". At this point, the function calls **PlayersScore** with the opponent as argument, in order to assess the board from the opponent's point of view. This is stored in the variable **OtherPlayersScore**.

Each of the eight possible moves is then examined again, in much the same way as in the function's "recursive case" clause. After each move is made with a call to **AlterBoard**, a value for the move from the player's point of view is gained by calling **PlayersScore** and subtracting from its result the **OtherPlayersScore** value. The move under consideration is then taken back, and its score is compared with the best so far. If it is the best, then **MaxScore** is given its value and **TheMove** is assigned to the column being checked. The loop then closes and the next column is checked.

Once all of the columns have been checked in either the recursive or base cases, **MaxScore** is assigned to the integer pointed to by **ScoreForMove**, and the column number of the move, **TheMove** is returned as a result. The pointer is necessary to communicate the score because we need **BestMove** to produce two values.

The function **PlayGame** is the glue that binds everything together. It calls **initialize** to set up the board, **setupdisplay** to create the display area, and **drawboard** to draw the empty board.

It uses a boolean variable called **TimeToQuit**. It is initially set to false, but is assigned a true value if the user clicks on the window's close gadget. Currently, the program doesn't recognise when it or the human has won – it just keeps on playing. You might like to try adding such a check in, and modifying **TimeToQuit** accordingly.

PlayGame uses two variables, **HumansMove** and **ComputersMove**, to store the columns in which the player and computer choose to make their moves. The variable **class** is used to store the **Class** field of an **IntuiMessage**.

The function enters a **do** loop, which exits only when the **TimeToQuit** flag is no longer false.

Immediately inside this loop is another, which is used to retrieve the user's move. It first of all, with calls to **SetAPen**, **Move** and **Text**, writes a message in the window indicating it's the user's turn to move. It then puts the program to sleep with the **Exec Wait** function discussed at the end of the last chapter.

When the program is re-awoken, it has received an **IntuiMessage** which indicates either a mouse click or a request to close the window. It finds out exactly what it is by calling **GetMsg** as discussed last chapter. The **class** of the message is found by taking the value in its **Class** field. This **class** and a pointer to the message are then passed as arguments to the function **getmove**, so the program can determine which, if any, column the player has selected.

The function then tells Intuition it has dealt with the message by calling **ReplyMsg**. It then examines **class** to determine how to react. If **class** doesn't equal **CLOSEWINDOW**, then it assumes that the user has attempted to make a move. After sending a message indicating that the user has clicked a mouse button, Intuition sends a second message, telling the program that the button has subsequently been released. We don't need this second message, so the bit of code that again sends the program to sleep with **Wait**, gets a message with **GetMsg**, and then replies to it, will absorb the unwanted input.

After that comes the close of the loop used to get the user's input. The loop continues for as long as an illegal move has been made *and* the user hasn't closed the window.

Once the loop is finished, the function checks to see if the user has clicked on the close gadget, and if so sets **TimeToQuit** to be **true**. Otherwise, it makes the move. It does this by calling **drawpiece** to place the user's new piece on the screen, and **AlterBoard** to place the piece in the board array and update the **NextFree** index for that column.

It then becomes the turn of the computer. It begins by putting a message on the screen to let the user know it is thinking. Otherwise, the user might make mouse clicks while the program was not ready to respond. These would be stored up by Intuition for such a time as the program was ready to receive them, resulting in the program making unwanted moves for the user.

It then calls `BestMove` and assigns the column number returned to the variable `ComputersMove`. This is used to aid in drawing the new piece in a call to `drawpiece`, and also in updating the board array and `NextFree` array with a call to `AlterBoard`.

The final function is `main`. It first of all calls `PlayGame`. When this has finished, it calls `ReleaseResources`, and then quits.

Further improvements...

That's about it for Four In A Row. There are a number of improvements you can make to the game: getting it to finish when somebody has won and speeding it up being two good places to start. Adding some sort of pruning to the `BestMove` function would certainly speed things up. You might also want to check for Intuition messages while the computer is thinking of its move, so the user can quit the game without having to wait. This would have the further advantage of absorbing any stray mouse clicks made while the computer is working out its move, as these currently get interpreted as the next move selected by the user.

Afterwards, you can use the Intuition and graphics functions listed here to create your own programs. Even just these few represent many possibilities. The functions presented here, though, make up just a fraction of those supplied with the Amiga. To use these, you really do need the proper documentation. You can gain some inkling by looking at the various header files in DICE's include directories, but sooner or later you'll need the Rom Kernel Manuals. With those, the knowledge you've just gained and your Amiga, there'll be no stopping you. Good luck.

Index

C

D

E

F

G

H

I

J

L

M

N

O

P

R

S

Epilogue

This book gives you everything you need to start programming your Amiga in C. It's not possible in a single book to explain everything there is to know about C, so we've concentrated on the basic C concepts, using examples and illustrations to demonstrate programming principles. We've also included the fully-registered version of what most people believe to be the best currently available shareware C compiler – DICE. This can be found on the four disks supplied with this book, and full installation instructions can be found in chapter 2.

There is much more to DICE – and advanced C programming – that we had space to explain. But we hope you will use 'Complete Amiga C' as a 'springboard'. DICE comes with its own documentation and, in conjunction with the advice and information in this book, we're sure this will provide all the information you need for your own programming experiments and projects. The registered version of DICE, supplied with this book, also comes with Commodore libraries and includes. These are the files needed to make use of the Amiga's special graphics and sound hardware. Although it's possible to write Amiga C programs without using these libraries, the results are basic and crude. In 'Complete Amiga C' we've provided you with the best start in Amiga C programming we can. The rest, as they say, is up to you. Good luck…

- The libraries supplied with 'Complete Amiga C' are for version 1.3 and version 2 of AmigaDOS. At the time of going to press, version 3 libraries were not available. Nevertheless, earlier libraries are designed to work on all subsequent machines, so owners of version 3 machines will have no problems – they will simply be unable to use version 3 enhancements. **Note that the license agreement overleaf refers solely to these libraries, and we are required by Commodore to print it. You are free to produce and distribute programs created using DICE and these libraries, but you must NOT distribute the libraries themselves. Note also that the version of DICE supplied with this book is the fully-registered version and is NOT shareware. Unauthorised copying and distribution of this software is illegal.**

STOP **PLEASE READ THIS FIRST!** **Commodore®**

License Agreement and Disclaimers

CAREFULLY READ ALL THE TERMS AND CONDITIONS OF THIS AGREEMENT PRIOR TO OPENING THE PACKAGE CONTAINING THE PRODUCT AND THE STORAGE MEDIA PURCHASED HEREUNDER ON WHICH THE PRODUCT IS STORED. IF YOU OPEN THIS PACKAGE OR OTHERWISE USE THE PRODUCT, THE STORAGE MEDIA, OR THE ACCOMPANYING DOCUMENTATION (HEREINAFTER "PRODUCT") YOU ACCEPT AND AGREE TO THE TERMS AND CONDITIONS OF THIS AGREEMENT. IF YOU DO NOT AGREE TO THESE TERMS AND CONDITIONS DO NOT OPEN THE PACKAGE OR OTHERWISE USE THE PRODUCT. If you do not agree to these terms and conditions, you may obtain a full refund by returning the unused and unopened PRODUCT along with your purchase receipt to the dealer where you purchased the Product, within fifteen (15) days following such purchase.

1. COPYRIGHT: THIS PRODUCT IS COPYRIGHTED AND OTHERWISE SUBJECT TO PROPRIETY RIGHTS. YOU MAY NOT USE, COPY, OR TRANSFER THE PRODUCT OR ANY COPY OR PORTION THEREOF EXCEPT AS EXPRESSLY PROVIDED IN THIS AGREEMENT. TITLE TO THIS PRODUCT (EXCLUDING THE STORAGE MEDIA) AND ALL OTHER RIGHTS AND USES NOT SPECIFICALLY GRANTED IN THIS AGREEMENT ARE RESERVED BY COMMODORE AND ITS SUPPLIERS.
2. LICENSE: Subject to the terms of this Agreement and the exclusive rights of the copyright holder as set forth in the Title 17 of the United States Code, you are hereby granted the personal, non-exclusive right to use this Product on and in conjunction with a single computer. You may (a) instal such Product onto a permanent storage device (e.g. a hard disk), (b) load the Product into temporary memory (e.g. RAM) and (c) copy the Product as required for reasonable backup purposes, provided the same are done solely in support of your use of the Product on such single computer, and provided the Product is not "copy protected". You must reproduce and include the Product's copyright notices on all such copies. You may not otherwise copy the Product. You may not decompile, disassemble or reverse engineer the Product or attempt to unlock or bypass any copy protection included within the Product. You may not make the Product available to multiple concurrent users unless you have purcahsed a version of the Product (if available) that is furnished by Commodore and specifically authorised for multiple concurrent users, and then only to the number of concurrent users so authorized. You may not rent, loan, lease or sublicense the Product. You may not transfer this Agreement or any of your rights hereunder without the express written permission of Commodore.
3. DURATION: This License is effective until terminated. If you fail to comply with any term or condition of this Agreement this License will terminate. You may also terminate this License at any time. Upon termination you will agree to immediately destroy all copies of the Product.
4. DISCLAIMER: THE PRODUCT IS PROVIDED "AS IS" WITHOUT WARRANTY OF ANY KIND, EITHER EXPRESS OR IMPLIED, STATUTORY OR OTHERWISE, INCLUDING WITHOUT LIMITATION ANY IMPLIED WARRANTIES OF NON-INFRINGEMENT, MERCHANTABILITY AND FITNESS FOR A PARTICULAR PURPOSE. THE ENTIRE RISK AS TO USE, RESULTS AND PERFORMANCE OF THE PRODUCT IS ASSUMED BY YOU AND IF THE PRODUCT SHOULD PROVE TO BE DEFECTIVE, YOU ASSUME THE ENTIRE COST OF ALL NECESSARY SERVICING, REPAIR OR OTHER REMEDIATION.
5. LIMITATION OF LIABILITY: IN NO EVENT SHALL COMMODORE OR ITS SUPPLIERS BE LIABLE FOR ANY PROPERTY DAMAGE, PERSONAL INJURY OR OTHER INDIRECT, INCIDENTAL OR CONSEQUENTIAL COSTS, EXPENSES OR DAMAGES. INCLUDING WITHOUT LIMITATION ANY DAMAGES FOR LOST PROFITS, BUSINESS INTERRUPTION OR DATA WHICH MAY BE LOST OR RENDERED INACCURATE, EVEN IF COMMODORE HAS BEEN ADVISED OF THE POSSIBILITY OF SUCH DAMAGES.
6. MISCELLANEOUS
   (a) This agreement shall exclusively be governed by the laws of the United States of America, Commonwealth of Pennsylvania, and represents the entire understanding regarding the Product, and supersedes any other agreement or representation, verbal or written. This Agreement may only be modified by a written amendment signed by an officer of Commodore.
   (b) This Product and documentation are provided with RESTRICTED RIGHTS. All use, duplication or disclosure by the U.S. Government is subject to the restrictions set forth in 252-227-7013, The Rights in Technical Data and Computer Software clause of the DOD FAR, or in 52-227-14, The Rights in Data General clause of the FAR. Such Product and documentation are also subject to compliance with the laws and regulations of the United States governing the export of technical information and must not be exported or re-exported in violation thereof.